W. H. AUDEN

a tribute

W.H.AUDEN
a tribute

Edited by Stephen Spender

MACMILLAN PUBLISHING CO., INC.

NEW YORK

Macmillan Publishing Co., Inc.
866 Third Avenue, New York, N.Y. 10022
Collier-Macmillan Canada Ltd.

Library of Congress Catalog Number: 74–15364

First American Edition 1975

Printed in Great Britain

Contents

APPENDIX

ILLUSTRATIONS

Editor's Introduction

When I was asked to edit this collection of writings about W. H. Auden I remembered that three years before he died, Auden had discovered that it was intended to publish a *Festschrift* for his sixty-fifth birthday. So far from being put off by a project which was to include reminiscences of him, he was pleased and took considerable interest in the volume. On two or three occasions he pressed me to write something for it and I would have done so had I not already written a poem for a previous tribute published on his sixtieth birthday.

Remembering his objections to the biographies of poets being written, I thought at first that *W. H. Auden – a tribute* should indeed be a tribute and that everything it contained should be completely new. Although practically everything in this book has been written especially for the occasion, I realized that there were several outstanding articles about Auden which are difficult to obtain and it was being unnecessarily dogmatic to exclude them simply on the grounds that they had appeared before. Out of the total of thirty-six contributions, only a handful have been published elsewhere and of these Christopher Isherwood, Lincoln Kirstein and John Hollander have all used the opportunity to add postscripts.

The emphasis throughout then has been to assemble a number of essays by friends, covering as much as possible of different periods of his life. I was fortunate in being able to obtain articles by Mrs Bulley, the headmistress of his (and Isherwood's) preparatory school and by a contemporary who was one of his friends there, Harold Llewellyn Smith.

There are, of course, gaps. For instance, there is nothing describing his first visit to Europe before he went up to Oxford or his visit to Spain during the Spanish civil war. If I had been very insistent I might have obtained these, but the main purpose of this book is to record friendship and trying to force articles out of friends who hesitated to put down their recollections would therefore have been contrary to the spirit of the book.

The question arises whether there may not be a few things which either Auden may not have wished quoted or said, or that solicitous readers may feel he would have objected to. There are, for example, some quotations, harmless in themselves, from letters, although Auden stated in a letter published by his executors after his death that he wished his friends to destroy his letters. The justification of this is really commonsense interpretation of his wishes, based on his own practice when he was living. Books and essays were written about him with his cooperation in which he allowed letters and other documents to be used. When a friend has died, there is always something questionable about saying: 'I know that if I asked him, he would have agreed to this, though it seems contrary to his expressed wishes.' But without claiming absolute knowledge of his wishes, one can be fairly confident that there are letters which he would really have wished destroyed and others about which he would have said: 'But of course I didn't mean that you shouldn't quote from that.' In the same way, based on knowing him, one can feel fairly sure that he would have been pleased with these tributes.

Reading them through, they do suggest a few conclusions. One is that he was more unrecognizably different when old from when young, than are most people. Something of the extraordinary spontaneity of the young man was sacrificed, which was a bigger price than most of us can pay, in order that he might attain the isolation out of which he wrote his later work. Another thing: the happiest period of his life was probably in the early 1930s, when he was a preparatory school master and the most easy and stimulating of colleagues. Inevitably he struck most of his contemporaries as being superior to them, but he had an extraordinary gift, revealed at that time, for being an equal among equals. Lastly, towards the end of his life, his intellectual and poetic ties were with America and Americans. His return to England was the attempt to return to the home of youth and childhood. He was torn between England and America. When he came back to live in Oxford, it was to New Yorkers that he wrote letters which contained poems he had just written. But times and places and English and American friends are brought together in this volume in one time and place.

I am particularly grateful to Auden's literary executor, Mr Edward Mendelson, who, in addition to providing his invaluable chronology and his article about Auden's texts, has read through the whole volume and made various corrections and suggestions.

STEPHEN SPENDER

London 1974

Chronology

Compiled by Edward Mendelson

1907 21 February: Wystan Hugh Auden born at York, third son of George Augustus Auden (1872–1957) and Constance Rosalie Bicknell Auden (1870–1941). His father was a physician, classicist and antiquarian. Bernard Auden (b. 1900), his eldest brother, became a farmer; his middle brother, John Bicknell Auden, became a geologist and mountaineer.

1908 The Auden family moves to Birmingham, and G. A. Auden is appointed School Medical Officer for the city and Professor of Public Health at the University.

1915 Enters St Edmund's School, Hindhead, Surrey, where he remains until 1920. Around 1917–18, at St Edmund's, he first meets Christopher Isherwood.

1920 'Period of ecclesiastical *Schwärmerei*.'[1]

Autumn: Enters Gresham's School, Holt, remaining until 1925. At Gresham's Auden studies biology, performs in plays, wins Latin prizes, arranges a concert of modern music, and is already reading Freud.

1922 'Discovers that he has lost his faith.'[2]

'One afternoon in March': Robert Medley first suggests that Auden write poetry.

16 December: His first published poem, 'Dawn', appears in *The Gresham*, unsigned.

1925 Summer: Travels through Europe, for the first time, with his father.

Autumn: Goes up to Oxford, where he remains until 1928, rooming at Christ Church. He begins as an exhibitioner (scholarship student) in natural science; then briefly studies politics, philosophy and economics; finally settles on English, with Nevill Coghill as his tutor.

1928 Summer: Poems, privately printed by Stephen Spender in an edition of 'About 45 copies'.

August: Begins a year in Berlin, where he learns German. He first rooms with a middle-class family who want to practise their English, so he moves to workers' quarters instead.

1929 Tutors in London after his return from Germany.

1930 Begins two years as schoolmaster at Larchfield Academy, Helensburgh.

18 September: Poems, containing 'Paid on Both Sides' and thirty shorter poems, published; second edition, replacing seven shorter poems, published 1933.

1932 19 May: The Orators published; second edition 1934; third edition 1966.

Autumn: Begins three years as master at the Downs School, Colwall, where he is a great influence on both pupils and teachers.

1933 'One fine summer night in June': 'I was sitting on a lawn after dinner with three colleagues, two women and one man. . . . We were talking casually about everyday matters when, quite suddenly and unexpectedly, something happened. I felt myself invaded by a power which, though I consented to it, was irresistible and certainly not mine. For the first time in my life I knew exactly – because thanks to the power, I was doing it – what it means to love one's neighbour as oneself.'[3]

9 November: The Dance of Death published; produced by the Group Theatre, 25 February 1934.

1934 11 September: American edition of *Poems* (including *The Orators* and *The Dance of Death*) published.

1935 30 May: The Dog Beneath the Skin, with Isherwood, published; produced by the Group Theatre, 12 January 1936.

15 June: Marries Erika Mann at the Registry Office, Ledbury, Herts, in order to provide her with a British passport.

Autumn: After leaving the Downs School at the end of the Summer term, Auden begins about six months with the GPO Film Unit as writer, assistant director, and worker in various projects. During this period, and, except for extensive travels, until his departure for America in 1939, Auden lives in London and Birmingham.

1936 July–September: Visits Iceland with Louis MacNeice.

24 September: The Ascent of F6, with Isherwood, published; revised American edition, March 1937; further revised second English edition, March 1937; produced by the Group Theatre, 26 February 1937.

22 October: Look, Stranger! published. Auden's title for this book appears to have been *Poems 1936*, but while he was in Iceland Fabers changed it. Auden said it 'sounds like the work of a vegetarian lady novelist' and titled the 1937 American edition *On This Island*.[4]

1937 January–March: Visit to Spain, where he works briefly broadcasting propaganda for the Republican government. 'On arriving in Barcelona, I found as I walked through the city that all the churches were closed and there was not a priest to be seen. To my astonishment, this discovery left me profoundly shocked and disturbed. . . . Shortly afterwards, in a publisher's office, I met an Anglican layman [Charles Williams], and for the first time in my life felt myself in the presence of personal sanctity.'[5]

29 May: Spain published; 'All the author's royalties from the sale of this poem go to *Medical Aid for Spain*.'

Summer term: Teaches again at the Downs School.

6 August: Letters from Iceland, with MacNeice, published.

1938 January–July: Travels to China with Isherwood, and returns via Japan, and across America by train; makes his final decision to move to America.

27 October: On the Frontier, with Isherwood, published; produced by the Group Theatre, 14 November.

1939 18 January: Departure for New York. From late 1939 to 1941 he lives in Brooklyn Heights, first alone, then in a house which he shares with other artists and writers.

2 March: Education Today – and Tomorrow, pamphlet written with T. C. Worsley, published.

16 March: Journey to a War, with Isherwood, published.

Spring: Meets Chester Kallman. Teaches for a month at St Mark's School, Southborough, Massachusetts.

(Probably 1939): 'Providentially – for the occupational disease of poets is frivolity – I was forced to know in person what it is like to feel oneself in the prey of demonic powers, in both the Greek and the Christian sense, stripped of self-control and self-respect, behaving like a ham actor in a Strindberg play.'[6]

1940 7 February: Another Time published.

Autumn: Begins a year of teaching at the New School for Social Research, New York.

October: Returns to the Anglican communion.

1941 21 March: The Double Man published; English edition titled (not by Auden) *New Year Letter.*

5 May: Paul Bunyan, operetta to music by Britten, performed at Columbia University.

Summer: Teaches at a writers' conference at Olivet College, Michigan.

Autumn: Begins a year of teaching at the University of Michigan.

1942 Autumn: Begins three years of teaching at Swarthmore College (also at Bryn Mawr College, 1943–5). During the summers, until he first stays in Ischia in 1948, he lives in a shack he owned on Fire Island, New York, which he reportedly names 'Bective Poplars'.

1944 6 September: For the Time Being published, including the title poem and 'The Sea and the Mirror'.

1945 5 April: The Collected Poetry (not Auden's title) published.

April–August: In Germany, and elsewhere in Europe, as a civilian research chief, with the equivalent rank of major, in the Morale Division of the US Strategic Bombing Survey; visits England for the first time since 1939.

Autumn: Moves to New York, where he lives in various apartments until settling at St Mark's Place in 1953.

1946 Spring term: Teaches at Bennington College.

20 May: Receives American citizenship.

Autumn: Begins teaching a one-year course in Shakespeare at the New School for Social Research.

1947 Spring term: Teaches as an Associate in Religion, Barnard College.

11 July: The Age of Anxiety published.

1948 Spring–summer: First visits Ischia, where, from 1949 to 1957, he rents a house, during the spring and summer.

Autumn term: Teaches at the New School for Social Research.

1950 9 March: Collected Shorter Poems 1930–1944 published; essentially a British version of his 1945 collection.

17 March: The Enchafèd Flood published; based on his 1949 Page-Barbour Lectures at the University of Virginia.

Autumn term: Visiting lecturer at Mount Holyoke College.

1951 21 February: Nones published.

11 September: The Rake's Progress, libretto with Kallman, music by Stravinsky, produced in Venice.

1953 Moves his New York flat to 77 St Mark's Place, where he remains until 1972.
Spring term: Research Professor at Smith College.

1955 21 February: The Shield of Achilles published.

1956 9 February: Elected Professor of Poetry at Oxford for a term of five years, during each of which he delivers three public lectures. His inaugural lecture, *Making, Knowing and Judging*, delivered 11 June and published 25 August.

1958 Spring–summer: Moves to a converted farmhouse in Kirchstetten, Lower Austria, which he had bought with the proceeds of an Italian literary prize. He spends the spring and summer of each year in Kirchstetten for the rest of his life.

1960 29 April: Homage to Clio published.

1961 20 May: Elegy for Young Lovers, libretto with Kallman, music by Hans Werner Henze, performed at Stuttgart.

1962 27 November: The Dyer's Hand published.

1964 April: Second visit to Iceland.

October: Begins six months in Berlin, as a member of an artists-in-residence programme sponsored by the Ford Foundation.

1965 13 July: About the House published.

1966 6 August: The Bassarids, libretto with Kallman, music by Henze, performed at Salzburg.

24 November: Collected Shorter Poems 1927–1957 published.

1968 14 October: Collected Longer Poems published.

25 November: Secondary Worlds published; first T. S. Eliot memorial lectures at the University of Kent.

1969 15 September: City without Walls published.

1970 20 June: A Certain World published.

1971 8 November: Academic Graffiti published.

1972 5 September: Epistle to a Godson published.

October: Returns to Oxford to live in a 'grace and favour' cottage at Christ Church.

1973 7 February: Love's Labour's Lost, libretto with Kallman, music by Nicolas Nabokov, performed in Brussels.

19 March: Forewords and Afterwords published.

29 September: After closing his cottage in Kirchstetten for the winter, and during a weekend spent in Vienna before returning to Oxford, Auden dies. On 4 October he is buried in a 'grave of honour' in the churchyard at Kirchstetten.

NOTES

[1] *Forewords and Afterwords*, p. 517.
[2] *Ibid.*
[3] *Forewords and Afterwords*, p. 69.
[4] *W. H. Auden: A Bibliography*, by B. C. Bloomfield and E. Mendelson, 2nd. edn. (1972), p. 26.
[5] *Modern Canterbury Pilgrims*, ed. James A. Pike (1956), p. 41.
[6] *Ibid.*

Geoffrey Grigson
A meaning of Auden

Geoffrey Grigson was Editor of New Verse *from 1933 to 1939 and published many of Auden's early poems. An earlier version of this article appeared in the* Times Literary Supplement.

I was one of those who welcomed the young, first Auden, and now after nearly fifty years I sit down on a cold half-sunny morning, the summer over, to write him a goodbye. No, I was not one of his intimate friends, many times as he befriended me. I knew him on and off, loving him, fearing him a little, as we often fear – and perhaps should fear – the great artists encountered by us on the outside of their inexplicable work. I revered him – 'him' including himself and his writing. I could offer my broad conviction that the English, and the English-speaking, are left now – only for a while, no doubt – without any master of verse, without a master in any kind of writing, of his wit, penetration and imaginative clarity. But I couldn't provide one of those confident surveys and assessments of the Land of Auden.

To be honest, their contemporaries are likely to be poor or only partial guides to the totality, including the middle works, and the late works, of great men. Contemporaries live most in the work they first recognized. I live – perhaps they are the best if not the most profound, profundity not being all – in the poems of his earlier books up to *New Year Letter*. I suppose that later on when he embraced more –

> How hard it is to set aside
> Terror, concupiscence and pride,
> Learn who and where and how we are,
> The children of a modest star,
> Frail, backward, clinging to the granite
> Skirts of a sensible old planet.

– he no longer composed so well.

Looking backwards then, I ask how do we first detect – or rather how do we so often miss – the new writer? The first poem I remember by Auden, never republished, and I have never hunted it out again, seemed to me to have risen out of an 'Englishness' (he was English, after all) until then unexpressed or not isolated in a poem. Auden was reading English; English at Oxford involved him in Old English, which involved him in *Beowulf*. In the poem he saw the blood-trail which had dripped from Grendel after his arm and shoulder had been ripped off by Beowulf. The blood shone, was phosphorescent on the grass – or so I remember the poem (in the *Cherwell* perhaps?). It was as if Auden, this untidy, untied up, short-sighted, pallid person from Christ Church, had given imaginative place and 'reality' to something exploited for the

Examination Schools, yet rooted in the English origins. It was the same with many of his early poems; a measure suggesting fatality, assonances and alliterations coming together to make a new verbal actuality as it might be of rock or quartz, a milieu of the profound Midlands, half aboriginal, half soiled or damaged, half abandoned; the very palpable truth of something, emotions and attitudes included, both anxieties and satisfactions, at once recognizable and pertinent, autochthonic and not provincial (though intimated a little in Housman, and more in Hardy).

In smart Oxford, and the smart Outside, a fashion then was for the frothy, vicious, aesthetic, and selfish; an aesthetical, excluding snobbery re-exhibited for us in the detestable diaries of Evelyn Waugh. The contrast. This is England, this is man: this is Us, this is our sensation. We only are. From Auden I first learnt what the trolls in *Peer Gynt* were up to, and amounted to, when they said 'To thyself be enough'; and how skilfully and suavely our trollishness disguises itself – like Auden's devil in *New Year Letter*.

Within a few years (*The Orators* and *The Dance of Death* and the first *Poems* already published) poems were coming to me from Birmingham or from the Malverns, and I was publishing them in *New Verse*. They came on half sheets of notepaper, on long sheets of lined foolscap, in that writing an airborne daddy-longlegs might have managed with one dangling leg, sometimes in pencil, sometimes smudged and still less easy to decipher. They had to be typed before they went to the printer, and in the act of typing each poem established itself. It was rather like old-fashioned developing in the dark-room, but more certain, more exciting.

> At the far end of the enormous room,
> An orchestra is playing to the rich.

– there at last on the white page, to be clearer still on the galley, the first entire sight of a new poem joining our literature.

> Earth turns over, our side feels the cold . . . .

England of a new generation beginning to widen into the world, the anxiety and the concern of the English individual; Wystan Hugh Auden, beginning to encompass the anxieties of man.

> August for the people and their favourite islands . . . .
> Dear, though the night is gone . . . .

A new poetry, poems to appear again in that wonder-book, *Look Stranger!*, in 1936.

The 'English individual' – what kind of a name was *Auden*? In the early Auden years I liked to think this name of his must be Old Norse, proper for a poet who knew about trolls running along the edges of the mind, liked Morris's *Sigurd the Volsung*, read the sagas, and visited (I had been there before him, impelled, I suppose, by the same kind of reading) the 'sterile, immature', cindery landscape of Icelandic dales and plains – the great plains 'forever where the cold fish is hunted'. The surname dictionary says *Auden* could be Anglo–Scandinavian, *Healfdene*, 'half-Dane'. That would do.

But it could also be English, from *Ælfwine*, 'elf-friend'. That, too, would serve for this Wystan Auden, the elf-friend, the magician, allowing that there are good and bad elves, good and bad magicians.

And 'Wystan'? I found that as well as a parish called Audenshaw, in Lancashire, there was a parish in Shropshire – Auden's Shropshire of the deserted lead mines – called Wistanstow; and didn't the guidebook to Shropshire by the Reverend John Ernest Auden – Auden's uncle, I think – relate the martyrdom of Wystan, son of Widmund, grandson of Wiglaf, King of Mercia, who wished 'to become an heir of a heavenly kingdom', not of an earthly one? Wystan's treacherous cousin – at Wistanstow – struck him down with a sword after giving him the kiss of peace. 'For thirty days a column of light extending from the spot where he was slain, was seen by all those who dwelt there, and every year on the day of his martyrdom, the hairs of his head, severed by the sword, sprang up like grass.'

Sentimental, beside any possible point, to connect the name-saint, the Half-Dane, the Elf-friend, the magician, the poet, and the poems? Well, this poet wasn't called Marmaduke Rees-Mogg, his names fitted his poems, they symbolized a depth of historical, local humus from which this poet could spread above and below ground from local into universal. For me more than a thirty days' column of light stood up from his poems:

> In the deserts of the heart
> Let the healing fountain start,
> In the prison of his days
> Teach the free man how to praise.

Picking through a folder, from these *New Verse* days, I found, on the back of a sheet of *New Verse* notepaper, a statement excerpted from Auden at this early time:

> When a poet is writing verse, the feeling, as it were, excites the words and makes them fall into a definite group, going through definite movements, just as feeling excites the different members of a crowd and makes them act together. Metre is group excitement among words, a series of repeated movements. The weaker the excitement, the less words act together and upon each other.

His feeling was already rising to its greatest power to excite. And the early article in which he wrote that, when he was twenty-five, to explain verse to children (and their parents), he called 'Writing, or the Pattern between People'. Between people – even then. Writers 'would like to be read by everybody and for ever. They feel alone, cut off from each other in an indifferent world where they do not live for very long. How can they get in touch again?' The wish for company, the desire to make – these, he said, are the respectable reasons for writing.

He had, when he began, no doubts of his vocation; he accepted his gifts, learning and admitting as well where he was limited or fell short. His Oxford tutor, Nevill Coghill, told me once, on a night drive between Reading and Oxford during which we talked the whole way of Auden, a story which might have appalled the Auden of his middle or later understanding. As usual Coghill had interviewed his new undergraduates, and he had asked Auden his stock question, after a while:

Tutor: 'And what are you going to do, Mr Auden, when you leave the university?'
Auden: 'I am going to be a poet.'
Tutor: (since something must be said). 'Well, in—in that case you should find it
    very useful to have read English.'
Auden: (after a silence). 'You don't understand, I am going to be a great poet.'

Not all of his writing – but who cares, except the pedant who hates and misunderstands both the arts and the readers he thinks he is serving? – is 'great' or free of dullness. The appalling uniqueness of each great writer includes the different proportions in him of fudge and gold. And what writer, Tolstoy, Hugo, Baudelaire, Melville, Shakespeare, is not a warning against demands for a sustained perfection in literature, as if the great writer's graph ascended steeply and at the worst flattened to a long high level? Zigzags are his condition. And Auden had to write for a living, in our indifferent Anglo–Saxony which gets its poems but expects its poets to live on book-reviewing and the free provision of stale air.

'I am going to be a great poet' – in that early essay I mentioned, he spoke of the writer as being the soil and the gardener: 'The soil part of him does not know what is going on, the gardener part of him has learnt the routine.' Better to be a bad gardener than bad soil, he went on. His soil proved deep and extensive as the Fens. If sometimes he gardened poorer patches of himself, he was a supremely able, dedicated gardener.

Not all of his poems are kind, but most of them are, and he was – exemplifying the unshiftably true fact that the great writer is always, in the base and inside the total of himself – the good man. A book about Auden (though I cannot bear to read such books) which was sent to me from Australia, ends with a note by Rex Warner mentioning Auden's great kindliness and the way he inspired 'great affection in all who know him'. To be kind – not to be cruel – isn't to be evasive, and I see as inseparable from his kindliness Auden's much debated Christianity. It has upset old faithfuls, it repels new readers. For me it demands too much of an 'as if' for intellectual assent; but I see it as wrung from Auden by his long look at the muddle, wickedness, goodness, and necessities of men; wrung from him by desperation about ourselves; not as backsliding, not as a contradiction, but as an enlargement, accepted or no, of his first, limited Marxist cures for our discontent.

Aren't poets, in one form or another, naturally religious men, or nothing? His Christianity may not be what we want, it may disappoint us, it may not be what we suppose is most effective, or most enjoyable; but is it discreditable for a poet to find himself – allowing this to have been Auden's location – outside and beyond poetry in the end?

What Auden doesn't do is opt either from us or from our primary world. I see that is why he turned from, rather than against, Hardy. When old, Hardy wrote, in strict continuation, that he had not cared for life, but that since life had cared for him he owed it some loyalty; which must have seemed grudging, and more than half defeated. It was unkindliness – unkindness to man, who has to live, and in this world. The unevasive Auden I revere and love, conceived, like Pasternak, that we are guests of

The Early Years

1 Auden's mother, the daughter of a vicar and the youngest of eight children.

2 Auden's father, Dr G. A. Auden, a distinguished scientist and physician, who was School Medical Officer in Birmingham.

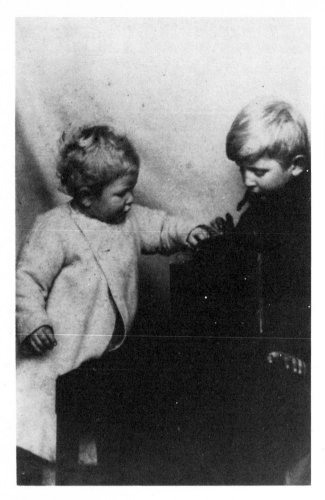

4 ABOVE The three Auden brothers in 1913. *Left to right* Wystan, John and Bernard (the eldest).

3 The earliest known photograph of Wystan Hugh Auden (*left*), taken *c.* 1910 and showing himself and his brother John inspecting a captive fieldmouse.

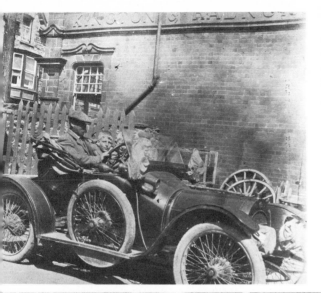

5 LEFT The three brothers with their mother in 1913.
6 ABOVE LEFT A family outing.
7 ABOVE The Auden family on a climb. Both Wystan and John's love of geology began in their youth.

8 A school photograph of St Edmund's in 1915 showing
Auden in front of Mrs Ivo Bulley. Immediately
behind her is Christopher Isherwood. (See Mrs
Bulley's contribution.)

during 1st Wald War   W. H. Auden

9 ABOVE Wystan (*right*) and John Auden.

4 YARMOUTH (*Isle of Wight*). — *High Street.* — LL.

Yarmouth, I. W. from the Bridge.

10 RIGHT Two pages from a holiday diary kept in 1917 by the Auden family while in the Isle of Wight.

a few hours and managed to get into Southampton under an escort. She was put into dry dock and it was found that she was torn from the bows to beyond the middle of the ship, but the sand ballast acted as a sort of cement and so the ship kept afloat. The chief officer shot himself. We arrived at Freshwater to find only an old growler which was engaged, but the man who engaged it said we could come too.

31st   M, W & J went out shopping at Totland and then walked over by the fields to Freshwater Church (All Saints) to find out the services. Came back home in time for dinner. After dinner we walked onto Headon Hill and after we had seen the Tumulus we walked down into what looked like an old disused fort but when we got in there an Orderly turned us out saying that it was an Isolation Camp.* There were two large muzzle-loader guns there. Then we walked down into Alum Bay but it was High Tide so we could not go and see the different coloured rocks. Then we came home. We had by that time almost discovered the shortcuts etc. It was a lovely evening and the sunset was beautiful. We saw some larks and Robins and several other birds. The rooms are very nice. For the sitting-room see drawing on the first page, Mothers room is a nice large one other the sitting room. JdW's room is a nice one also with 2 beds in it. B's room is a small one about the size of

* . M. heard it was cerebro-spinal meningitis . so felt anxious !

12 ABOVE LEFT Auden in 1924, a year before his first visit to Europe.

13, 14 ABOVE and LEFT Two pictures of Auden in 1928, the year his first book, *Poems*, was privately printed by Stephen Spender in an edition of 'about forty-five copies'.

existence, which must be honoured with delight. If that is one reason why he has been a rhythm and a revolving or shifting fixture in our lives, I shall insist that Auden's Long Mynd and Malverns became the hills of the world. He saw man and the world as Langland saw them from the Malverns.

Our English fortune is to share particularities with him, as Americans share them with Whitman or Russians with Pasternak, or the French with Hugo. He is for everyone, for us he is extra, by language, by keepings, and milieu. In *A Certain World*, which he published in (and which by dedication was my ultimate gift from Auden), I was delighted to encounter so much, so late in him, of our primary world, whether, with everything else, in extracts from Cobbett, a winter and mountain poem by an Irishman of the tenth century, or a poem on roads by Edward Thomas. Who else would have known, say, about Ivor Gurney making delight of the world, in his distress, out of the Malverns or the Cotswolds:

> Cotswold's farther early Italian Blue arrangement. . . .

> Up in the air there beech tangles wildly in the wind. . . .

If we follow him round, as he celebrates, investigates, discards, adds, re-attempts, we find in him, I declare, explicit recipes for being human. And implicit ones, in poems, stanzas, lines, again and again, which give us in sonority and movement the additional bonus of what their language cannot say – the bonus of great poetry.

John Auden
A brother's viewpoint

Dr John Auden is an elder brother of W. H. Auden and a distinguished geologist

---

As a brother of Wystan, older by just over three years, but lacking the craggy landscape of his face, and far removed from the catholic compass and depth of his intellect, to write of our youth brings back ancient friendships and jealousies. Right from childhood he was clearly exceptional and, although then with only a child's knowledge, he was often aware of the wrong logic of his elders and brothers, who would take care in accusing him of bumptious precocity. He mentions somewhere his scorn and anger when an aunt incorrectly pronounced 'pyrites' as 'pirritz', he evidently having recently had the correct pronunciation from our father. Wystan was the youngest of three brothers and many years later maintained to my wife that, as in the fairy stories, being the youngest he was the most loved and was destined to find great treasure. Jealous no doubt of affection and attention being transferred to a new arrival, I remember being happiest between 1908 and 1911 while staying with my two aunts and an uncle who lived during vacation time in three houses at Wyesham, near Monmouth. I had been escorted there from Birmingham by a Swiss nanny. Wystan recently became interested in the role of the nanny in Victorian and Edwardian life; he was too young to remember that I was the only one of the three brothers who had a friend of my own, and all the way from Switzerland. Alas, sixty-three years later even her name is forgotten.

My father was a GP in York. We had a coachman who did not live in, as well as a cook and two maids who slept in the attic which, although I was only four, appeared even then to smell of inferior soap. There was a benign paternalism, but obligatory church for them on Sundays and house prayers every morning before breakfast. My father's interests went beyond medicine, especially to archaeology, the Classics, and Icelandic sagas. He edited the handbook on York for the 1907 meeting there of the British Association for the Advancement of Science. We had the impression in later years that our mother slightly disapproved of his proficiency in gynaecology. At any rate, in 1908 he gave up general practice in York and became the first School Medical Officer in Birmingham, on a modest salary. This, together with some private means, sufficed to send his three sons to preparatory and public schools; Wystan and I were at the same two preparatory schools although the age difference was too large to bring us much together there. It was during the summer holidays especially that we saw most of each other, that of 1913 being spent at Rhayader in Wales, where we became interested in the tannery, a ginger beer factory and the three dams of the Birmingham waterworks (this was long before the Claerwen Reservoir was constructed). My elder brother Bernard and I had bicycles. Wystan rode pillion on my father's machine. In Easter 1914 we climbed Cader Idris from Arthog, descending to Dolgellau, Wystan being carried part of the way.

On the outbreak of war my father joined the RAMC and our Solihull house was sold. He was in Gallipoli, Egypt and France for four years, and my mother lived during term times with relatives and friends. From 1915 to 1918 our holidays were spent in Dyffryn, Rhayader, Monmouth, Bradwell in Derbyshire, Clithero, Cleeve Hill and Totland Bay, with occasional visits to Horninglow, near Burton-on-Trent, where our paternal grandmother lived in a house surrounded by poplars. There were long walks over the moors and bicycle rides. We studied menhirs and stone circles, gold and lead mines, blue-john caverns, pre-Norman crosses and churches. When my mother felt the call of nature she would retire behind a wall and invariably demand that whatever we did we should not look. Wystan once asked across a wall what in fact would happen if we did look, and was told not to be cheeky and rude. We had to go to church twice on Sundays which created a side interest as we had developed a graded scale of degrees of Anglo-Catholic ritual; most of the churches, especially in Wales, alas from our point of view, falling far below the practice of St Albans, Holborn, which was the church we attended while visiting the aunts in their Brooke Street apartments, and which had become the standard.

The wide interests of our parents, their books, and the many holidays spent amongst the hills, had a great influence on us. They gave rise to an intellectual curiosity about natural phenomena. In Wystan's case this developed into a Goethe-like interest in the inter-relationship of different aspects of knowledge, in mine leading me to spend twenty-seven years in India in an attempt to understand the structure of the peninsula and Himalaya. Limestone landscapes became Wystan's chosen environment, a passion originating at the time we were at Bradwell, although, when he had seen more of the Pennines, he probably came to love Alston Moor in Cumberland more than any other place. He preferred those gentle slopes to the precipices of the Dolomites, although I think that he would have liked the karstic Taurus mountains, north-east of Antalya.

We seldom discussed our attitudes to nature, but I did once suggest that a life spent almost entirely in north-west Europe and on the Atlantic sea-board of the United States created an impression in marked contrast to the crisis physiognomy of Asia. Indeed, the seven Bucolic poems, and a later one entitled *River Profile*, have little connection with the drought, cyclone, flood and earthquake which almost annually change the face of the earth in Asia.

It was K2, the second highest mountain in the world, which I must have mentioned to Wystan in Berlin in 1929 when on leave from India, that provided the title of *The Ascent of F6*, and also, I suppose, the dedication to me. Eight years later, in 1937, the peak K2 was our only fixed point while exploring along the Shaksgam in the Sinkiang Karakoram with Eric Shipton, H. W. Tilman and Michael Spender. Our anxieties were not then connected with Oedipus but with remaining alive between food-dumps and the crossing of torrents swollen every afternoon with glacier-melt water.

Our mother was a Bicknell, the youngest of eight children born in rapid succession to the Vicar of Wroxham – so rapid that our grandmother retired to the sofa in 1869 which gave some degree of immunity from importunate demands. In about 1881, when my mother was twelve, my grandmother died, and thereafter my mother stayed frequently with her bachelor uncle, Charlie. They were together in Bordighera when he died suddenly, and the whole business of the death and burial fell on a girl of eighteen on her first trip abroad. Later, with her sisters, she graduated from London University, specializing in French. With the idea of joining a Protestant medical mission in Africa, she took up nursing at St Bartholomew's Hospital and there met my father who was then an intern. So the medical mission did not materialize. She frequently attended retreats in Anglican convents, and we have one of her anthologies of prayers in her beautiful handwriting, with capitals in Gothic red.

Wystan was puzzled by the mystery of our parents, with their contrasted backgrounds and outlooks coming together in marriage, maintaining that each should have had different spouses. But of course he had to continue with the truism that if they had not met and married we three brothers would not have been born. This was a particular case of general speculation on the apparent incompatibilities of most marriages; in making it he did not overlook that the marriage of our parents was indeed blest with happiness and understanding, and that ours was a family in which there was love and encouragement to many activities.

He became fond of music when quite young and used to play duets with his mother, recalling with some amusement both of them often singing the love song between Tristan and Isolde, Wystan taking the part of Isolde, with implications of which she was evidently totally unaware. Wystan never did escape from his mother, for right to the end he would continue, almost as her deputy, to say of any particular action, 'Mother would never have allowed that.' He developed a fetish about punctuality which he attributed to an imaginary Bradshaw image of gongs and peremptory summons to the table by mother. I never recall pained admonitions on late arrivals at meals, and certainly walks on the fells from our Lake-District cottage near Threlkeld could seldom be timed with exactitude. All of us attempted to be punctual, but no one except Wystan would have curtly told some guests who had arrived late to dinner two years ago in our London apartment, where he too was a guest, that they were not on time and should have been. All our family had a fear of missing trains and flights so that many a half hour was spent shivering on wind-swept platforms – Penrith being one of the draughtiest – but this was no foible peculiar to our mother.

After 1926 he and I saw very little of each other, except during my periods of leave from India and, after 1960, on duty trips from the FAO, Rome. We met in Berlin in 1929, Bruxelles in 1938, New York on several occasions, Ischia twice, Kirchstetten once. It was in Bruxelles that we discussed his wish to become an American citizen, and my feelings towards the British Raj in India. His reasons for going to America were not then so much disgust with Chamberlain as a dislike of the narrow intellectualism of the English establishment, and the desire not to become a 'court' poet. His convictions were confirmed no doubt on arrival in America whence he could see in clearer perspective aspects of English life which he disliked, and the progressive capitulation of Britain and France to Hitler's demands during 1939. Notwithstanding the covert sneers of Evelyn Waugh, in going to America he made the right decision, and few people have so bridged the Atlantic, and so combined the American vitality and inventiveness with the long roots of European culture.

In August 1941 our mother died in England while Wystan was in New York and I in Calcutta. He said that he could never open those few of her letters which arrived after her death. In my case the letters took even longer to reach India, up to three months on account of the war. Golo Mann has suggested that Wystan's sudden return to religion may have been influenced by Reinhold Niebuhr's *The Nature and Destiny of Man*. This is quite possibly so, but Wystan told me after the war that the primary reason was our mother's death, and he once more accepted the Anglo-Catholicism of his childhood, while I after some years went over to Rome in 1951. Wystan was surprised by that decision, for he had come across the effects of a rigid hierarchic discipline on a friend of his who was a Catholic priest, which made him tend to see the outward structure rather than the spiritual content. To anyone long resident in India it seemed anomalous that the established church should be a paid organization of the British Raj, and Catholicism then and there cut right across dominions and powers. There were also dogmas to which Wystan took strong exception; the Immaculate Conception in his view making an honorary Arian of the Blessed Virgin, a bizarre idea which he repeated every time we met.

In Kirchstetten there was no Protestant church, and Wystan worshipped regularly in the Catholic one, giving the *Pfarrer* a collection of his poems. When we visited him in 1963 he insisted on indicating to me in an avuncular manner the sequence of the Latin ritual, although since 1951 I had not in fact been totally unaware of the liturgy. This was years before the Mass became troubled with unhappy vernacular renderings and disorientation, and had called in hippies to take the place of the lost cadencies. Now indeed one might well ask for guidance to the peculiarities of local usage.

Gradually our ways became more set, and neither of us liked contradiction. He developed many of the minor economies of our father – one of which was not to waste toilet paper, and he would observe the diameter of the roll in the guest room. Water was scarce in the volcanic island of Ischia, and economy in its use was very necessary. At great expense he had had installed a flush system, of which he was very proud, which was fed by a tank that was filled periodically from goat skins carried by donkeys. Our two daughters were staying with him as he had kindly thought that my wife and I might like a short holiday on our own. He brought Cyril Connolly to their room to demonstrate the modern addition to his home just as the flush had been pulled; there was a torrential flow carrying away, as was indeed desired, all that had to be removed, but not then obeying Jehovah's command to desist, so that the overhead tank was exhausted with precipitant haste of its contents. The resulting shame and anger at the failure of the mechanism quickly evaporated, and then entirely slipped his memory. That was one side of Wystan, a side which Stephen Spender once remarked was Wystan enjoying being Wystan. Another side was his great generosity and kindness. I do not know how many young students he helped financially through college; and he was good to his nieces, whom he loved dearly. He opened book accounts for both our daughters with Blackwells in Oxford, and he attended their weddings (that of Anita in Florence while still recovering from a broken shoulder blade after a car accident in Kirchstetten) and gave them handsome presents. The poem entitled *Epithalamium* was the result of the Rita–Peter wedding in 1965.

He maintained frequently the advantage which we had had in being born into a white Anglo-Saxon Protestant background, which was conducive to work and fundamental research and left him in the fortunate position of never being bored. But he had of course to admit the profundity and excellence of so much that had arisen from totally different environments. While we were born with the prejudice common to that background, he was from his youth singularly devoid of prejudices about class, religion and race (with the possible exception of the French). What he detested was expediency and evil in high places, whether in the Kremlin, Berchtesgaden or Whitehall.

In spite of his fame and wide friendships throughout America and Europe, he was lonely, lacking as a result of his personal psychology, a family of his own, but remembering our own happy early years. Recently he wanted more and more to see his family, to be met at airports, and to spend a few days with us in Thurloe Square, when in transit between America, Austria and Oxford. Seen unawares in an armchair, with *The Times* crossword puzzle on his knee, a vodka martini by his side and cigarette-ends covering large dishes, there was an isolation and sadness which arose from his uprooted and solitary existence. Whatever he may have said about the dangers of thuggery in New York, the main reason we are sure for his return to England was loneliness, and the prospect of a quasi-monastic existence among colleagues at Oxford. However since his professorship there in the 1950s Oxford had altered and the dreams of mellow common-room interchange did not appear to have been quite what he had hoped. He also complained that Oxford was noisier than New York.

Although strictly disciplined in regard to work every morning, and with only a beer or a plain martini at lunch, the evenings brought stiff vodkas and martinis from the freezer, which we would drink measure for measure. This sometimes led to a slight clumsiness of movement and blurring of speech. The last time he stayed with us in April 1973 he was called at about eight o'clock for a television recording, and we were uncertain how this would be undertaken. We need not have worried. Surrounded by the whole paraphernalia of broadcasting techniques he sat alone, as if on the moon's vacant surface, and recorded from unaided memory, movingly and with absolute confidence, a complex suite of poems.

He and I corresponded between Austria and France on our respective gerontic symptoms, and he admitted that just recently there had been a diagnosis of a defective heart; 'Whatever that means', he added. He had not long previously addressed himself with the words:

> Time, we both know, will decay You, and already
> I'm scared of our divorce . . . .

and he wanted to know exactly what was wrong with me which made me feel tired too quickly. An undated letter reached us on 27 September asking as usual to be met at Heathrow and to be put up on 2 October, but he died on the night of 28 September, after having given a very successful reading to the Austrian Society of Literature at the Palais Palffy. He was then offered supper but declined because of tiredness. He asked, however, to be sent back to his hotel in a *nice* car. His own was a Volkswagen which he used, notwithstanding his distaste for everything to do with motor cars, because it did have certain advantages in mobility (he often asserted that no cars should be allowed to exceed 30 mph and that they should all run on batteries). But this time, and quite out of normal character, he wanted something elegant.

On 3 October, together with a great friend of his from Ischia days, Thekla Clark, I collected his small bundle of belongings from the American Consulate in Vienna – his suit, pyjamas, a worn pair of bedroom slippers and a wrist watch, with little more than which he always travelled.

It was fitting that he should have been buried in the place which he had come to regard as his home, with its cats and dogs, books and records, and appropriate that the funeral was ecumenical, German prayers of the Catholic rite alternating with those in Cranmer's English. A lovely autumn day on a hillside close to the Wienerwald.

Amongst those things which will always remind us of him is the shy smile of recognition as he would come through the airport gates in his lopsided slippers.

Rosamira Bulley
A prep school reminiscence

Mrs Bulley was the daughter of the headmaster of Auden's preparatory school, St Edmund's

I have in front of me a school group of 1916 with Wystan Auden, sitting at my feet, and, behind my left shoulder, his life-long friend, and my cousin, Christopher Bradshaw-Isherwood (illustration no. 8). St Edmund's, the prep school that Wystan came to, was started a hundred years ago by my grandfather the Reverend John Morgan-Brown in Norfolk. It was continued by his son Cyril Morgan-Brown who had come down from Oxford with a First in Mods and Greats and who was headmaster at this time, the school having moved in 1901 to Hindhead. There were many who thought him a fine headmaster: a gentle person occasionally mistaken for the odd-job carpenter by prospective parents who caught a fleeting glimpse of him. I myself arrived in the school in the year of Queen Victoria's Golden Jubilee, but was not actively engaged with the boys until I joined the bottom form as a pupil at the age of seven. I lived in the school all my life and loved every minute of it until my husband, Ivo Bulley (head-master 1937–1952) and I retired in 1952. Since 1914 I had helped my father. As it was wartime my two aunts, who had fulfilled this function, felt it was their duty to make their precipitate departure and start a soup kitchen in the East End of London.

The group also includes two young mistresses of my own age and Miss Bertha Lowe, who was to teach Wystan the piano – and which she did, it has been said, by wielding a large red pencil over her pupils' knuckles, and which perhaps led to a rather staccato style of playing. She also played the organ. She had become decidedly deaf, but couldn't bear to retire until a parent, Field-Marshal Sir William Robertson, CIGS, who when he heard us shouting at her during drawing-room tea, said incredulously: 'Does Miss Lowe really teach the piano?'

The school itself, in front of which this photograph was taken, is a late Victorian country house, converted to our needs, surrounded by large and hilly grounds, very wild in those days. The school timetable had been unaltered from time immemorial. Classics, maths, French and divinity were there and of course music. English, it is interesting to note, was only represented by two hours of geography and two hours of history a week, out of which a few minutes were devoted to spelling, derivations and synonyms.

It was in the September term of 1915 that Wystan came to the school, one of four-teen new boys, including his elder brother John. I have a snapshot of twelve of those fourteen, in their Sunday Eton suits and stiff collars, sitting on a sunny bank among pine trees in the school grounds, and Wystan's face and figure bear out my remem-brance of him as a very fair-haired and plump small boy. I was very interested in looking up a number of the St Edmund's school chronicles to read the first mention of

Wystan. He first appears in December 1916, Volume VII. A holiday competition was held at the beginning of each autumn term, and this always resulted in a large exhibition, which was arranged in the drawing room. The entry reads '. . . in the first class all the exhibits were distinctly above average. Auden (1) showed a very good collection of shells. . . . His brother's notes on the prehistoric remains in that part of Wales where their holidays were spent were also very neat and good!' In that same competition Bradshaw-Isherwood got an honourable mention but it doesn't say for what. In the next competition Auden (2) presented a collection of 'insects, beetles, bees, flies and the like' and Isherwood achieved a first class for 'a carefully kept journal illustrated with postcards and photographs'.

Christopher had joined the school three years earlier. According to some of his writings he did not seem to have been as happy as Wystan was at St Edmund's. In fact, when he described how I slapped his face in the extracts of his book, *Kathleen and Frank*, published in *The Times Saturday Review* (16 October 1971), I felt impelled to write to the Editor of *The Times* in time for the publication date of the book to say that 'the Miss Rosa who is alleged to have slapped Bradshaw-Isherwood, C.W., fifty-seven years ago sincerely hopes that he has imbibed enough of the Morgan-Brown ethos to be ready now to turn the other cheek and to reciprocate the many happy memories she has of those far-off days!' Sure enough, there was an agreeable sequel. A cheerful reply came to me from Christopher in distant California, bearing no grudges and saying that he was attempting to give an objective impression or rather a guess at the feelings of people far, far away from him in time – including his ten-year-old self. 'As for the slap,' he wrote, 'I am sure it did nothing but good!'

Before looking in detail at the school chronicles of those days I must mention one vivid memory I have of Auden. A young man invalided from the army joined the staff and with enormous zeal organized the school into a military force which seemed to have considerably more officers and NCOs than privates. The great occasion was a Field Day in the Punch Bowl at Hindhead when Corporal Auden, waving a police rattle wildly over his head, represented a whole machine-gun corps. It was only one of the things that we did in the countryside around, so beautiful and unspoilt in those days. The highlights were the annual blackberry picnic, when 'firms' competed for the largest pickings – the smell of fresh blackberry jam at school tea was a memory of the Michaelmas term – and the carefree Ascension Day picnic when we were free to wander where we would.

However it will be of interest to wander through the chronicles. I don't remember that Wystan took much interest in games, but it was recorded that in the 1917 swimming races, 'Auden – won the Novices' Race, one length in eight seconds'. But in lifesaving in his last term the report of the Examiners of the Royal Life Saving Society reads, 'Very fair. Rather slow!'

Wystan always enjoyed music and acting. I quote from a passage about the variety entertainment put on by the Fourth and Upper Fourth, the top forms, in October 1919: 'Robinson, Fagge and Sant performed with much grace in a country dance which would have been excellent if the accompanist, Auden, had not taken the bit between his teeth and bolted. However, he recovered later and played his next accompaniment with much skill . . . he also recited.'

Auden must have been present at the Armistice Day memorial service in the Chapel in 1919 when the thirty-seven boys who had died were remembered in the first two minutes' silence. The flag on the field on its newly-erected flag pole was flown at half-mast; in the evening a bonfire was lit on the playground and, joining hands, we sang 'Auld Lang Syne'.

That Wystan was musical there is no doubt. 'Musical Notes', June 1920: 'the prize in Division 1 was gained by Auden, whose work was excellent both in quality and quantity, not only in the more attractive sections, such as the learning of new music, but also in the more humdrum but essential matter of care and accuracy in scale playing.' When an enlarged choir assisted by grown-ups gave a rendering of Lisa Lehmann's *Fairy Cantata* . . . 'A word of praise must be given to Auden, to whom fell the arduous task of leading the choir and to whom in great part the success of the attack was due.' The school chapel, where Auden at this time led the choir, had been opened in 1901 by Talbot, Bishop of Rochester, with the assistance of Cosmo Gordon Lang, who later became Archbishop of Canterbury. Wystan's mother later gave a fine crucifix for the chapel. Other prizes, besides music, came his way that term. He got the Form Prize for the top form and First Prize for mathematics.

On my marriage in 1919 my sister Winnie, who after coming down from Oxford with an honours degree in history, taught for ten years at Downe House, took over my tasks. Therefore Auden was in her care for his last term at St Edmund's. This set the scene for the following excerpts from the chronicle reporting the formation of the St Edmund's School Literary Society: 'It was most extraordinary that Miss Winnie should be planning, simultaneously and independently, the same thing as Auden and Llewellyn Smith – namely the foundation of a literary or Shakespeare reading club. Their united efforts produced a club, afterwards always known as the Lit. Soc. The society was composed of Miss Winnie, Auden (President), Llewellyn Smith (Hon. Sec.) and seven members.' It was a stately affair; members addressed each other with formality as 'Mr' and on the last meeting of the term they partook of ginger wine and biscuits. The meetings were lovingly described in the *Times Literary Supplement* of 5 November 1971, where it was remembered that there was a short-lived Literary Society journal, whose first and only number contained a great variety of matter, such as 'The Religion of India', 'A Clever Parody' and 'An Account of the Growth of the South East and Chatham Railway.'

Wystan left for Gresham's School, Holt, in September 1920. He just missed getting a scholarship and as a result was placed in too low a form and found the work easy. The next term another old St Edmund's boy, Timberg, wrote from Holt, 'There are really very few St Edmund's boys at Holt at present. I suppose that one can put this down to the fact that Holt is essentially a modern school: Harrow, Rugby, Winchester and others are more appealing to the ear!' Wystan himself wrote that he was enjoying himself very much. 'The buildings are excellent and also the teaching. We all have studies. Your first few terms you share with about three others, then less; finally you get a single study. John [his brother] is in the Science Sixth at Marlborough . . . he has just joined the English Literature Society and enjoys it very much.'

The last entry in the chronicles reads: 'A note from Mrs Auden gives us some welcome news of W. H. Auden (1915–1920). He has just won the top scholarship at Holt (which he had missed the year before). He has also been acting and took the part of Miss Ashford in *The Private Secretary*. This was in the house play and his acting was such that he has been chosen for a part in the school play which comes off in July.'

This was as far as I know the last time that we heard directly from Auden in the following years and it was all the more of a pleasant surprise, when we heard from two other old boys and former members of the Lit. Soc., Harold Llewellyn Smith, contemporary and old friend, and John Willett, of a younger generation, that Auden was anxious to hold a lunch party when he was in England, to honour Miss Winnie as co-founder of the St Edmund's School Literary Society and to celebrate its jubilee. And so it was that in October 1971 in a corner of Odin's restaurant, off Marylebone High Street, Wystan Auden took his place beside Miss Winnie Morgan-Brown and in company with various old boys, past members of the Lit. Soc. – Harold and Jack Llewellyn Smith, John Willett, Christopher Cornford, John Fennell, Ronald Hope-Jones, Michael Walker, David Edwards, and finally myself and my daughter, Anne Maier, both of us 'old boys'. Sadly no present St Edmund's boy was there as the Lit. Soc. ceased to exist in 1960. The luncheon was a delightful and convivial affair and it was rather nice to hear Wystan, shouting down the table and trying to draw my attention by calling, 'Miss Rosa'. He told me that his schooldays seemed like yesterday. Eventually towards four o'clock the party began to break up and John Willett returned from seeing Wystan in his new long overcoat and carpet slippers off down the street, saying 'I think I have pointed him vaguely in the direction of home!'

Harold Llewellyn Smith
At St Edmund's 1915-1920

Harold Llewellyn Smith was Auden's contemporary at his preparatory school

You must picture a rather chubby, smooth-cheeked little boy, with very fair hair, who stared you in the eye and whose nickname, 'Dodo', didn't suit him, being merely inherited from an elder brother, whom it did.

What sort of a child was he? What were his tastes and interests? Was there anything about them which hindsight can perceive as pointing to a poet's calling? Although I suppose I was about his closest friend during our years as boarders at St Edmund's, and though more than once we stayed in each other's home during school holidays, I find it difficult, after the lapse of half a century, to give assured answers to such questions.

It is said that Wystan, aged eight, signalled his arrival at the school by announcing that he looked forward to studying the different psychological types! I cannot personally vouch for this legend, although I am perfectly ready to accept its authenticity. Wystan, as a small boy, was not only clever and precocious, but was also well aware of the fact. He liked talking for effect; but he was not insincere and there was never anything cynical or hard-boiled about him, though there was a strong sense of fun. He was essentially warm-hearted and a good deal more sensitive, and even thin-skinned, than he cared to appear. He could have been unhappy at boarding school, but he was immediately made 'at home' by the headmaster's daughter, 'Miss Rosa', to whom he became and remained devoted. When Rosa was married and her role in the school passed to her elder sister Winnie, it took a little time for Wystan to accept the change; for Miss Winnie came to us from Downe House, a celebrated girls' school, and there were dark forebodings that practices like putting us 'on our honour', which we considered only fit for girls, might insinuate themselves! However Miss Winnie soon cast her own magic spell over all of us and Wystan was captivated with the rest. With the headmaster, Cyril Morgan-Brown himself, I think Wystan was never wholly at ease. He held 'Ciddy' in high respect, as we all did, for the gentleman and scholar that he was; but he was wary of him too, for Ciddy had an uncomfortable knack of deflating bumptious little boys. So it was that, when an incident occurred at the beginning of Wystan's last year, which a question to Ciddy might have cleared up, the question was never asked. Wystan had counted upon being head of the school, but Ciddy passed him over to begin with, against all precedent and unfortunately without a softening word of explanation. Wystan digested his mortification in silence and though, in the following term, he duly became head boy, the original wound left its small scar.

There is no doubt that Wystan was extremely fortunate in his family, and not in the matter of genes alone. Their home at Harborne, though comfortable, was one in which the arts (especially music) and the sciences were valued far above material luxuries. He greatly revered his father – a man of wide scholarship – and he adored his mother, a devout Anglican of high church inclinations. The latter spoilt 'Witny' somewhat, as being the youngest of her three sons. The eldest, Bernard, had gone to Canada quite early in life; the second, John, was, like Wystan, at St Edmund's. Conversation at home was stimulating; books were plentiful; the piano was daily in use and there was a much-loved terrier called Vigi to be exercised. I remember with gratitude how I myself was first introduced to the translations of Gilbert Murray, the architecture of Chartres and the crags of Tryfan through visits to the Auden home.

Wystan was certainly happy at St Edmund's. He had no aptitude or liking for games, on which popularity at a prep school so much depends; yet he made friends easily, lessons presented few difficulties and he enjoyed his music. He played the piano well, by the not very exacting standards of the day, and he had a good treble voice. He took a frank delight in displaying his remarkable general knowledge. On one occasion, when two forms that were accustomed to share a single room for prep were sundered for disciplinary reasons, he dubbed the event 'The Great Schism' and treated us to a short discourse on the late fourteenth century. He was then aged ten. No less remarkable and doubtless more important was his relatively mature sense of justice. Those were the days when, in the estimation of schoolboys, cheating was an offence hardly less heinous than stealing, and Wystan certainly did not take a permissive attitude on the subject himself. But he saw things in better proportion than most of us. Once, when a case of cheating had been exposed, and there was a move to 'take it out of' the culprit, I remember Wystan speaking up and declaring that cheating to avoid punishment, though wrong, was less wrong than cheating to obtain a prize and that, in any case, both of them were less wrong than lynch-law.

I would say that throughout his years at the school the bias of Wystan's many interests was scientific – mining engineering being prominent among them – but he became increasingly fascinated by words, so that, by the time he left, he knew that his future lay with the humanities. He was always fond of poetry, though he found no more joy in Latin prosody than the rest of us. His favourite poems, I remember, included Christina Rosetti's 'Uphill', and R. H. Barham's 'As I laye a-thynkynge'. But that he was destined to become a poet himself neither he nor any of us guessed. A second interest of his, which deepened as he grew older, was his Anglo-Catholicism. His attraction towards high church doctrines and practices was no doubt in the first place due to the influence of his mother; but in his last year at the school it was fortuitously strengthened by the avdent on the school staff of the Rev. G. G. Newman, whom we boys believed, quite erroneously, to be some sort of nephew of the cardinal. We duly went to confession – Wystan leading, I following, not without hesitation.

Wystan was one of those boys who set the tone of their group. In trying to recall his special friends, it is natural to think first of Christopher Isherwood, who became his valued collaborator and close friend in later years. But Isherwood was some three years older than Auden, which limited their contacts, and there were others, like Leslie Hutchinson, who were nearer contemporaries. I remember the planning of an ambitious historical novel between Auden, Isherwood and myself, which was carried out surreptitiously while we should at least have been going through the motions of playing cricket. It was to have been in the manner of Harrison-Ainsworth, to whose works Wystan was at the time addicted, and its 'Gothic' scenario was shamelessly derived from Marple Hall, the ancestral seat of the Bradshaw-Isherwoods. I can still gloat over Christopher's luscious descriptions of tapestried galleries where suits of armour alternated with shelves of books bound in leather 'inlaid with great lozenges of velvet'. Needless to say, the project did not get far.

In our last year (by which time Isherwood had left) we jointly planned the School Literary Society which Rosa Bulley recalls in her contribution. This time the venture was not only launched, but, thanks to Miss Winnie's sponsorship, remained afloat for many years to come. Papers were presented, plays were read – I remember Wystan playing Peter Quince; in short a good time was had by all in Winnie's hospitable room. The last time I saw Wystan was in October 1971, at the reunion of some of the Society's members with Winnie and Rosa in London, and for a few happy hours time rolled back more than fifty years.

Two years later came the news of his death and I felt impelled to take down the volume of poetry, presented to me by the Society, and to read again the final stanzas of those two poems which he had so loved as a child.

Robert Medley
Gresham's School,[1] Holt

Robert Medley went to the same public school as Auden and designed the sets for the original productions of the Auden-Isherwood plays

Wystan arrived at Gresham's School, Holt in the autumn of 1920, exactly one year later than me. Gresham's then, when Wystan and I were there, was a new kind of public school: it had modern ideals and was based on modern curricula; very little Latin was taught and no Greek. Corporal punishment and bullying were practically unknown and there was an absence of snobbery about social class. If the buildings were too recent to harbour age-old customs, like torturing new boys and other tribal habits, we were constantly reminded that the tradition at Gresham's was a moral one – Greshamian boys were *ipso facto* kinder and more virtuous than any others. Progressive but not cranky, it was exactly designed to appeal to cultured parents of the liberal professional classes; it is therefore not surprising that we both landed up at the same school.

What was good and what was amiss with Gresham's stemmed directly from Howson, a forward-looking headmaster who had come to the school in 1905 and who had died the year before Wystan arrived; his creed was that 'boys could be trusted to behave, if put on their honour to do so'. The sting, as we shall see, was in the tail.

When Wystan arrived he was put into the lower third, but fortunately it was soon noticed that he was an exceptionally bright boy and in the following year was given an open scholarship and promptly moved up two forms. Thereafter he floated up the senior school without effort; he never bothered to make a show in class, and many thought him lazy. When he came up to London and stayed with my parents while taking his matriculation in 1923, he astonished my sister by going over John Ireland's *The Holy Boy* on the piano, before breakfast on the day of the exam, explaining to her exactly how it should be played. He left Gresham's in 1925 with the expected scholarship: 'Natural Science – Christ Church – Oxon.'; a fact duly recorded in gold lettering on the black honours board.

On his death Howson was succeeded by his trusted lieutenant, J. R. Eccles, whose mission it was to carry on the teachings of the 'master'. A compulsively precise bachelor, J.R.E. bustled about like an energetic scout-leader in gown and mortar-board and usually carrying an armful of books. He had an effective style of public speaking either in school or chapel and his peculiar mannerisms of delivery and phrasing are exactly caught, and made use of, by Auden in his 'Address for a Prize Day' (*The*

---

[1] All quotations, unless plainly otherwise, are from: W. H. Auden, 'Honour – Gresham's School', in *The Old School*, ed. Graham Greene (Jonathan Cape, 1934).

Orators) and later in Ransom's opening speech in *The Ascent of F6*. I have never known an old boy of our generation fail to recognize the original. Over-conscientious, lacking in humour, and, I suspect, a bit of an actor, J.R.E. was not the Olympian figure that Howson must have been. He not infrequently misjudged the sophistication of his audience and so, from the boys' point of view, he could be made fun of: as when he addressed the upper sixth divinity class (Monday mornings) on a pamphlet entitled 'Jesus Christ Cuts No Ice in California'; 'Question number one: Who cuts no what – where?' Wystan, who was a good mimic, lived off this one for several weeks.

Owing to the shortage of younger men during the war, there remained a number of seemingly elderly teachers on the staff. They are those whom I remember the best, particularly Walter Greatorex (The Ox), who had charge of the music.

We never penetrated the mystery of how it was that Greatorex whom we regarded as one of the great musicians of the land, came to be stranded in Holt. He combined haughty indifference with the greatest kindness and tact. Of Greatorex, Wystan wrote:

> I owe not only such knowledge of music as I possess, but my first friendship with a grown-up person, with all that that means. As a musician he was in the first rank. I do not think it was only partiality that made me feel, when later I heard Schweitzer play Bach on the organ, that he played no better.

On consecutive Sundays one term, Greatorex treated us to most, if not all the preludes and fugues. Wystan sang in the choir. The Psalms were done to Gregorian chants.

We were encouraged to form societies in extension of our interests, and Wystan took an active part for us, out of school hours, in the Arts and Archaeological Society. Early in 1923 with Mervyn Roberts (my other close friend and an exceptional pianist) Wystan promoted a recital of modern music which was introduced by Greatorex (the programme included Delius, McEwen, Bax, Ireland and Elgar). Later the same year he gave a talk on 'Comparative Folklore'. Wystan is also remembered 'as a small boy from "Farfield" [his house] talking about Psychology'.

There were of course official school concerts and lectures. Myra Hess (1922) played for us; of this concert the ecstatic young reviewer (not Wystan) wrote 'We were so carried away on the wings of music that we forgot all about her.' G. L. Mallory, the mountaineer, gave an illustrated lecture about Everest. Finally, that autumn, there was the hilarious occasion when Mrs Watts-Dunton, dressed in pale, sea-green Liberty silk and hung with moon-stone necklaces, gave a lecture on the celebrated deceased Theodore without mentioning Swinburne; she read a lot of poems about gypsies. Subsequently we went to Putney and looked at the outside of The Pines.

During 1921 I was absent from Gresham's for the best part of a year, recovering from a road accident (my bicycle skidding in the snow of a cold Easter, I had been thrown under a steam-wagon). It was not, therefore, until March 1922, that Wystan and I met for the first time, by Wystan's contrivance, in the bus that took the Sociological Society to visit a boot factory in Norwich. I was then sixteen and Wystan just fifteen.

The term following that of our meeting, the summer of 1922, found us together in the annual Shakespearian production in the 'school woods' where there was an open-air theatre. In these 'idyllic' surroundings, strewn with leaves which were usually so damp that sitting on the ground was a discomfort, we played that year *The Taming of the Shrew*. Wystan was cast as Katherina and played opposite that excellent and now professional actor, Sebastian Shaw, as Petrucchio. I played Biondello. Of this production the reviewer in *The Gresham* writes: 'Another delightful setting in the theatre, a cast of exceptionally high standard, a splendid Petrucchio. Auden struggled nobly against overwhelming odds to give Katherina her rightful dominant position in the play, but was completely swamped by Petrucchio's all pervading personality the moment he appeared. To do justice to the character Katherina is an extremely trying task for a mere male, and Auden was far from assisted by a poor wig and clothes that can only be described as shocking. Under so many adverse circumstances, however, it reflected the greatest credit on him that he contrived to infuse considerable dignity into his passionate outbursts and, moreover, by his spirited performance showed that determination can overcome almost insurmountable difficulties.' This review was, I suspect, written by Armand Trêves, the sharp-witted French master (another mystery, whom some credited with being an extreme left-wing political exile).

Sebastian Shaw recalls 'a small, slightly puffy little boy with pink and white cheeks and almost colourless hair', not very good at being a girl, 'red wrists projecting from frilly sleeves and never knowing what to do with his hands. His voice however was clear and his diction excellent.'

Schoolboy friendships develop fast, and though we rapidly became close and intimate companions I was totally unaware of the real extent of Wystan's feelings for me. That I remained so obtuse, so innocent as to be insensitive, is a fact that can only be explained in terms of my own adolescent problems which I had short-circuited by identifying my longings with the unattainable, a friend of mine at Gresham's, whom my imagination had endowed with the purity and sanctity to which I aspired, and which I supposed him to possess by a gift of nature.

It was not until I was visiting Wystan, at his parents' home in Harborne, a year after I had left Gresham's to become an art student in London, that his father discovered among Wystan's poems, through which we had been privately going the previous night, one which described me at the school swimming pool and in which he suspected an erotic content. The following morning we were put 'on the mat'. Dr Auden gently explained that he himself as a young man had also enjoyed a close friendship, but that it was not desirable, nor had it ever gone 'that' far – had we in fact gone 'that' far? It was with relief that we were truthfully able to assure him that our relationship was purely platonic. In this way our friendship was allowed to survive without parental interference from either side.

With regard to the subject matter of the poem I recall that as a boy I was a very good swimmer and diver, and during the summer term spent much of my time at the swimming pool. Wystan, soon after our meeting, seeing me larking around with other boys and taking them on double-dives, off the top diving-board, asked me to do the same with him. This elementary trick, which had never caused me the least concern before, was done by taking your partner either on your shoulders, or 'pick-a-back'. I explained to Wystan his part in the operation, particularly to keep his head down. After some difficulty in getting him to grip firmly with his legs and not to strangle me with his arms, all was declared ready and off we went to disaster. Wystan emerged from the water with a badly bleeding nose. Feeling responsible, I was very upset, but it was the first time I had encountered his innate physical clumsiness. Also I suppose it was as near as we, or most of us, ever got to an embrace at Gresham's.

Wystan visited me and my family regularly either in London, or in Yorkshire, where my parents leased a house, and which was very much Wystan's kind of country. In London we used to go to Harold Monroe's Poetry Bookshop (of Chap-Book fame), to the theatre, Basil Dean's productions of Capek's *The Insect Play* and *R.U.R.* (the early Robot play) and inevitably to Rutland Boughton's opera *The Immortal Hour*. We also visited mutual school friends like Chris Bailey, the electronic genius of Farfield who, with his own home-made apparatus, broadcast the private fatuities of the speeches on Prize Day to the passers-by on the high road to Sheringham.

My parents, who were not easy to please, were fond of Wystan and he fitted very well into a family of six – except that he won too frequently at card games like Slippery Ann or at paper games. We had to sleep in the same bedroom with my youngest brother and we sometimes wondered how much he had heard of the conversations that went on, as it seemed, for half the night; or what my father really felt about Beethoven symphonies on the gramophone before breakfast.

Wystan differed from the more artistic friends like Mervyn Roberts, whom I had known before I met Wystan, in being very articulate. He already had that clinical imagination which surveyed areas and experiences unfamiliar to me. After my accident I had returned to Gresham's disillusioned with school, and this would have appealed to him. I now considered myself already very well informed in all those matters that concerned me most, and therefore school seemed to me a phase of life to be got through as quickly as possible. I did not belong to Gresham's any more.

We had plenty to talk about. To summarize my attitudes to life at that time, I would say they consisted of a romantic and muddled mixture of William Morris's Guild Socialism, the social anarchy of Kropotkin's *Mutual Aid*, Shelley and Blake's *Marriage of Heaven and Hell*. I had recently refused Confirmation.

Walking one afternoon towards the woods which lay about a mile and a half on the far side of the Sheringham Road, I made an attack on the Church and discovered to my surprise that Wystan was devout. An argument followed and to soften what I feared might become a serious breach, after a pause, I asked him if he wrote poetry, confessing by way of exchange, that I did. I was a little surprised that he had not tried and suggested he might do so.

At the end of the year (1922) when I was barely seventeen, I left Gresham's to study at art school. Then followed the period of letters from him and sheaves of poems. My opinions being called for and his handwriting taking so long to read, I took them about with me in various coat pockets to study on buses or walking over Primrose Hill to the Academy School or later the Slade. In this way Wystan's *juvenilia* became eroded. I fear, moreover, that I did not always answer him promptly; years later I was reproached for this. Wystan of course had kept copies, and when he allowed a few to appear in Christopher Isherwood's *Lions and Shadows*, I recognized them as those which I had received years previously.

Meanwhile for Wystan, back at Gresham's, there was a crisis that had to be resolved and, more importantly, lived through. In many ways Gresham's was an excellent school, but, if we are to give roundness to his experience, the shadow must be taken together with the light.

In a climate far less favourable to discussion than now, Wystan had become fully aware of his sexual nature by the time of my leaving school. The moral problem which this set him was complicated by the operation of the 'honour system' (now long abandoned) whereby Howson, in a particularly nasty and underhand way, sought to guarantee our behaviour by repression of the growth of our instincts. Every new boy was seen by the headmaster, privately, about two weeks after his arrival and made to promise: (1) not to smoke or drink; (2) not to swear; (3) not to say or do anything indecent. Your agreement was then called for (refusal would have been impossible) to the following: (1) if you broke any of these promises you should report this breach to your housemaster; (2) if you saw anyone else break them you should endeavour to persuade him to report and if he refused you should report him yourself. This pernicious system whereby the new boys' ardent emotions of loyalty were enlisted and identified with the honour of the school (i.e. to the community as seen by those in authority) we now recognize as the trick played by totalitarian dictators. Also, as Wystan afterwards wrote, 'I believe no more potent engine was ever devised for turning boys into neurotic innocents.' This acute emotional and moral problem, which struck at the very roots of his being, Wystan resolved with great perception, in terms of a conflict of loyalties: 'what do you owe to the community'; 'what do you owe to yourself'. The experience of this struggle with himself was the catalyst that precipitated the moralist and the didactic in him. The first part of his double question was certainly made clear – Who am I?; and the second implicit question – What should I become? – occupied the poet Auden for the rest of his life.

In his final term at Gresham's, summer 1925, a production of *The Tempest* was to be the annual school play. Wystan was determined to play Caliban and succeeded in being chosen for the part. The significance of the role for him was that when the play ends Ariel is dismissed, Prospero puts on his old clothes to go home in, and Caliban, who has learned only to curse his masters, inherits the island. With extraordinary psychological insight Wystan perceived that, implicated in Caliban, was a protest against the honour system, under which he had suffered so much; the occasion for making a witty, personal and deeply felt 'send-up' of the system was not to be missed.

Equally revealing was Auden's contribution to the *Grasshopper* (1955) (the fiftieth anniversary memorial to Howson) entitled *'Qui e l'uom Felice?'* It invites the reader in the form of a question-and-answer game (the rules are carefully set) to get to know himself. He told me at the time that he thought he had solved the problem rather neatly and that he considered it was the only valuable advice he could give to Greshamians. It is the only contribution that makes no reference whatsoever to the school.

Described at school as 'alone but not aloof', Wystan was found on several occasions by R. P. Bagnall-Oakley, the school naturalist and a local scholar, in the early hours of the morning as far away from Holt as Weybourne, standing alone, looking at the sea; this confirms Wystan's own account of his habits like watching a 'June dawn at Hempstead Mills'. Of this period I remember that he sent me a book of Edward Carpenter's and a little later *Poems of Edward Thomas* (which I still possess).

Certainly Wystan was and felt himself to be alone; set apart by the crucial experience of the self-realization that he had had to face up to, and in which he had refused to deny his nature and the source of his creative being. With his self-knowledge characteristic modes of thought found their place and the moral certainty about himself, which matched up to his exceptional and precocious intellect, was formed.

I should mention here that the house-prefect referred to by Wystan in his article on Gresham's for *The Old School* as 'Wreath', was Michael Fordham, who later in life became a well-known Jungian psychoanalyst. Fordham helped Wystan to reconcile himself somewhat to school life, and also, no doubt, to the control of his intense dislike of Mr R—, his housemaster who was also the producer of *The Tempest*. The origin of this dislike was the earlier occasion when Mr R— caught Wystan writing a poem during prep and remarked, 'You should not waste your sweetness on the decent air like this, Auden.' For many years Wystan could not think of this incident 'without wishing him evil' and it is referred to again in a fine, early poem in the line 'The death by cancer of a once-hated master'.

As a senior, Wystan served on the school library committee, an appointment which afforded him much satisfaction; there would, I fear, be no records remaining of a time so long ago to indicate if his own personal preferences were included.

It was less understandable, to me, that Wystan, the most unlikely of soldiers, should voluntarily choose to go to the Annual OTC (Officers' Training Corps) Camp where the Gresham's contingent would join up with those from other public schools for a week's training under professional army officers; but of course I did not then understand his appreciation of parochial life, or his need to live in contact with small and understandable communities. It also appealed to his sense of the absurd; he pointed out afterwards that I had missed a lot of fun, and also the chance of witnessing the unexpected and surprising behaviour of some of the 'pure and virtuous' when in close contact with the 'rude' from less inhibited schools.

Wystan later claimed that the honour system was generally known as 'half-watt hypnotism'; it may have been so, but not until after I had left Gresham's. The phrase anticipates the kind of clinical terminology he used so effectively in *The Orators*.

In many ways Gresham's was a good school for his parents to have chosen and Wystan confessed that 'Taking all things into consideration I was very happy throughout my time there.' It had the advantage of being a relatively small school, and as most of us came from comparable backgrounds, it had a certain homogeneity. Setting aside the crucial exception of our sexual education, the atmosphere was accommodating rather than prohibitive.

That none of us at Gresham's, including myself, realized that we had among us an outstanding human being and a great poet is excusable since he never indulged in the vanity of sharpening his wits at other people's expense; he also took care to nurture his genius and his ambitions in secret. Though I was privileged to share many of his secrets there were naturally others that remained shielded from premature inspection. However precocious his intellect, he was not precocious in the exhibition of his genius; unlike Shelley, perhaps, or Mozart – or indeed, Benjamin Britten who came to the school some years later and for whom special arrangements had to be made.

It would be true to say that by the time Wystan went to Oxford his character and all that went with it, was already formed. Disciplined and unafraid, he was able to make full use of the opportunities that the university could offer.

As soon as Wystan was settled enough to invite a guest I went to Christ Chuch for a weekend. It was now my turn to envy him his life there; he was free whilst I, after three years at art school was still living at home. I did not know that within a matter of months I would be in Paris with Rupert Doone.

Inevitably we now saw each other less regularly though he came to Yorkshire on several occasions; if my memory serves me rightly, the last was soon after his return from Berlin. It was therefore no accident that shortly after the formation of the Group Theatre, Rupert and I should write to Wystan, then teaching in Helensburgh, to ask him to stay with us in Fitzroy Street. It was on this visit, in the autumn of 1932, that he suggested writing *The Dance of Death* for us. This we received during the summer of 1933. It was put into rehearsal in the autumn and given a first performance on a Sunday late in February 1934. Later that year the Group Theatre season, at the Westminster Theatre, opened with the first public performances of T. S. Eliot's *Sweeney Agonistes* and *The Dance of Death*; the forthcoming production of *The Dog Beneath the Skin* was also announced.

The history of this period until 1939, during which I became, as designer, the servant of two masters, if not more, does not properly belong here, with its intricate pattern of divergent ambitions and divided loyalties; but I felt honoured and very touched when, after the war, Wystan proposed that I should design *The Rake's Progress*. That, in the upshot, I did not do so, was a matter of some relief to me, because I did not consider I was the most suitable choice. Moreover I needed to get back to painting and to have done with the stage. However, I never spoke to Wystan of my doubts or confessed that I was glad that his judgement had never to be called into question, because I knew from experience how easily he could be hurt. Anyway, the age of discussion was over.

Sir John Betjeman
Oxford

Sir John Betjeman, the Poet Laureate, was a friend of Auden's at Oxford

When we first met we were Oxford undergraduates. I was adolescent enough to think that learning was the accumulation of facts and getting dates right. I greatly reverenced dons and thought that schoolmasters were men who were not full enough of facts to be made fellows of an Oxford or Cambridge college. When at Marlborough I had had the run of a little-used part of the library which contained, bound in leather, the whole run of Alfred H. Miles' *Poets and Poetry of the Nineteenth Century*. The short biographies and clear criticisms of these excellent volumes, together with the selected examples of the poets, are still fresh in my mind. At school and at Oxford I generally had with me the *Oxford Book of English Verse* and Quiller-Couch's still unsurpassed *Oxford Book of Victorian Verse*. I felt I knew as much about poetry as a schoolmaster, nearly as much as a don and certainly much more than my fellow undergraduates. Witness then my horror on being introduced to a tall milky-skinned and coltish member of 'The House' (Christ Church), who contradicted all my statements about poetry, who did not think Lord Alfred Douglas was a better sonneteer than Shakespeare, who had read Ebenezer Elliott and Philip Bourke Marston and other poets whom I regarded as my special province and who was not in the least interested in the grand friends I had made in the House – such as John Dumfries, Christopher Sykes, Edward James, Harold and William Acton and Bryan Guiness; who dismissed the Sitwells in a sentence and really admired the boring Anglo-Saxon poets like Beowulf whom we had read in the English school; and who was a close friend of John Bryson and Nevill Coghill, real dons who read Anglo-Saxon, Gutnish, Finnish and probably Swedish and Faroese as easily as I read the gossip column of the *Cherwell* of which I was then an editor. And yet there was an oracular quality about this tough youth in corduroys that compelled my attention. He was very attractive and quite unselfconscious and already a born schoolmaster and lecturer.

He would not come to the fashionable luncheons with peers and baronets and a sprinkling of dons which I liked to attend and sometimes gave myself. He was not a member of the 'Georgeoisie' like Alan Pryce-Jones and Mark Oglivie-Grant who dined every night at the George restaurant to the strains of a string band. (Mark Oglivie-Grant once came into the restaurant in a bathing dress with seaweed in his hair and carrying a looking-glass.) He didn't belong to the OUDS like Osbert Lancaster or Peter Fleming. He belonged to no clique. When he asked me to tea in his rooms high up in the north-west corner of Peck (Peckwater Quad) I felt I was district-visiting, so snobbish was I, so other-worldly he. There it was that I found out where his heart was. He had quite enjoyed his life at Gresham's School, but did not seem to have retained Greshamian friends in Oxford. At this time it was fashionable, in my set, for undergraduates to regard their parents as brutal philistines. Auden, on the other hand, much reverenced his father. They lived in Edgbaston and his mother was high church as I was. He often spoke with affection of his parents and brother, of Birmingham and the country around it and was very proud of a relation who had written the decidedly antiquarian Methuen *Little Guide to Shropshire*. He was interested in sanitation as his father had been and was, even after I had gone down from Oxford, always asking me for the return of a book with coloured illustrations of soil-pipes and domestic privies for the working classes which he had lent me and which I had lost.

Wystan (the name is that of a Saxon saint whose church Wistanstow is fully noted in Auden's *Little Guide to Shropshire*) was unaware that he represented the new type of Oxford undergraduate. I was the old type, trivial, baroque, incense-loving; a diner with a great admiration for the landowning classes and the houses and parks in which they were lucky enough to live. Wystan was already aware of slum conditions in Birmingham and mining towns and docks. But he combined with this an intense interest in geology and natural history and topography of the British Isles. He liked railways and canals and had a knowledge of Bradshaw's timetables. He liked visiting churches old and new. He loved the Isle of Man, its railways, trams and trains, and first encouraged me to go there. Above all he liked poetry, chanting it aloud after tea. In this he enjoyed the complicated internal rhymes in Irish hedge poetry and the alliteration of Anglo-Saxon poetry. The alliteration of Swinburne seemed false by comparison. The two friends of his I recall meeting in his rooms at this time were Gabriel Carritt (later Bill Carritt the politician) and William McElwee who became a schoolmaster at Stowe. They must have been interested in the music, a side of Wystan's life I was never able to share except in the appreciation of verbal rhythm.

Wystan and I much enjoyed discovering unknown poets, preferably of the last century and the Edwardian age and reading out our discoveries to each other. This was how we stumbled on the works of the Reverend Doctor E. E. Bradford, D.D., whose lyrics, innocent and touching about the love of 'lads', as boys were so often called by scout-masters in those days, used to bring us uncontrollable mirth.

> Once a schoolboy newly come,
> Timid, frail and friendless,
> Feared to face a footer scrum
> Oh! the taunts were endless.
>
> Suddenly he drew apart
> Soon they heard him crying.
> With a penknife in his heart
> Home they brought him dying.

This was the Auden I knew at Oxford and whom I was to meet later in the documentary film world and at home, when I was first married, in Uffington, Berkshire, where he rapidly wrote in some parts for a village play which my wife was producing. We never lost touch with him. The last two times we met were in the Refreshment Room of the Great Central Railway on Marylebone Station, before it was ruined by re-decoration and, more conventionally, at a poetry recital given by the BBC.

Gabriel Carritt
A friend of the family

Gabriel Carritt was an Oxford friend of Auden's. This article was written in conjunction with Rex Warner, the poet and critic, who was another Oxford contemporary

These are the reminiscences of Rex Warner and myself. Rex was at Wadham College, two years senior to Wystan, I was with him at Christ Church, but one year his junior. I went to Christ Church with a scholarship from Sedbergh School, well known for its rugger XV, of which I had been captain.

I remember him in various circles, sometimes with the friends who were senior to me, Rex, Cecil Day Lewis, Louis MacNeice, and, from Cambridge, Christopher Isherwood and Edward Upward. They were all writing then and intended to make that their life. More often I met him with my own contemporaries, Stephen Spender, Sidney Newman, organist scholar at Christ Church, and Dick Crossman.

These are our first impressions of Wystan. Rex writes: 'I first met Auden towards the end of my second year. My impressions of him were of a more than ordinary boyishness, a fresh, unwrinkled, pink face and an amazing intellectual ebullience. His appetite for facts and ideas was voracious. His rapid voluble conversation, full of delightful twists and turns, had always a kind of positive character which distinguished him from most of us.'

On the contrary, as a freshman, I was full of awe. I did not understand much of what Wystan said, when I first met him at the college Essay Club, but I felt certain it was important because of the portentous manner in which he said it. Although I had grown up in a don's family, my life at Sedbergh and preoccupation with success at football had kept me green, so it was not surprising that his Johnsonian manner, his questing, mocking, emphatic talk overwhelmed me. It took me some while to realize that Wystan was exploring his own ideas and experimenting with words. Rex said he often assumed different roles, his favourite being that of a headmaster, or a school prefect, and examples of this role playing appear in *The Orators*.

My impression of his appearance differs from that of Rex. I remember him as loosely put together, flat-footed, with big chubby hands and well-bitten nails, fumbling with a cigarette, and a big mobile face good at expressing contrived emotions. He was conventionally dressed and tidy, but wore his clothes as if they did not fit.

Rex sums up very well the general impression he made on his contemporaries: 'He differed profoundly from his contemporaries in several respects. Most of us whatever face of confidence we might put on, were at a loss. Faced with the apparent absoluteness of crisis of the thirties, Wystan always had or thought he had, some curative or specific, often based on some medical or psycho-analytic theory, things which at that time were somewhat strange and consequently exciting. He used to snatch up ideas, information, scraps of conversation with the assiduity of a jackdaw and would neatly label and catalogue his findings with enormous rapidity.'

Our friendship grew during the walks we took in Wytham woods above the Thames and on the downs above Wantage and later among old workings on the fells. He admired nature poets, such as Thomas Hardy and Edward Thomas and the way the Anglo-Saxon poets created the atmosphere of the northern land and seascapes, but he himself was not interested in nature; unless nature was reclaiming old mines and derelict machinery. His fascination with these scenes is often apparent in the small volume of poems published while he was at Oxford. Rex writes of this attitude to nature as follows: 'We used to go for long and talkative walks in the neighbourhood of the gasworks, a locale already sanctified by a phrase in *The Waste Land*, and I can remember expeditions in canoes with Wystan and Cecil Day Lewis up evil-smelling tunnels. He was somewhat disappointed in the canals I was able to show him near my home in Gloucestershire. In so far as these waterways were disused and overgrown they got high marks, but the vegetation and fairly rare birds left him unmoved.'

Wystan was attached to the fells round Sedbergh but chiefly as the background of the tough boys and masters I used to describe to him. Some of these appeared later in the *The Ascent of F6* and he wrote a very funny poem about the Sedbergh football xv, which he dedicated to me as its one-time captain. This appeared in the first edition of *The Orators* and was, I think, subsequently omitted, and it may therefore be of interest to quote some stanzas:

> Walk on air do we? And how
> With panther's pad, with his lightness
> Never did members conspire till now
> In such whole gladness:
> Currents of joy incalculable in ohms
> Wind from the spine along the moving arms
> Over the great alkali wastes of the bowel, calming them too.
>
> Success my dears – Ah
> Rounding the curve of the drive
> Standing up, waving, cheering from the car,
> The time of their life:
> The fags are flushed, would die at their heroes' feet;
> Quick someone tug at that handle, get
> At them shouting, shoulder them high, who won by
> their pluck and their dare.

At that time, I used to ride to the Berkshire hunt and Wystan was always asking me for news of my latest fall in front of the assembled meet. Rugby and hunting set Wystan dreaming of heroes, successful but vicious. When he met these people he was mostly shy, but sometimes rude.

A rather odd aspect of him which I am told he retained in later life, was his belief in fate and that he could intervene with the Almighty. Once walking on the downs, he discovered that he had lost three pounds which he had stuffed loose into his trouser pocket. 'Never mind,' he said. 'We will pick them up on the way back.' Four hours later, in the dusk, as we followed the ridgeway above Letcombe Bassett, we saw three notes fluttering along the grass. He picked them up, put them back loose in the same pocket and said nothing.

On another occasion we were walking along the Roman wall and late at night were reluctantly received at a small inn. When we went to our room, Wystan found under his crumpled pillow a half-full bottle of brandy. He took a drink as if he had just ordered it and passed it on.

My room at college was on the top of the Meadows Building looking out over the elm trees to the college barges on the river. Wystan's was one of the beautifully proportioned, oak-panelled rooms on the third floor of Peck Quad. He became extra-talkative and paid visits late at night and if I was too sleepy to talk, he would hold a monologue about what he had been reading or writing. In these talks I was introduced to many poets whom I had never heard of before, three I can especially remember, none of whom were well known at the time: Emily Dickinson, Wilfred Owen and Laura Riding.

He was vastly read and greatly interested in prosody and the mechanics of poetry. How he came to get a third class degree, no one could comprehend, least of all his tutors. We all took it more as a joke than a serious matter and I cannot remember Wystan ever talking about it at all.

Sometimes he read his poems aloud. They sounded exciting as he intoned them in his sonorous, rather deadpan voice. But I never really understood them at first reading and hearing. Sometimes he gave me the various drafts which preceded a poem, yet I had not then much appreciation of him as a poet, certainly not as Stephen Spender had, who collected and published the small volume of his Oxford poems.

Of his writing, during the Oxford period, Warner says: 'He was writing incessantly. For some weeks on end, T. S. Eliot would be the model, then Gerard Manley Hopkins or Anglo-Saxon verse. Yet even when these influences were most marked, there was always something distinctly and recognizably his own. Everything that he admired was absorbed and with increasing felicity changed according to his own image.'

I thought of him as my most interesting, serious, dotty friend, who like me, happened to like writing poetry. Once when I showed him some of mine, he said 'Gabriel, you are good at rugger.'

Sometimes with mischievous intent, I used to introduce some of Wystan's more unusual ideas into essays for my tutor, C. S. Lewis, and waited with curiosity for the reaction. I do not think that C. S. Lewis, then, had a very high opinion of Auden. I admired Lewis enormously and was pleased that he shared at least one eccentricity with Auden. They both enjoyed going for walks in Oxford fog and declaiming poetry in a loud voice.

Besides believing in fate, Wystan had his own principles of behaviour. For example he did not on principle wear a raincoat or walking-shoes when he went on the hills. On principle, he said, 'No gentleman should admit to sickness.' He had strong likes and dislikes of food. When he liked it, he liked quantity and ate it like a hungry dog, in a hurry to light up the next cigarette. In public places he either behaved as if he was not there, hardly talking and then in undertones, or he made shocking remarks in a loud voice. On one occasion in a public bar full of agricultural workers he ordered 'best bubbly' to 'celebrate the anniversary of my birth', he then proceeded to pour drinks all round talking complete nonsense until he had got them all to take part in the farce. In pubs, as in people's homes, he would sometimes go to the piano and play Bach partitas or sing Brahms songs.

Some of the best times we had, were spent at my home on Boars Hill near Oxford and at the farm we took on the Pembrokeshire coast. After the initial shock at his manners, my parents took to him warmly. It was the same at Rex's home. He writes: 'His considerate behaviour to old people who came to tea-parties won him golden opinions and more than atoned for some minor eccentricities, such as wandering about in the middle of the night to raid the larder or take down the curtains to pile on his bed. I think my parents realized earlier than I did, that Wystan had, to a marked degree, what Jane Austen would call "right principles".'

My father, a philosophy don at University College, had learned to accept unserious students like Stephen, but he found Wystan's role-playing and sham-arrogance difficult. He thought it was wrong that Wystan would not bathe in the sea before

The Thirties

15 *Left to right* Auden, Isherwood and Spender in the early thirties. At this time all three were making their names in the literary world.

16 Auden, Spender and Isherwood.

17, 18 BELOW and OPPOSITE Illustrations from *Letters from Iceland*, published in 1936, showing Louis MacNeice and Michael Yates. (See Michael Yates's contribution for an account of the trip.)

Louis

Michael

Letter to William Coldstream, Esq.

And *I was* so frightened, my dear.
And we all rowed on the lake and giggled because the boat
    leaked
And the farmer was angry when we whipped his horses
And Louis had a dream—unrepeatable but he repeated it—
And the lady at table had diabetes, poor thing
And Louis dreamt of a bedroom with four glass walls
And I was upset because they told me I didn't look
    innocent
(I liked it really of course)
And the whaling station wouldn't offer us any coffee
And Michael didn't speak for three hours after that
And the first motor-boat we hired turned back because of
    the weather
'A hot spot' he said but we and the vice consul didn't
    believe him
And that cost an extra ten kronur.
And it was after ten when we really got there and could
    discover a landing
And we walked up to the farm in the dark
Over a new mown meadow, the dogs running in and out of
    the lamplight
And I woke in the night to hear Louis vomiting
                    Something like a ship siren
And I played 'O Isis and Osiris' on the harmonium next
    day
And we read the short stories of Somerset Maugham
    aloud to each other
And the best one was called *His Excellency*.
And I said to Michael 'All power corrupts' and he was very
    angry about it.
And he ate thirty-two cakes in an afternoon
And the soup they gave us the last day tasted of hair oil
And we had to wrap the salt fish in an envelope not to hurt
    their feelings

19 RIGHT The cover from one of the programmes of the Group Theatre, which first staged the Auden-Isherwood plays.

20 ABOVE Pamphlets concerning the Group Theatre and the first production of *The Dog Beneath the Skin* on 12 January 1936.
21 OPPOSITE TOP LEFT The programme of the first production of *The Ascent of F6*, by the Group Theatre in 1937.
22, 23 TOP RIGHT and BOTTOM The cast list and a scene from the Old Vic production of *The Ascent of F6* in 1939.
Left to right Alec Guinness, Frederick Paisley, Arthur Macrae, Laurier Lister and Ernest Hare.

Feb. 26th 1937

MERCURY THEATRE

(Licensee : C. M. Dukes.   Lessee : New Mercury, Ltd.)

Directed by Ashley Dukes

2 Ladbroke Road *at* Notting Hill Gate

THE ASCENT OF F.6

'The price of this
programme is sixpence

There is no charge
for our cloak-rooms

Cars are to be Parked down the middle of Kensington Park Road

---

THE ASCENT OF F.6

BY W. H. AUDEN AND CHRISTOPHER ISHERWOOD

Directed by RUPERT DOONE

Characters

Michael Forsyth Ransom	Alec Guinness
Sir James Ransom	Gyles Isham
Lady Isabel Welwyn	Barbara Couper
General Dellaby-Couch	Frederick Bennett
Lord Stagmantle	Ronald Adam
David Gunn	Arthur Macrae
Ian Shawcross	Laurier Lister
Edward Lamp	Frederick Peisley
Dr. Williams	Ernest Hare
	(By kind Permission of Tyrone Guthrie and the Old Vic)
Mrs. Ransom	Barbara Everest
The Abbot	Francis James
An Acolyte	Stephen Bate
Blavek	John Moody

*   *   *   *   *

Mr. A.	John Moody
Mrs. A.	Helen Horsey
An Announcer	Stuart Latham
Chorus	Stephen Bate, Nella Burra, Wallas Eaton

THE PLAY IS PRESENTED IN TWO PARTS, WITH ONE INTERVAL OF 15 MINUTES

Scenes in Part I   Summit of the Pillar Rock, Wastdale.
A Room at the Colonial Office.
An Inn Parlour in the Lake District.

Scenes in Part II   A Monastery on the Great Glacier of F.6.
The Foot of the West Buttress.
Camp B.
The Arête.
The Summit.

Musical Director : BRIAN EASDALE.

Pianos : *BRIAN EASDALE* and *FRIDA EASDALE.*   Percussion : *PHYLLIDA GARTH.*

The Music specially composed by BENJAMIN BRITTEN.

Costumes, Masks and Scene by ROBERT MEDLEY.

The Abbot's Costume kindly lent by Mrs. C. KAHLER.

Miss Everest's Dress by CHARLES H. FOX, 184, HIGH HOLBORN, W.C.I.

Climbing Equipment kindly lent by ROBERT LAWRIE, LTD., 38, BRYANSTON ST., W.I., and
BOY SCOUTS' ASSOCIATION, 25 BUCKINGHAM PALACE ROAD, S.W.I.

Furniture by J. S. LYON, LTD., 112, HIGH HOLBORN, W.C.I., and
OLD TIMES FURNISHING CO., 125a, VICTORIA STREET, S.W.I.

Electrical Equipment by STAGE ELECTRICS, 24, HIGH HOLBORN, W.C.I.

Camera kindly lent by SANDS, HUNTER & CO., LTD., BEDFORD STREET, STRAND, W.C.2.

Telephones by courtesy of the POSTMASTER-GENERAL.

Scenery built by JACK HILL, 40, MARLBOROUGH GROVE, S.E.I, and
FRED CAREY, MERCURY THEATRE, LADBROKE ROAD, W.II.

Pianos supplied by GRIFFITHS, HANSEN & CO., 32, GOSFIELD STREET, W.I.

Wigs by "BERT," 46, PORTNALL ROAD, W.9.

Stage Director		STUART LATHAM
Stage Manager	FOR THE	GUNDE VON DECHEND
Assistant Stage Manager	GROUP THEATRE	STEPHEN BATE
Wardrobe Mistress		CONSTANCE FOLJAMBE.
Press Representative		RONALD J. HARRISON
Business Manager		DORIS THELLUSSON.
Master Carpenter		FRED STUBBINGS.
Property Master	FOR THE	WILLIAM THORNBY.
Electrician	OLD VIC	JACK EGAN.

While smoking is permitted, it is requested that the convenience of non-smokers be considered and that it be limited to the intervals.
Members of the audience are requested not to take photographs during the performance.

Fire Curtain. The design on the fire curtain is by Robert Medley, and won the prize in the competition organised by the Sadler's Wells Society and judged by Winston Churchill, Sir Kenneth Clark, and C. B. Cochran.

In accordance with the requirements of the Lord Chamberlain.

1.—The public may leave at the end of the performance by all exit doors, and such doors must at that time be open.

2.—All gangways, passages and staircases must be kept entirely free from chairs or any other obstruction.

3.—Persons shall not in any circumstances be permitted to stand or sit in any of the gangways intersecting the seating, or to sit in any of the other gangways. If standing be permitted in the gangways at the sides and rear of the seating, it shall be strictly limited to the numbers indicated in the notices exhibited in these positions.

4.—The safety curtain must be lowered and raised in the presence of each audience.

24, 25 Two pictures of the original production of *The Dog Beneath the Skin* at the Westminster Theatre in 1936. ABOVE '*Have you seen Sir Francis Crewe?*' BELOW Mad masks in the red light district of Ostnia.

Night Mail

This is the night mail crossing the border,
Bringing the cheque and the postal order,
Letters for the rich, letters for the poor,
The shop at the corner and the girl next door.
Pulling up Beattock, a steady climb—
The gradient's against her but she's on time.
Past cotton grass and moorland boulder,
Shovelling white steam over her shoulder,
Snorting noisily as she passes
Silent miles of wind-bent grasses;
Birds turn their heads as she approaches,
Stare from the bushes at her blank-faced coaches;
Sheep dogs cannot turn her course,
They slumber on with paws across.
In the farm she passes no one wakes,
But a jug in the bedroom gently shakes.
Dawn freshens, the climb is done.
Down towards Glasgow she descends
Towards the steam tugs, yelping down the glade of cranes
Towards the fields of apparatus, the furnaces
Set on the dark plain like gigantic chessmen.
All Scotland waits for her;
In the dark glens, beside the pale-green sea lochs,
Men long for news.

26 The first half of Auden's commentary to a GPO film. The leaflet was issued by the Post Office in 1938 to celebrate the centenary of the Travelling Post Office.

27 RIGHT Auden and
Isherwood in 1938 about
to leave for China, later to
result in *Journey to a War*.
28 BELOW The couple
later in the year, after
their return from China,
making a radio programme
for the BBC.

breakfast and then enjoy a good bowl of porridge. My mother, an unconventional woman, loved to have talented, amusing, handsome young men around, and it was she who kept them coming to our uncomfortable house and wild garden.

Wystan, Stephen, Sidney Newman and Dick Crossman were regular members of the family circle and a laughter-making mixture they were, with all of us slightly envious, slightly admiring, of Dick's handsome, ambitious bearing. From the first, Wystan established himself as one of the few who spoke his mind to my mother. On the second day, arriving late for breakfast, he tasted his tea and said in his flattest voice 'Mrs Carritt, my tea is like tepid piss.' My mother looked outraged, but she burst out laughing, and I noticed next day they were calling each other Winifred and Wystan.

On another occasion he made himself briefly unpopular by throwing up his breakfast over the geraniums in the post office garden. He then went into the post office and said to the postmistress, 'Excuse me, Madam, it is the Carritts' porridge.'

Just as at the Warners', so at the Carritts', he raided the larder at night and wolfed the cold potatoes and leg of lamb. In our case he took up the stair-carpet to put on his bed.

I think my mother felt his unconventional behaviour became our unconventional family. In *The Orators* there is a passage describing a summer holiday Wystan and Dick Crossman spent with us on the coast near St David's in Pembrokeshire. It must be unintelligible to anyone not in the circle, but to those who were, it is very evocative.

> I'm afraid it sounds more like a fairy story.
> There was a family called Do:
> There were Do–a, Do–ee and other Do–s
> And Uncle Dick and Uncle Wiz had come to stay with them
> (Nobody slept that night).
> Now Do–a loved to bathe before his breakfast
> With Uncle Dick, but Uncle Wiz . . .
> Well?
> As a matter of fact the farm was in Pembrokeshire.
> The week the Labour Cabinet resigned
> Dick has returned from Germany in love.
> I hate cold water and am very fond of potatoes. . . .

Do–a was my father's nickname, and Do–ee that of my youngest brother.

Among Wystan's friends outside of the Oxford circle was Olive Mangeot, wife of André Mangeot, the leader of a well-known string quartet. She was the secretary of the Chelsea branch of the Communist Party and used to make a round of the Chelsea pubs in a flowing black cloak and black hat selling the *Daily Worker*. Wystan characteristically managing his friends' lives, arranged for Olive and me to meet in a Soho restaurant where we spent a hilarious evening, with Wystan playing the role of pander. Later with a group of Wystan's friends, including Sally Bowles and Mr Norris himself, I became a lodger at Olive's Chelsea home.

In two ways Wystan initiated interests that greatly influenced my life. Talking about Homer Lane he made me want to study adolescent deviance and later I went to New York and enrolled as a student at the School of Social Research. Secondly he introduced me to Brecht and Toller and set me on the road to study Marxism, so that later I joined the Communist Party while I was in USA at the time of the Wall Street Crash.

After the Second World War, I met Wystan in Oxford and we spent the evening discussing my Marxism and his Anglo-Catholicism with much humour. He was not a political person, but nevertheless he became the spokesman of the feelings that turned so many of our generation towards revolutionary movements of one kind or another.

I conclude with a characteristic story, funny and revealing. We were travelling to limestone country and stopped at Oxenholme. We went to wash in the Gentlemen's and the towel was filthy, so I took out my handkerchief. Wystan remonstrated with me, saying I showed disgust for my fellows. He washed and dried his face in the towel. Absurd, laughable, yes, but something else as well, which was essentially Wystan Auden.

Sir William Coldstream
A portrait

Sir William Coldstream has been the Professor of Fine Art at the Slade school of art since 1949 and has painted Auden's portrait. This article appeared in the New Statesman *after Auden's death*

I first met Wystan Auden when I was seventeen, just before I went to the Slade. He was in his first year at Oxford and I was introduced to him by a journalist friend who had talked a lot about him and wanted us to meet. During that visit of Auden's to London, we spent most of several days walking through the streets while he talked without stopping and in a most exhilarating way about poetry and psychology, about his family and his childhood. He had a lot of his own poems in his pockets. He made an extraordinarily striking impression: I had never met anyone with so much vitality, enthusiasm, warmth and directness.

It was nine years later that we met again when I was working for the GPO Film Unit in Soho Square, and Auden joined the staff. It was at that time that he wrote the verses for the film *Night Mail* and the poem 'O lurcher-loving collier' for *Coalface*. During this period of about a year, he lodged in my house in Hampstead and we saw a great deal of each other. Shortly after this, both he and I left the Film Unit, he to return for a period to his teaching in a preparatory school in the country and I to painting. I went and stayed with him at the school, where he sat for me for his portrait. His pupils would sometimes come and watch, among them a tall boy, then twelve years old, with a prodigious knowledge of the history of art, Andrew Forge. Wystan was always in very high spirits at this time and would particularly like to play and sing hymns to groups of boys and staff.

He had me to stay in Birmingham with his mother and father and there his mother kindly sat for me. She was very tall and severe-looking and highly intelligent. Her influence always remained with Wystan, who often towards the end of his life would say, half-jokingly, about something, 'Mother wouldn't like it!' Mrs Auden had kept some of Wystan's poems dating back to when he was seven or eight years old and was very proud of him, and so was his father. He was at this time much more taken up with political ideas than formerly, though I do not think he ever had any real appetite for politics. It was, I think, curiosity as well as social conscience that made him go to Spain in the civil war. I remember seeing him off at the station. After he came back, it was my impression that his Spanish experience had slightly shaken his faith in revolutionary solutions.

After he went to America in 1939, we corresponded occasionally and after the war I saw him from time to time on his visits to Europe. As he grew older some of his early habits and opinions became increasingly emphasized: his passion for going to bed early, for instance. He was angry if someone was late for dinner because it might keep him up, and at 9.30 sharp he would pad upstairs in his bedroom slippers, leaving the rest of the company behind to get on with it.

As a very young man he was, I think, extremely good-looking, tall and slim, with a smooth, pale complexion and fair hair, and now in his sixties one could somehow still see all this concealed under the extremely craggy surfaces which overtook his features. Throughout his life there was to me – and I think to many – a real magic and glamour in his presence and he somehow made one feel that life was more than usually worth living.

Michael Yates
Iceland 1936

Michael Yates was a schoolboy when he first met Auden and remained a lifelong friend

In the summer of 1936 I was at Bryanston School in Dorset. A year earlier, it had been rumoured that W. H. Auden was to join the staff. Concurrently with the rumour, a letter arrived from him addressed to one of his ex-pupils from The Downs School, Colwall. In the letter Auden had remarked 'I hear G.H. [Geoffrey Hoyland] is coming to preach next Sunday. Put an onion in the chalice for me.' The recipient imprudently allowed this letter to reach the headmaster. Auden did not join the staff at Bryanston.

In spite of this he visited Blandford from time to time. One weekend that summer term he came down to see the late Wilfred Cowley. I saw him on Sunday morning and he suggested we drive to Shaftesbury for lunch. I put my bicycle in the back of his battered car and off we swerved. Although in the main he was a safe driver he could be carefree, also impatient. There was an occasion when in exasperation he deliberately bumped a leisurely cow into the ditch. This time we reached Shaftesbury without incident.

During lunch he asked me if the family were as usual going to the Isle of Man for the holidays. I said yes, except that I myself with three other boys and a master were going to Iceland. He became excited, and only a short time later I received a letter saying his publishers, Faber and Faber, had agreed to finance him on a visit to Iceland. Although he would be there some weeks ahead of us, would I ask the master if he might join our expedition when we started out, as he would like to include an account of it in the book. This then is the origin of his visit, why I was with him, and how *Letters from Iceland* in collaboration with Louis MacNeice came to be written.

He was there three months altogether. The first six weeks on his own, after which Louis MacNeice joined him, followed soon by the school party for ten days. The last two weeks were spent with Louis and myself.

Iceland and its sagas had been part of his imagination ever since his father used to read him Icelandic fairy tales. Moreover, his own ancestry could be traced back to the island, hence his christian name Wystan. This fascination for the sagas was to continue to the end of his life; as was shown in his conversation, writing and in one particular Kent Lecture at Canterbury on 'The Primary and Secondary Worlds'.

His visit was therefore to satisfy him in two ways: his liking for travel when he could observe political, historical and cultural trends; and his need for purely visual impressions – landscape, architecture, and geology. He took a positive pride in knowing about the sagas and the island's history but found no echo of these in the Icelanders' present way of life. The geography of the island, with the exception of its architecture, often fired his imagination, exciting or repelling him. It still seemed a setting for that 'gangster' society of centuries past.

The purpose of this essay is to recall my own visit there and my memory of him at that time – the memory of a schoolboy. Although my visual impression is as keen now as in 1936, I have had to refer to *Letters from Iceland* for some details and names; I hope without plagiarism. Further, I found I had kept my diary of the second part of the visit after the school party had returned to England. Nevill Coghill referred to this with charm as 'just what you would expect from a nice English schoolboy'. Claustrophobic family life and the cocoon of public schools at that time did not exactly condition one to develop unusual powers of observation on one's travels. I think Wystan would have agreed.

The school party sailed from Hull on the *Godafoss* in early August with W. F. Hoyland in charge. The fare was £4 10s plus five kronur a day for food. The voyage took four days, stopping briefly at the Vestmannaeyjar islands, subsequently obliterated by volcanic eruptions in 1973. It was a rough sea passage.

The object of the expedition was to circle one of the central icefields, the Langjökull, on horses. The party was told that we would be joined by two poets, W. H. Auden and Louis MacNeice.

They were on the quay at Reykjavik to meet us. That same day, after leaving our main luggage at the *studentagardur* (the university hostel) and purchasing oilskins, we were at Gullfoss, the starting point of our journey.

In the book, Louis gives a full and 'camp' account of the following ten days in the form of a letter from Hetty to Nancy. I say 'camp' because he chose to transform us into a party of schoolgirls in the charge of their mistress, with himself and Wystan as two young spinsters. Some may not find this amusing. Some, indeed, did not do so at the time of publication. However, it remains a fact that a mass of acute observation is incorporated in this spoofy account, not just of our progress but also more particularly of our individual characters and our reactions to rough conditions.

At Gullfoss there is a spectacular waterfall, a mini-Niagara. Wystan's view was that one waterfall was much the same as another, whatever its size or shape. That night he was to regret this theory.

We met our guides here, Stengrimur and Ari, who had assembled our seventeen horses along with provisions for ten days. A large part of the detailed organization had been done by Wystan. Indeed he was so efficient that he was the only person with a stove! A further feat, less laudable but to our advantage, was that all our horses had been destined for another party. He had merely commandeered them leaving the other party mount-less and stranded.

That first night was classic. The route round the Langjökull was a regular but rough one. Where there were no turf-roofed huts of a very primitive kind for shelter (and there were in fact only three) we slept in tents. That night we did sleep in tents and the only place to pitch them was to the windward of the falls. The school party, as you would expect, was properly equipped. So was Wystan, although he only had a small conical tent with an opening but no 'door flap' and one piece of the central pole missing. Louis, except for an oilskin bought in Reykjavik, was totally unprepared in all other respects which made Wystan rather cross. We stripped down to pyjamas and had a dry full night's sleep. Even Wystan wore pyjamas, which in retrospect I find amazing.

We rose at six, no slacking or lying about being permitted. On emerging we saw no sign of them, just a flattened tent on the ground. Perhaps they had sneaked off to the nearby tin hut for a final cup of coffee. Then the tent undulated and two wet cross faces appeared.

According to Louis they had pitched it on a patch of prickly bilberry bushes, with their heads running downhill; fortunately the opening was not facing the waterfall although their feet were sticking out. It was raining. Wystan had brought with him a large yellow and blue pneumatic mattress – hard surfaces never suited him for sleeping. In Louis' words he looked like something out of Brueghel when blowing it up. It took up a lot of space and his habit of sleeping in the foetal position left Louis little room. Added to this was the absence of the one length of pole and the fact that they had set up the tent with both skins touching. With the rain and their lack of expertise the tent began to subside and close in on them 'like something in Edgar Allan Poe'. Wystan declared he was going down with all hands; Louis merely hid deeper inside his wet sleeping bag. The final moment arrived when all had collapsed flat on the ground. There they remained for the rest of the night, clammy canvas on their faces, whilst the rain fell and a strong spray from the falls blew steadily across them, seeping in wherever possible.

With the exception of Wystan who had ridden a little during the earlier part of his visit, and one boy from the school party, none of us had ever been on a horse – or pony to be more exact – in our lives. After breakfast with a sharp word of command from Stengrimur we started, almost vertically up the side of the valley. It was terrifying, but we were on our way.

The whole of this central part of Iceland is quite barren, consisting mainly of lava, brown or grey rock, occasional hot springs, and the putty-coloured river Hvita spreading into a large area of pools, tributaries and quicksands towards its source at Hvitanes – perhaps the most beautiful place we saw. Here the main glacier of the Langjökull falls vertically into a lake. There were however unexpected glades and patches of grass and moss in this wilderness. Wystan was not insensitive to landscapes but not only was he less impressed by this than by what he had already seen, he was also more interested in us and our reactions to the tough life. To me the vast panoramic views, the clarity of the air, and the colours ending in distant piercing blues, were incredibly beautiful.

There were of course many moments when this enchantment was obliterated as the sky blackened and blinding rain with biting winds bent our heads low to the horses' necks. Or on the days when we rode or walked over miles of lava. And one particular time when we walked, leading our horses, all day over an endless desert of sharp brown stones, a part apparently never crossed before. Wystan likened it to 'the uninteresting and useless debris of an orgy'. His view of the great open spaces was that they were 'a closed book' and that much of it was 'like after a party which no one had tidied up'.

The changing weather governed what we wore, which was basically a lot. Wystan chose to be more extraordinary than anyone. I can see him to this day in his full vile-weather regalia. According to his own account he wore flannel trousers over his pyjamas topped by riding breeches, two shirts, a golf jacket under his tweed jacket, and enormous brown gum-boots. When it rained he put on a long black oilskin and a bright yellow sou'wester with an old felt hat fastened on over it with a safety pin. When the weather was at its most vile he also put on yellow oilskin trousers reaching to the waist. The first time he tucked them into his gum-boots which immediately filled with water. Having pulled them out he looked, to quote Louis, as though he had webbed feet – 'wisps of hair straggle over his forehead and when he walks he moves like something that is more at home in the water'. This extraordinary apparition seen from behind, jogging along on a pony scarcely as large as its rider, with his right hand hovering near his mouth as though smoking a cigarette, was a sight I was always to remember with affection.

In the forty-one years I knew him, except during the war, the happiest were probably the earliest when he was making his first great impact on modern poetry; when he was bursting with ebullience and quite outrageous fun; when he was teaching young people, especially at that remarkable prep school The Downs; and when he was a colleague among colleagues. On this expedition the same spirit carried him forward.

His energy was amazing. The discomforts did not deter him – though he was far from indifferent to comfort as long as it did not look *tidy*. He observed us boys shrewdly, teasing us when we complained, telling us that if we had come here to demonstrate our toughness then 'children, it is time you did so, though heaven knows why you want to!' But on Bill Hoyland saying that 'when roughing it in this way it is always a good thing to think of the discomforts of the people climbing Everest', he said he would much rather think of people dining at the Ritz!

Bill was of course in charge of the expedition. In Louis' account he is christened Miss Greenhalge (*La Paloma* to the girls in their more private conclaves). Wystan was a great support. The guides could only speak Icelandic and a few words of German. With his fluent German he became the liaison between Bill and them. Called Maisie in the letter from Hetty to Nancy, he loved 'playing every girl her own billican' and would be the first at the end of the day to start preparations for supper, getting our one and only stove going. Just as well, considering its age and that it needed the comfort of his personal touch in the endless pumping required.

He did not like cold food very much. But he resigned himself to the fact that all our meals were to be cold. These were confined to rock-hard bread, excellent tinned mutton, cheese, smoked mutton, and a dried fish which he described as being 'like skin off the soles of one's feet' – we were spared the other fish which he compared to toe-nails. The only hot sustenance was coffee or cocoa.

Our days followed a regular pattern. Up at six o'clock with a brief breakfast. We would then saddle our own horses. The horses often took revenge on us for not being good riders (I am sure they knew it) by breathing out when we tightened their girths. On mounting, the saddles would slither sideways finishing under their bellies with us on the ground. Hardly a day passed without one of us flying over their heads or falling backwards over their tails, but no serious injury was suffered. At noon we would stop briefly to rest the horses. We would be allowed a few squares of chocolate, occasionally some bread with smoked mutton. The latter we had to gnaw and savage like animals; Wystan said it tasted like soot.

He never believed in wasting a moment so at each stop out would come his camera. Bill Hoyland who was an extremely good photographer was amazed by his methods. He would stumble about the lava like some amphibious monster taking the most extraordinary art shots: the backside of a horse followed by the guide Ari's bottom, a boot, distant views or half-hidden faces between our legs or under the horses' bellies. He clicked away regardless although I think he did at least adjust the focus. He had a definite theory which he wrote down in a letter to Erika Mann. 'It's a pity I am so impatient and careless, as any ordinary person could learn all the techniques of photography in a week. It is the democratic art, i.e.: technical skill is practically eliminated – the more fool-proof cameras become with focusing and exposure gadgets the better – and artistic quality depends only on choice of subject. There is no place for the professional still photographer, and his work is always awful. The only decent photographs are scientific ones and amateur snapshots, only you want a lot of the latter to make an effect. A single still is never very interesting by itself.' As always, a sweeping final statement!

Before our arrival Wystan had succumbed to one Icelandic passion, playing cards –

in this case rummy. Unlike bridge he found he could talk whilst playing. It was to become a minor enthusiasm to the end of our stay on the island. The fact that he could talk and joke made it less serious, although he found he was a bad loser. It is possible that had he talked less he would not have lost so often.

After Hveravellir, which incidentally is noted for its valley of hot sulphur springs which are very beautiful indeed when looked at closely, shortage of time and worsening weather compelled us to make that appalling trek across the desert of stones, all seventy kilometres of it. As yet unexplored, the guides using compasses and setting up cairns, got us safely across to the north of the Langjökull, but not without Louis having hallucinations: 'I thought I saw Greenhalge in the distance but it turned out to be a cairn.' It was also on this trek that Wystan added to his disgust in Icelandic deserts by remarking that 'anyone would be an optimist who expected to find anything as human as a dry bone in these parts'.

Reaching Arnavatn with its miraculous emerald green grass and white sheep beside a silver lake, unrelieved gloom descended when we discovered our only stove in shattered pieces. Beautiful as the site may have been it was the coldest; having no hot drink we cut short our game of cards. We put on our lunatic pyjamas, crawling into our tents, whilst Wystan and Louis settled in the smallest and most primitive hut yet. By this time I think he had had enough of the pioneering spirit – it could hardly have been his chosen way of travelling. That night he said to Louis: 'Never again' and went to sleep with a cigarette in his mouth, his mattress 'sighing like something out of A. E. Housman'.

The wind roared down off the ice-field all night and the next day, with slanting hail adding to the paralysing cold. But evidently we seem to have felt heroic and even Wystan, now in his full vile-weather regalia, gave no sign of 'Never again'. We rode for twelve hours that day and at six o'clock in the evening reached Kalmanstunga, a real farm isolated in the wilderness. As we sat in this haven drinking wonderful coffee with the rain beating against the window panes, he turned to me and said: 'Isn't that a nice sound; just like the Lake District.'

Timing was a little eccentric. The following day we had a large breakfast at nine o'clock and an enormous lunch at ten. But apparently farm time is two hours ahead of Reykjavik time. Before the meal he announced that Icelandic cooking 'made him think of a little boy who had got loose with mother's medicine chest'. In fact the food was very good and we were spared those brilliantine and almond flavoured soups he described with stewed rhubarb to garnish them, followed by sweet potatoes. It would be ungrateful to leave Kalmanstunga on such a note. As on all farms, indeed every-where throughout Iceland, people were very kind and hospitable.

We had three more days riding ahead. To Brunnar by the lake where we camped on marshy ground; Thingvellir the site of the ancient parliament, the *Thing*; and finally Laugarvatn where there was a hotel, The Gleneagles of Iceland but a school in winter. The continual drizzle combined with mist hid the Langjökull and mountain called Ok between which we rode. Wystan and Louis had their final traumatic experience at Brunnar. The lie of the land and the wind forced them to sleep with their heads outside the tent. We also lost the horses because they made off during the night. Whilst waiting for their recapture Wystan rushed about photographing our misery.

On the last day of our expedition Louis wrote: 'And so the game is ended that should never have begun.' Although this part of my memoir has been properly concentrated on Wystan it would be an ungenerous omission if I did not say that none of us would have been there if it had not been for Bill Hoyland. However, even he would admit that without Wystan's presence, inimitable personality and humour we might well have been left with no more than a fine factual impression, highlighted by the memory of staggering landscapes.

We rode to Laugarvatn, sleeping there in tents, and next day returned by bus to Reykjavik. The school party stayed at the *studentagardur* whilst Wystan, Louis and I went off to the lunatic asylum at Kelppur. It might be thought: 'No wonder!' In fact we were to be guests of Dr Sveinsson and his family. Apart from their great kindness our night's visit was marked by three incidents. The Doctor insisted on talking in Latin which was difficult even for the others let alone myself who had given it up at fifteen. When having baths in the lunatics' bathroom to faint cooings in the distance, the door burst open and we expected to be thrust naked and dripping into straitjackets, but all was well. Finally, Wystan completely demolished the camp bed he slept on; perhaps he dreamt he was still on the hard unyielding barren ground.

The following evening the others sailed for England and the three of us prepared for two short trips: first to a farm in the area centred on Reykholt and then to Isafjördur not far south of the Arctic Circle.

We remained for one day in Reykjavik where, apart from a remarkable painting on wood of the Last Supper in the museum, the only worthwhile sights in Wystan's opinion were: Arni Pāllson, Professor of Icelandic History, a vast man in height and girth shuddering with mirth; Oddur Sigurgeirsson who haunted the harbour; Vladimir who imagined spirits about his head; and Kjarval the painter!

At this time, indeed throughout his life, Wystan had an unerring instinct for recognizing those who had talent. There was no place for the fake or insincere. He would declare his views with an absolute finality. So I was taken to meet Kjarval, an enormous but gentle man. Wystan admired his drawings of heads, reminiscent of Dürer and Cranach. His oil paintings on the other hand were of the utmost abandon, even ferocity.

The National Theatre was still a concrete shell so he was disappointed in seeing no plays which might have reflected the sagas. He was intensely interested in the theatre at this time. He was steering me towards it, ultimately helping me to study and become a scene designer. The fact that years later I ended up successfully in television was not a consolation to him. He considered it a wicked medium which should never have been invented, having no value beyond the coverage of sport and news. He tempered his antipathy only by agreeing to work for it as long as he did not have to watch. Once he did look and saw his own face. This led to his famous statement which likened his craggy features to 'a wedding cake which had been left out in the rain'.

In his last years at Kirchstetten where my wife and I would stay each summer he had become slower, often withdrawn, though the greatness of his mind remained unquestioned. Many will not know that under that tough, uncompromising, domineering exterior was a real kindness and generosity; and not confined only to those close to him personally. And so it was in 1936 except that his energy was then irrepressible, his mind darting from one subject to another, unyielding in his views, yet quite capable of changing them with equal conviction – there was always to be a present pet theory. He would exaggerate outrageously, clouding serious opinion because it was fun. No wonder he was called 'Uncle Wiz'.

We sailed on the motor-ship *Laxoss* for Borganes and so by bus to a farm at Hraensnef near Hredavatn. He had stayed there earlier. He wished us to enjoy his own experience of Icelandic hospitality, especially on farms. It was, as he predicted, warm and generous. Not dissimilar to England, the parlours always had two special features: a glass bowl of family photographs which it was obligatory to look through, and a harmonium. He adored harmoniums and in a moment would be seated playing the inevitable hymns and psalms, singing in a strong but not very melodious voice. His favourite stop was the *Vox Humana* which alas did not work here. But there was consolation in finding Brahms's *Sapphic Ode* and *Moonlight in the Sahara*.

During these last weeks – on the farm, at Reykholt, the North Pole Café in Isafjördur, or at Melgraseyri – we were to drink more coffee accompanied by cream cakes than I remember before or since. Cakes are an essential part of Icelandic life, even starting the day with them at breakfast, a final plate before going to bed. Wystan did not like cakes, adding 'a sweet tooth is a bad thing!'

A short ride from Hraensnef brought you to Hredavatn with its small lake, an island in the middle. We found a boat, Wystan sitting in the stern playing cox and adding dangerously to the displacement. Louis and I did our best which was not much. The boat went round in circles, filling slowly with water whilst we rested on the oars helpless with laughter. Somehow we reached the island. Whilst idly looking at the view he launched into a lecture on the wickedness of some aspects of public schools, especially the power of the prefect, beating and fagging. He knew I was to be head prefect next term. He concluded by looking at me, saying: 'All power corrupts.' I was very angry and he grinned with pleasure.

The following day, accompanied by the farmer, we rode on to Reykholt, staying briefly at its modern school classified by him as 'Corbusier goes all northern'.

The rooms there were hot. Heated by water from sulphur springs the temperature was never below seventy degrees and often higher. Looking in on him before bed you would have thought we were back at Arnavatn. His bed was heaped with anything to hand. All his life regardless of temperature his bed was piled with a suffocating load – not for warmth but because he liked weight. Once when staying with my family he even put a large picture on the bed in addition to a loose rug snatched from the floor. At Kirchstetten his bed looked like a blanket store.

We returned briefly to Reykjavik. With one exception this was to be the last extended holiday he was to take for the rest of his life, discounting odd short visits. The remainder of his days became an increasingly strict time-table of work. But he remembered this visit clearly and with pleasure to the end.

During our passage to the far north on the *Dettifoss* we berthed for one day at Patreksfjördur for moving cargo. We had the crazy idea of walking in gum boots sixteen miles over the lava-strewn headland to a whaling station. The very long tiring toil brought us to the top where the view of the deep blue fjörd was unsurpassed. No good. We continued wearily down to the scene of carnage. To Wystan whales were one of the most beautiful sights. Having watched the brutal destruction on the slimy slip-way he remarked: 'It is enough to make one a vegetarian for life. It gives one an extraordinary vision of the cold, controlled ferocity of the human species.' We turned away and sought food and coffee but were refused. We were numbed and left in disgust. I behaved very badly, refusing to speak for three hours. At the top of the watershed he turned and said: 'Picture of a person in a fucking awful temper!' It did not help.

Next morning we were in Isafjördur, to him the most beautiful area he had visited. The Salvation Army hostel seemed the only place in which to stay. A more unlikely trio with Wystan at its head could scarcely have crossed such a threshold. So whilst waiting to cross to Melgraseyri we ate and slept there making the North Pole Cafe our daytime base.

The moment came when we thought some alcohol would be a change from our eternal coffee. The days of lethal vodka martinis were a long way off when, at Kirch-stetten, in his last years he would pad off at nine o'clock in those carpet slippers, a bottle of wine in his fist, looking like the back side of an elephant, to have his bubble bath. He would, I imagine, then lie in bed – whilst the rest of us listened to opera – sipping a final glass and smoking one more cigarette. It is a wonder that he survived this routine. On at least two occasions there Chester Kallman rushed to his room to find the poet lost to the world and the mattress on the point of bursting into flames. Sleep had taken him but that last cigarette had burnt on.

In Iceland the aftermath of prohibition prevented any such possibility. Alcohol could be obtained legally or otherwise but only with difficulty. Wystan approached the helpful Mr Joachimsson, the British Vice-Consul. Like a conjurer he whipped a bottle of Spanish brandy from under the counter. Almost kissing him we stumbled in our gum-boots as fast as we could to the Salvation Army where we behaved most disreputably. In one of our bedrooms, beneath a notice on the wall saying NO CARD PLAYING, we swiftly dealt our cards for rummy, the brandy in tooth mugs by our sides, 'feeling like school boys hiding our sins from the maid'.

When at last we got a reliable motor-boat we sailed for Melgraseyri. A high sea was running, the sun was bright, the wind cold and strong. Wystan stood perilously on the heaving deck looking like a nineteenth-century lifeboat man clicking away with his Zeiss, the lens blurred by spray. Eventually, the wildness of the sea, extreme cold and nightfall drove us below amongst coils of rope and the smell of tar. Given up for lost we arrived at midnight farm time 'on a newly mown meadow, the friendly dogs barking as they ran in and out of the lamplight'.

Morning revealed the emerald green *tún*, the specially cultivated meadow which even in barren country is a characteristic surrounding to all farms. It was a soothing sight at the end of our wide travels. Although Louis had been violently ill during the night, our final three days there, unsurpassed in its position, were wonderful. Wystan played the harmonium and sang 'O Isis und Osiris' – transposed up a little! All our usual farm pastimes filled the hours.

We walked and rode on the unaccustomed grass. Louis' endless dreams defeated Wystan's Freudian theories. And on Sunday we visited on horseback all the neighbours. After so many teas I had by the end of the day eaten thirty-two cakes. Wystan did not behave well. He swallowed, surreptitiously, the remains of a jug of cream in spite of the many sweet bilberries wrapped in wafer-thin pancakes which he had just consumed – all that nonsense about a sweet tooth!

It is a sad but unavoidable record that our last meal consisted of a soup flavoured seemingly with hair-oil and eau-de-Cologne with whites of eggs floating on top. This was followed by salt fish so nauseous that we had to wrap it in paper and later throw it in the sea – all had been meant as a compliment but it was in fact the nastiest meal we had ever had. Be that as it may. We had enjoyed a degree of hospitality I have not known excelled. We walked over the *tún* to the edge of the water where the motor-boat waited, and there we stood, looking back at the assembled family.

Many years later he returned and stood alone on that exact spot gazing across the immense fjörd out towards the arctic sea. He thought of Louis and me and our days there and felt very sad. It was less than a year after Louis' death.

Cyril Connolly
Some memories

Cyril Connolly was the Editor of Horizon *magazine from 1939 to 1950, in which Auden published many poems*

> Personal song and language . . .
> Thanks to which it's possible for the breathing
> Still to break bread with the dead. . . .

A few years ago it would have been easier: memories would have come crowding in, it remained only to sift them and bring them up to date with our last meeting, for I still saw him regularly when he came to England. But since he had made his home in Oxford we hardly met, except through Stephen Spender. Age still finds me devoted to my old friends but increasingly reminded that it is a one-way traffic so that I anticipate their rebuffs from an instinct of self-protection. I used to imagine the old as yarning away together or locked in pregnant silence like Tennyson and Carlyle. But age is not like that: the old are diminishing universes racing further and further apart, piling up space between them, unable to cope with the simplest mechanics of meeting. Artists can be touchy, frivolous and unforgiving, and often the only way to catch a glimpse of our old friends is at a memorial service or a literary award. 'O yonge freshe folke' be warned; friendship is for those who strenuously pursue the same goal; cultivate it now and do not put it off 'for when there will be more time' – time there may be but also death, weariness and estrangement.

I endangered our relationship at a recent meeting by telling Wystan that I could not agree to destroy his letters, that I did not think it scandalous that Keats' love-letters should have been published or the sonnets of Shakespeare, nor rejoice in the burning of Byron's journal. I could not wholly deplore the public's curiosity about artists' lives (better than none at all). But Wystan saw himself by now as a great gentleman, 'I am afraid I have become very square in my old age,' he answered:

> The class whose vices
> he pilloried was his own,
> now extinct, except
> for lone survivors like him
> who remember its virtues.

I have disobeyed his wishes by keeping his letters; worse still, I shall want to quote from them.

I have to hew my way back through the wilderness of time to rediscover the dazzling adornment of my youth, the one indisputable genius – 'water-fluent tea-drinking' – whose friendship I could once enjoy on an equal footing. I should perhaps mention in passing that when I am moved by the work of a contemporary my instinct is to wish to get to know him, and that once we have become acquainted, he can do no wrong. Some, like George Orwell and Evelyn Waugh, were already my friends before they revealed their talent, others like Dylan Thomas proved too alien to assimilate, or, like Hemingway, were always somewhere else.

At that time (the early thirties), poetry seemed to have exhausted itself; Eliot had gone religious, the Georgians moribund; Edith Sitwell appeared to be resting after giving us her *Collected Poems* of 1930 and Geoffrey Grigson had not quite started *New Verse*. *New Signatures*, *New Writing* – everything *new* but the *New Statesman*, was still in the womb.

I first heard of Wystan through Tom Driberg's column in the *Daily Express* when he required of his large public 'Awareness of Auden', referring, I think, to the *Poems* of 1930, but it was the *Orators* (1932) which deeply moved me, while I found the chilly Marxism of *The Dance of Death* rather intimidating. But it was not Auden but Spender whom I was to meet after he wrote me a long letter from the island of Mlini about *The Destructive Element* which I reviewed in the *New Statesman*. We became firm friends and still are. Isherwood also I was to get to know well and it was he who told me to look up Auden at his hotel in Valencia where I was to return in my reporting on the Spanish war; I went there with my wife and Ran Antrim, who at that time described himself as 'me good pink peer', and we were rather cosseted except for a strict examination by the Comintern agent for whom I produced a letter from Harry Pollitt, the Secretary of the Communist Party. Auden, who was working for the government radio, seemed overjoyed to meet us and ordered a bottle of Spanish champagne, a detail which delighted Isherwood, who said it would have convinced him that it was the real Auden and not some impostor. I was at once obsessed with his appearance which penetrated deep into my subconscious so that I often dreamt about him. (The last time was January 1973.) Fortunately there are many photographs of the youthful Auden, as he remained till the end of the last war; the solid cragginess came later. He was tall and slim, with a mole on his upper lip, rather untidy tow-coloured hair in a loop over his forehead with extraordinary greenish eyes suggesting that iceberg glare he liked to claim from his Norse ancestors. His voice was unforget-table, with no trace then of an American accent, he was charming but ruthless, and certainly, like Isherwood, a Marxist of sorts, but less close to Communist orthodoxy than Day Lewis or Spender. My feelings towards him were entirely platonic: I was passionately fond of his poetry and desired his friendship but my subconscious demanded more and I was put out by a dream (based on his ballad) in which, stripped to the waist beside a basin ('O plunge your hands in water') he indicated to me two small firm breasts; 'Well, Cyril, how do you like my lemons?' Though not homo-sexual, I was, I hope, without any prejudices, and so was my wife Jean who became one of Wystan's closest women friends, the first, I believe, to call him Uncle Wiz and whom he described in her copy of his *Epithalamium* as the only woman who could keep him up all night.

After Valencia (May 1937), we soon met again in Barcelona where he took a photo-graph of Antrim playing chess and where, after a good lunch with much Perelada Tinto, we went for a walk in the gardens of Monjuich. By the remains of the old International Exhibition Auden retired to pee behind a bush and was immediately seized by two militia men – or were they military police? They were very indignant at this abuse of public property and it took several wavings of Harry Pollitt's letter to set him free. I think the incident was important for it revealed the misunderstanding between the revolutionary poet who felt disinhibited by the workers' victory and the new bureaucracy to whom the people's gardens deserved more respect than ever before. I suppose we were in as much danger then as we had been during the shelling of Valencia. By the time we left a few days later it was clear to all of us that the govern-ment could not win. I see, by the way, that I reviewed *The Dog Beneath the Skin* for the *New Statesman* on 12 February 1936, and 'Spain' on 5 June 1937 whose ending:

> History to the defeated
> may say 'alas' but cannot help nor pardon

he has crossed out in my copy and written 'This is a lie.' The first contemporary inscription I possess is in *Look Stranger* with an unpublished quatrain sometime in 1937. I did not much like *The Dog Beneath the Skin* perhaps because I had found the hero, Francis Turville Petre, a little too much.

> I raise myself upon an awkward elbow
> and mourn beside the open window
> those two who fell at Pressan Ambo

The Ascent of F6 seemed to me a far better play.

One of the drawbacks of being a professional critic is that one sometimes cannot get out of reviewing a friend's books although one is disappointed. I once apologized to Wystan for one of these infrequent disparagements, 'O that's all right', he answered, 'I didn't mind. I thought "It's just Cyril".' 'And is that what you would have said if I had praised it?'

I have said that he was ruthless and I do not mean only that he was intellectually tougher; he was uncompromising in his feelings, in his coherence of idea with action. He was hard-edge and unmellowed, wanting the benevolence of his later years. I remember once discussing my father and my difficult relationship with him. Wystan was adamant. 'Those people just batten on one, real emotional harpies, they've got to be taught a lesson. Stand up to him, make him see you don't need him any more.' ('From the immense bat-shadow of home deliver us.') Shortly afterwards my father lunched with me in Soho, a treat he always enjoyed, and on the way back I stopped the taxi outside my door in Chelsea (he lived in South Kensington). He clearly expected to be invited in for a talk and a brandy but I bade him an abrupt farewell and gave the driver his address. Clutching his two thick cherrywood sticks with the rubber ferrules, his legs crossed, his feet in pumps, for owing to arthritis he could not stoop to do up laces, he fingered his grey moustache while a tear trickled down his cheek. I don't know which of us felt more unhappy.

Freud's way-out colleague Dr Groddeck was to blame here, for Auden took him more seriously than Marx; he was more at home then among biologists and doctors than humanists; he knew German but little French and he was insularly devoted to northern England.

How much more difficult it is to write about a poet than his work. I keep trying to describe Wystan yet I feel I am but making a grotesque waxwork because I cannot communicate the mysterious certainty of inspiration that covered old envelopes with his tiny crabbed writing. He never seemed to erase and never to be at a loss – 'nothing superfluous and nothing wanting'.

To experience the impact of his early poetry one should re-read it in the magazines in which it first came out. *Oxford Poetry*, *New Country*, *New Signatures*, *New Writing* ('Lay your sleeping head my love') above all, *New Verse*. Grigson's little sixpenny, so well-printed and composed, was a joy right up to its special Auden number but editorial enthusiasm was counteracted by the spleen of his *alter ego*, who saw himself as a *chef d'école* like Breton. But he admired and loved Auden who got no worse chastisement than a comment that 'there was a smell of light verse in the air' (1938).

I always felt that the influence of Shakespeare's sonnets (later to be dismissed by the old Anglican arbiter as the height of bad taste) was extremely stimulating to the younger poet seeking to revive a convention in which it was possible to celebrate homosexual love. Hence those five sonnets, which he never reprinted, among the loveliest he has written I have always thought (*New Verse* No. 5, October 1933):

> I see it often since you've been away:
> The island, the veranda and the fruit;
> The tiny steamer breaking from the bay;
> The literary mornings with its hoot;
> Our ugly comic servant and then you,
> Lovely and willing every afternoon.
> But find myself with my routine to do,
> And knowing that I shall forget you soon.
> There is a wound and who shall stanch it up?

> Deepening daily, discharging all the time
> power from love. . . .

These magical first lines of his!

> The latest ferrule now has tapped the curb

or

> August for the people and their favourite islands

or

> Out on the lawn I lie in bed
> Vega conspicuous overhead

or

> A shilling life will give you all the facts

In a brief list of my friends in 1937 (I am a compulsive list-maker) I end with
'?Wiz' – and one of my pleasantest moments was when I lent him my tails to go to the
Palace to receive his gold medal from the King and he came straight back to tell us
about it. I shared with Brian Howard the position of his social adviser but Brian, more
assiduous, soon cut me out. The next year witnessed his departure with Isherwood
for China and in October the publication of my *Enemies of Promise* so eulogistic of
his prose and verse. *4 February:* 'The Indian Ocean is crashingly dull. We take the
best part of a week to cross it. You're to get that book finished before we return or
there'll be big trouble . . . '.
Hong Kong: 'We are living in a baking hut, but move to the Vice-Chancellor's house
today. The ambassador saw us while he was dressing, and tomorrow we call on the
bishop. Love Wystan.' 'It's Uncle Wiz's birthday. This evening we're giving a big
Chinese supper-party. We're off to Canton next week. Love C.'

15 November 1938 [Birmingham]: I have just finished reading *Enemies of Promise*
. . . . As both Eliot and Edmund Wilson are Americans . . . . I think *E. of P.* is
the best English book of criticism since the war, and more than Eliot or Wilson you
really write about writing in the only way which is interesting to anyone except
academics, as a real occupation like banking or fucking with all its attendant egotism,
boredom, excitement and terror. I do congratulate you on a brilliant but also solid
and moving book.

On their way home from China they had passed through America and had both
made friends whom they found they had missed more than they had expected. Abruptly they struck camp and migrated to the USA sufficiently near the outbreak of war to
incur some hostile criticism. Soon afterwards the intellectual ties reasserted themselves
and Auden began to send his American-based poetry to *Horizon* and *New Writing*. (I
published his elegy on Freud in March, 1940.) It soon became clear from his important
transitional poem, *New Year Letter* (first published in the USA as *The Double Man*)
that Auden had undergone a change of heart as well as of scene. *On this Island (Look*

Stranger) is British, *Another Time*, transitional, *New Year Letter*, American, prelude to *The Age of Anxiety* and the Christian poetry of *For the Time Being*. We had met again, briefly, in 1945 when he passed through London in his pale American officer's uniform and his flat 'a's' ('gas' rhymed with 'mask').

28 November 1946, New York: Wystan charming, though very battered-looking. More American than ever and much less self-conscious than in London .... On to chez Chester. At last the luxury of poverty, stairs (no lift), leaking armchair and an exquisite dinner – with really good European conversation; arguments about poetry and Lorca. Mysticism and fucking, according to Wystan, are the two extremes where man forgets himself and art consequently can't be made. Much conversation about the USA and Wystan continues to propound his point of view (see his Intro-duction to Henry James' *American Scene*), he is quite pro-British and defends this also. He always reverts to the same argument which I think is true for him – in the USA he receives anonymity, more money (he made ten thousand dollars this year and bought a mortgage) and his desire is gratified for a large, open, impersonal new country.

Away from the 'bat-shadow', Auden warns us of the perils of the big city, hold-ups, the proper use of the subway system, and jumping to it at the traffic lights, his welcome is like that of the town mouse to the country one.

Dearest Cyril,

Chester and I sail from here on 7 April [1948]. I hope very much you will be in London then to look after us. It would be lovely if you could meet us at Victoria (you can be the town mouse this time). By the way have you ever read *Tender is the Night?* I did for the first time this summer and found it magnificent – probably the best American novel since H.J. It made me bawl like a baby.

This return visit was after the appearance of the American number of *Horizon* which contained *The Fall of Rome* which he dedicated to me. I believe or rather I hope that it is true that I had asked him to write me something that would make me cry. It is a beautiful poem and like all the true expressions of his genius there is something totally unpredictable about it (those reindeer) yet even so one finds, as once his scientist was Groddeck, that now Sheldon had taken over – 'Cerebrotonic Cato . . .'. I also published *In Praise of Limestone*.

I think this is the moment to stop, just before Auden's private face grew, through no choice of his own, irrevocably public, finally to settle into that striated Roman mask of luminous authority which it became harder and harder to penetrate. In 1972 I was invited by Alasdair Clayre to the All Souls *Encaenia* where, resplendent in cap and gown, Wystan was made a Doctor of Letters. 'Why Cyril, what on earth are you doing here?' 'I came to find *you*,' I answered. It was the only time I had ever seen him at a loss.

Christopher Isherwood
Some notes on the early poetry

Christopher Isherwood was one of Auden's oldest friends. The first part of this article appeared in the 1937 Auden double number of New Verse

If I were told to introduce a reader to the poetry of W. H. Auden, I should begin by asking him to remember three things.

First, that Auden is essentially a scientist: perhaps I should add, 'a schoolboy scientist'. He has, that is to say, the scientific training and the scientific interests of a very intelligent schoolboy. He has covered the groundwork, but doesn't propose to go any further: he has no intention of specializing. Nevertheless, he has acquired the scientific outlook and technique of approach; and this is really all he needs for his writing.

Second, that Auden is a musician and a ritualist. As a child, he enjoyed a high Anglican upbringing, coupled with a sound musical education. The Anglicanism has evaporated, leaving only the height: he is still much preoccupied with ritual, in all its forms. When we collaborate, I have to keep a sharp eye on him – or down flop the characters on their knees (see *F6 passim*): another constant danger is that of choral interruptions by angel-voices. If Auden had his way, he would turn every play into a cross between grand opera and high mass.

Third, that Auden is a Scandinavian. The Auden family came originally from Iceland. Auden himself was brought up on the sagas, and their influence upon his work has been profound.

Auden began writing poetry comparatively late; when he had already been several terms at his public school. At our prep school, he showed no literary interests whatever: his ambition was to become a mining-engineer. His first poems, unlike Stephen Spender's, were competent but entirely imitative: Hardy, Thomas and Frost were his models:

THE CARTER'S FUNERAL

Sixty odd years of poaching and drink
And rain-sodden waggons with scarcely a friend,
Chained to this life; rust fractures a link,
  So the end.

Sexton at last has pressed down the loam,
He blows on his fingers and prays for the sun,
Parson unvests and turns to his home,
  Duty done.

> Little enough stays musing upon
> The passing of one of the masters of things,
> Only a bird looks peak-faced on,
>   Looks and sings.

ALLENDALE

The smelting-mill stack is crumbling, no smoke is alive there,
Down in the valley the furnace no lead-ore of worth burns;
Now tombs of decaying industries, not to strive there
    Many more earth-turns.

The chimney still stands at the top of the hill like a finger
Skywardly pointing as if it were asking: 'What lies there?'
And thither we stray to dream of those things as we linger,
    Nature denies here.

Dark looming around the fell-folds stretch desolate, crag-scarred,
Seeming to murmur: 'Why beat you the bars of your prison?'
What matter? To us the world-face is glowing and flag-starred,
    Lit by a vision.

So under it stand we, all swept by the rain and the wind there,
Muttering: 'What look you for, creatures that die in a season?'
We care not, but turn to our dreams and the comfort we find there,
    Asking no reason.

The saga-world is a schoolboy world, with its feuds, its practical jokes, its dark threats conveyed in puns and riddles and understatements: 'I think this day will end unluckily for some; but chiefly for those who least expect harm.' I once remarked to Auden that the atmosphere of *Gisli the Outlaw* very much reminded me of our schooldays. He was pleased with the idea: and, soon after this, he produced his first play: *Paid on Both Sides*, in which the two worlds are so inextricably confused that it is impossible to say whether the characters are really epic heroes or only members of a school OTC.

Auden is, and always has been, a most prolific writer. Problems of form and technique seem to bother him very little. You could say to him: 'Please write me a double ballade on the virtues of a certain brand of toothpaste, which also contains at least ten anagrams on the names of well-known politicians, and of which the refrain is as follows. . . .' Within twenty-four hours, your ballade would be ready – and it would be good.

When Auden was younger, he was very lazy. He hated polishing and making corrections. If I didn't like a poem, he threw it away and wrote another. If I liked one line, he would keep it and work it into a new poem. In this way, whole poems were constructed which were simply anthologies of my favourite lines, entirely regardless of grammar or sense. This is the simple explanation of much of Auden's celebrated obscurity.

While Auden was up at Oxford, he read T. S. Eliot. The discovery of *The Waste Land* marked a turning-point in his work – for the better, certainly; though the earliest symptoms of Eliot-influence were most alarming. Like a patient who has received an over-powerful inoculation, Auden developed a severe attack of allusions, jargonitis and private jokes. He began to write lines like: 'Inexorable Rembrandt rays that stab . . .' or 'Love mutual has reached its first eutectic. . . .' Nearly all the poems of that early Eliot period are now scrapped.

In 1928, Spender, who had a private press, printed a little orange paper volume of Auden's poems. (This booklet, limited to 'about forty-five copies', is now a biblio-phile's prize: the misprints alone are worth about ten shillings each.) Most of the poems were reprinted two years later, when Faber and Faber published the first edition of their Auden volume: here is one of the few which were not:

> Consider if you will how lovers stand
> In brief adherence, straining to preserve
> Too long the suction of good-bye: others,
> Less clinically-minded, will admire
> An evening like a coloured photograph,
> A music stultified across the water.
> The desert opens here, and if, though we
> Have ligatured the ends of a farewell,
> Sporadic heartburn show in evidence
> Of love uneconomically slain,
> It is for the last time, the last look back,
> The heel upon the finishing blade of grass,
> To dazzling cities of the plain where lust
> Threatened a sinister rod, and we shall turn
> To our study of stones, to split Eve's apple,
> Absorbed, content if we can say 'because';
> Unanswerable like any other pedant,
> Like Solomon and Sheba, wrong for years.

I think this poem illustrates very clearly Auden's state of mind at that period: in this respect, its weakness is its virtue. Auden was very busy trying to regard things 'clinically', as he called it. Poetry, he said, must concern itself with shapes and vol-umes. Colours and smells were condemned as romantic. Form alone was significant. Auden loathed (and still rather dislikes) the sea – for the sea, besides being deplorably wet and sloppy, is formless. (Note 'ligatured' – a typical specimen of the 'clinical' vocabulary.)

Another, and even more powerful influence upon Auden's early work was non-literary in its origin – in 1929, during a visit to Berlin, he came into contact with the doctrines of the American psychologist, Homer Lane. (*Cf.* Auden's own account of this, in his *Letter to Lord Byron*, Part Four.) Auden was particularly interested in Lane's theories of the psychological causes of disease – if you refuse to make use of your creative powers, you grow a cancer instead. References to these theories can be found in many of the early poems, and, more generally, in *The Orators*. Lane's teachings provide a key to most of the obscurities in the *Journal of an Airman* (Mr John Layard, one of Lane's most brilliant followers, has pointed out the psychological relationship between epilepsy and the idea of flight.)

The first collaboration between Auden and myself was in a play called *The Enemies of a Bishop*. The bishop is the hero of the play: he represents sanity, and is an idealized portrait of Lane himself. His enemies are the pseudo-healers, the wilfully ill and the mad. The final curtain goes down on his complete victory. The play was no more than a charade, very loosely put together and full of private jokes. We revised the best parts of it and used them again, five years later, in *The Dog Beneath the Skin*.

It is typical of Auden's astonishing adaptability that, after two or three months in Berlin, he began to write poems in German. Their style can be best imagined by supposing that a German writer should attempt a sonnet-sequence in a mixture of Cockney and Tennysonian English, without being able to command either idiom. A German critic of great sensibility to whom I afterwards showed these sonnets was much intrigued. He assured me that their writer was a poet of the first rank, despite his absurd grammatical howlers. The critic himself had never heard of Auden and was certainly quite unaware of his English reputation.

The scenery of Auden's early poetry is, almost invariably, mountainous. As a boy, he visited Westmorland, the Peak District of Derbyshire and Wales. For urban scenery he preferred the industrial Midlands; particularly in districts where an industry is decaying. His romantic travel-wish was always towards the north. He could never understand how anybody could long for the sun, the blue sky, the palm-trees of the south. His favourite weather was autumnal; high wind and driving rain. He loved industrial ruins, a disused factory or an abandoned mill: a ruined abbey would leave him quite cold. He has always had a special feeling for caves and mines. At school, one of his favourite books was Jules Verne's *Journey to the Centre of the Earth*.

A final word about influences – or perhaps I should say, crazes. For Auden is deeply rooted in the English tradition, and his debt to most of the great writers of the past is too obvious to need comment here. The crazes were all short-lived: they left plenty of temporary damage but few lasting traces. The earliest I remember was for Edwin Arlington Robinson. It found expression in about half a dozen poems (all scrapped) and notably in some lines about 'a Shape' in an Irish mackintosh which malice urges but friendship forbids me to quote. Then came Emily Dickinson. You will find her footprints here and there among the earlier poems: for example,

> Nor sorrow take
> His endless look.

Then Bridges published *The Testament of Beauty*, and Auden wrote the poem beginning: 'Which of you waking early and watching daybreak. . . .' which appeared in the first Faber edition, but was removed from later impressions. Finally, there was Hopkins: but, by this time, Auden's literary digestive powers were stronger; he made a virtue of imitation, and produced the brilliant parody-ode to a rugger xv which appears at the end of *The Orators*.

POSTSCRIPT

I am asked to comment on 'Some Notes on Auden's Early Poetry', an article which I wrote for the 1937 'Auden Double Number' of *New Verse*.

As I have already said in my book, *Exhumations*, I now find the tone of these 'Notes' somewhat aggressive and patronizing. But I won't be too hard on the Christopher of 1937. It must be remembered that he had first met Auden as a seven-year-old schoolboy and that he was nearly three years Auden's senior. A sense of seniority is important in one's schooldays and it is apt to persist if the senior and the junior continue to see each other in later life. By 1937, Auden had become the most famous British writer of his generation. He was also, temporarily, a hero in the eyes of many young people because he had offered his services to the Spanish Government in the civil war and had gone to Spain for several months, earlier that year. No wonder Christopher felt that his status as Auden's senior and mentor was threatened! I don't think he was ever seriously envious. Indeed, he was lovingly proud of Auden's achievements – so proud that his pride embarrassed him: he masked it in irony. But his pride was possessive. He wanted to let the world know that he still claimed to be Auden's best friend and chief interpreter. At the same time, he was aware that Auden was no longer anybody's property: he was in the public domain. Hence Christopher's patronage and aggression.

Observers were sometimes slightly shocked when they saw how Auden would ask for Christopher's literary advice and follow it without question, rewriting lines and even whole poems of which he had disapproved. Perhaps they did not realize that Auden's apparent passivity was an aspect of his creative strength. A powerfully fertile imagination often finds it amusing to subject itself to somebody else's commands. Like an Arabian Nights genie, it rejoices in overcoming all obstacles and fulfilling all wishes, however ill-advised.

In his 'Notes', Christopher makes a mistake which I can't account for. He states that *The Dog Beneath the Skin* was evolved out of *The Enemies of a Bishop*. This is not so. *The Enemies of a Bishop* was a play which Auden and Christopher had written together, probably in 1930. In 1934, Auden wrote another play, *The Chase*, independently. He sent it to Christopher, who made some suggestions for additional scenes. Thus they found themselves collaborating, for the second time. *The Dog Beneath the Skin* was a thoroughly revised and much enlarged version of *The Chase*.

Another, less important mistake: Auden must have met John Layard in Berlin in 1928, not 1929. I am sure of this because Auden told Christopher about Layard and Homer Lane when he came back to England for Christmas in 1928.

Referring to Auden's taste for stories of the subterranean, Christopher mentions only Jules Verne's *Journey to the Centre of the Earth*. An even greater favourite of his was, as I recall, Verne's less well-known *The Child of the Cavern*.

When Christopher discusses the writers whose work influenced Auden as a young poet, he makes the word 'influence' sound pejorative. He even uses 'craze' as a synonym for it. He seems to regard the influencing writers as seducers who tempted Auden to deviate from the Auden line – that is to say, the line of Auden's proper poetic development, as ordained by Christopher. But Auden always knew instinctively what he was about. By learning to speak with the tongues of other poets, he was continually enlarging the range of his own strongly individual poetic language. Christopher writes disparagingly of a poem by Auden which resembled the late work of Robert Bridges. He implies that this was an unfortunate lapse; the deviant composition even managed to sneak into Faber's first edition of the *Poems*. However Christopher reports, with stern satisfaction, that it was removed from later impressions. What the 'Notes' neglect to mention is that, while Auden was in the throes of his Bridges craze, he gave Christopher a copy of Bridges' *The Testament of Beauty* which he had inscribed with four lines of the very purest Auden:

> He isn't like us
> He isn't a crook
> The man is a heter
> Who wrote this book.

Anne Fremantle
Reality and religion

Anne Fremantle, author of The Protestant Mystics, *had many religious discussions with Auden*

I first met Wystan in the autumn of 1931, at Helensburgh. He was teaching at a private school there. I was on my first and only visit to a cousin of my father-in-law, Helen Campbell, widow of the Episcopalian bishop of Glasgow and the Isles. I had gone there to read a manuscript diary of Helen's grandmother, Eugenia (née Wynne) whose sister Betsey's diary I had just found at Swanbourne, in the house where my husband, Christopher Fremantle, was born. Wystan was twenty-four, I, just down from Oxford and married the previous year, was twenty-one. Cousin Helen asked Wystan over for supper. He was pale, with egg-white skin and straight yellow hair. We began right away talking about religion, and, whenever we met again (the last time in April 1972) we continued. We must have overlapped at Oxford – I was a contemporary of Stephen Spender, Louis MacNeice, Arthur Calder Marshall and Brian Howard – but, though I belonged to the Poetry Society, I never met Wystan there.

He seemed happy at Helensburgh, and I remember wondering why, it seemed to me a dour place. He told me: 'I enjoy teaching. And I like teaching small boys best.' I asked why, and he replied that they could be taught to concentrate, and that one of the few things the human animal can learn to do is to learn to concentrate. 'Can anyone learn?' I asked, and he replied, 'Everyone has a chance.' Stephen Spender, at the memorial service for Wystan at Oxford on 27 October, noted that his 'happiest poetry' was written while he was teaching at prep schools. Forty years later, I reverted to the subject of teaching children, and Wystan added: 'Yes. I think what is important is to teach them the technique of prayer. That is, the technique of paying attention and of forgetting oneself. . . . I think one has a chance with *every* child to teach them to concentrate.' I then commented that Bertrand Russell had told me he found the techniques of prayer enormously useful, and used them, though he didn't believe in God. 'That has nothing to do with technique,' Wystan remarked. Mention of my father's beautiful but awesome relation, Mrs Sidney Webb (Aunt Bo) who meditated daily, preferably, though an agnostic, in church, brought us back to discussing the Church. In 1931 we had discussed the Patripassian heresy, which I, then, passionately believed: that God the Father shared in the (human) sufferings of his Son. Wystan, always more theologically sound than I, was doubtful, not just because the first of the Thirty-Nine Articles claims that God is 'without body, parts or passions'. I argued that if God didn't suffer for us, for our Redemption, how could Christ's passion help us any more than that, say of St Peter or John Huss or any other holy martyr? Wystan stuck to his guns, however, and in 1941 his Christmas Oratorio *For the Time Being* contained, in Mary's lovely lullaby, the lines:

> Sleep: what have you learned from the womb that bore you
> But an anxiety your Father cannot feel?

Cousin Helen produced, that 1931 evening, the Anglican's alphabet, which delighted Wystan. I copied it out for him. It seems pawkish now, beginning with:

> A was the Anglican given to gas
> B was the breakfast he ate before Mass

and ending with:

> Z was the zeal that he shewed for religion.

In turn, Wystan quoted the *Song of the Deposited Book* (of Common Prayer) which, with 'apologies to Gilbert and Sullivan' had appeared in October, 1927, in the St Mary's Graham St Quarterly. I took it down, and still have it, on Helensburgh notepaper. The first verse goes:

> A bait-on-the-hook new book
> A bring-in-the-Jesuit book
> A plainly-papistical, grossly-sophistical
> Most anti-scriptural book

The last verse went:

> Our please-be-good-boys new book
> Our don't-make-a-noise, new book
> Our why-can't-you-risk-a-bit, trust-the-Episcopate
> Save-the-Establishment Book.

During the following years Wystan and I met mostly at political meetings. We never discussed politics as it seemed as though all our generation at Oxford held the same views. I don't know where he was teaching after Helensburgh, but he was in London for the production of his three plays, written with Christopher Isherwood for

The Forties

29 Auden with Tania Stern in 1945 shortly before leaving for Germany as a member of the US Army. (See James Stern's and Nicolas Nabokov's contributions.)

30 Auden in May 1945, in the ruins of Nuremberg. In the background is a statue of Durer which miraculously survived the bombing.

31 OPPOSITE Auden in 1946, reading Tolkien for the first time.

32 LEFT *Left to right* James Stern, Rhodda Klonsky and Auden at Fire Island in 1949.
33 BELOW Auden, Isherwood, anon, George Davis at a New York fairground in 1949.

34 OPPOSITE FAR LEFT
Auden, Spender and
Isherwood on Fire Island.
35,36 OPPOSITE TOP AND
BOTTOM Two photographs
of Auden taken in the late
forties when he won the
Pulitzer Prize for *The Age
of Anxiety*.

37 LEFT Auden at his villa
in Ischia in 1949, where he
spent a large part of each
spring and summer until
1957.

38 ABOVE *Left to right* Auden, C. Day Lewis and Stephen Spender in Venice during the PEN club conference there in 1949. This is believed to be the only photograph of the three together.
39 BELOW Another picture, taken on the same occasion, of Auden with Chester Kallman. The two collaborated on the writing of the operas, *The Rake's Progress, The Bassarids, Elegy for Young Lovers* and *Love's Labour's Lost.*

the Group Theatre: *The Dog beneath the Skin* (1935) *The Ascent of F6* (1936) and *On the Frontier* (1938). We also met at Unity Theatre performances, and at meetings to raise money to send a hospital ship to Spain, which was largely financed and organized by Gavin Faringdon.

Wystan came to the USA in the spring of 1939. I was working in Washington, at the British Embassy, from 1942 to 1945, only coming to New York after VJ Day. I had been received, in 1943, into the Roman communion. When we met, I asked him what made him come back to God, and he replied 'I was always very lucky with God. You see, I was a choirboy, and so I always enjoyed singing, and I was a boat boy. So even when I got bored with God, I always enjoyed his worship.' 'What made you come back?' I repeated, and he replied 'Partly Charles Williams, though we never discussed it. And then Hitler. At sixteen I had no need of a theological basis for my nice liberal views – everybody had them. But then when Hitler came along there had to be some reason why he was so utterly wrong. Also, when I was in Spain during the Civil War and all the churches were shut, I realized I didn't like it. I wanted them to be open. I didn't at that point want particularly to pray myself, but I wanted people to be able to.' My own reasons for 'verting' – that I am an historical and a linguistic snob, preferring a faith that goes clear back nearly two thousand years to one which stems from around 1500, and to sing the liturgy, that is, public worship, in an unchanging language, rather than in a language subject to the vagaries of slang and fashion – were approved by Wystan. In fact, he was as heartbroken by what he called the 'mucking up' of the Book of Common Prayer as I was by the change from Latin to the vernacular. Almost his last article was one in the September 1973 *Vogue*, in which he declared that the Book of Common Prayer should now be used only in Latin, since there is a perfectly respectable translation extant, instead of being transliterated into contemporary jargon. We both raged over the twittering owls ('you-who, you-who') in the *Gloria*, and both refused under any circumstances to say '*We* believe in one God'. '*Credo* cannot become *credamus*', he said, and I mournfully recalled to him some of those who had died for such single words as the *filioque*. No two human beings, Wystan declared (and I agreed, and agree) ever believed in the same God: the Nicene Creed (as also the Apostles and the Athanasian) are affirmations of *my* faith, *my* adherence to the Church, not yours, or ours.

I asked him whether he no longer felt himself a political animal and he replied: 'I know that all the verse I wrote, all the positions I took in the thirties, didn't save a single Jew. These attitudes, these writings, only help oneself. They merely make people who think like one, admire and like one – which is rather embarrassing.' Asked whether he ever still wrote political – or *engagé*, as he preferred to call it – verse, he replied 'In 1968 I wrote a poem on the invasion of Czechoslovakia. My spies tell me it is very well known in the USSR.' He did not, however, believe that poets could affect the political climate:

The social and political history of Europe would be just the same if Shakespeare, Dante and Goethe had never written. The only people who affect the political climate are journalists who try and produce the truth, and writers in countries where there is no freedom – so any statement from any writer carries weight. But the poet is really like Dr Johnson: 'I write a little better to endure the world and a little better to enjoy it.'

On another occasion, Wystan spelt out to me that: 'The duties of a writer as a writer and a citizen are not the same. The only duty a writer has as a citizen is to defend language. And this is a *political duty*. Because if language is corrupted, thought is corrupted. Karl Kraus is right, that speech is the mother and not the handmaid of thought.'

When Christopher and I moved to Princeton, Wystan came to stay. It was a small house, with only one bathroom, and we always told our three boys that guests had an absolute priority. The first time Wystan came, only our youngest, Hugh, who loved Wystan and called him 'the other Hugh', was home. He tore up the stairs at about seven o'clock next morning shouting 'Mama, Mama, the other Hugh is taking a bath.' It was an amusing visit, as we invited Father Jean de Menasce, the Dominican Sanskritist, then a fellow at the Institute for Advanced Study, and Dom Aelred Graham, at that time Prior of Portsmouth Priory, to supper. As the first evening was a Friday in Lent, I provided lentils, which neither of the good Fathers had ever eaten. Wystan, Christopher and I, to whom they were very familiar, were rather shocked. On a subsequent occasion Wystan came (to give a talk, I think) and agreed to write an introduction to a new edition I was preparing of George MacDonald's visionary novels, *Phantastes* and *Lilith*. He had been raised on George MacDonald, whom he thought 'one of the most remarkable writers of the nineteenth century'. His favourite of MacDonald's stories was *The Princess and the Goblin*, 'the only English children's book in the same class as the Alice books', and he considered *Lilith* as the equal if not superior to the best of Poe.

After I had published an anthology of the Fathers, called *A Treasury of Early Christianity*, I was asked to compile a similar collection of the Protestant mystics. My first thought was to get Dr Reinhold Niebuhr's wife Ursula, who had been at Oxford with me, and is the only woman I know to get a First in theology, to do it with me. But she turned me down, in a letter I still treasure as it reflects what I later found was a fairly common Protestant reaction to mysticism.

> To be absolutely honest [she wrote], I am rather allergic to what is usually called 'mystical'. The mystical structure, I question. I am inclined to think more and more that theologies and idealogies can be classified according to whether one is a monist or, if I may coin a word, a 'bi-polarist'. I mean by this, a point of view which expresses both foci of reference: 'this is' and then 'this is not'. I think this is what the ancient Hebrews got hold of and many others in our western tradition. Over against this there is the Perennial Philosophy, whether expressed in Eastern or Western forms. The problem about what I am now calling the monist, is the philosophy of identification, whether it is the identification of the self with God or the identification of the person with ideology or theology with the Divine purpose of things. . . . Because of all this I am much more anxious to work at something that is unmystical or even anti-mystical.

Wystan, next approached by me, was equally firm that 'I am not mystical.' But he professed himself pleased to collaborate, and wrote, I think, one of his best essays as an introduction to our book and was endlessly helpful in choosing worthy mystics and endlessly hardworking, reading all possible candidates, and constantly sending in suggestions on postcards. Though professedly not mystical, he said that: 'Every important experience tells you something about reality. One must beware of calling moods of euphoria mystical encounters. I have had encounters with numinous objects,' he admitted, 'and the whole of poetry depends on that. But I avoid the word mystical.' 'Yet,' I countered, 'you wrote that "There is no other want . . . all actions and diversions of the people, their greyhound races, their football pools, their clumsy acts of love . . . what are they but the pitiful, maimed expression of that entire passion, the positive tropism of the soul for God".' 'Yes, yes,' he said, 'but Augustine said it first, and better.' So I quoted *irrequietum est cor nostrum donec requiescat in te* and went on to ask if he agreed with my favourite of all Augustine's remarks, that *Virtus est ordo amoris* – wasn't that absolutely true for a writer above all? 'I think,' Wystan said, 'that the ideal for the writer is to find that he has a view of reality he shares with everyone else, but knows he sees it uniquely and can express both the unique vision and the shared view and feel he knew this all the time. And the writer must remember – as Augustine also said – "that the truth is neither mine nor his nor another's, but belongs to us all, and that we must never account it private to ourselves, lest we be deprived of it".'

I had always found it impossible to believe both in immortality and in eternity. It seemed to me (and still does) that they are contradictory: any extension to beyond time of what was or is *in* time, makes nonsense of the *tota simul*. Wystan disagreed. 'One has an analogy. One has to believe that both are possible' he said:

> For instance, when one hears a Mozart symphony, the means are all material – and the result is beyond the material. What's so silly about B. F. Skinner is when he says that all behaviour is conditioned, including thought; he can't say that what he says is true, or any truer than anything else, because his thought is as equally conditioned as any other – so how can it possibly be true? It's the same with Jacques Monod. Monod is wrong, because the moment you introduce the word random, you can't be objective in stating the theory that you weren't meant to be – except in the case of autistic children. In fact, if everything is random, you cannot possibly be objective about something that is random. I prefer to believe that the invention of photosynthesis is not random but just luck. And I'm sure that Monod must just once in his life have believed, when he heard a voice saying to him 'Thou shalt serve science.'

For about two years, Wystan was very drawn to the Church of Rome. One night, returning from a meeting of the Third Hour (a Catholic-Protestant-Orthodox group that only meets when someone interesting theologically turns up in New York) Wystan said, 'Do you know why I don't become a Roman Catholic?' 'Can't guess,' I said. (It was very late indeed, especially for Wystan who generally insisted at nine o'clock on going home; 'beddybyes' he would say, and leave, whatever the company.) 'Because I think I bear better witness where I am,' he said. I left him at his door without comment.

When I went to stay with him at Kirchstetten, I found he was *regelmässig* indeed.

It was a nondescript house, on the edge of a wood, too near a highway, in dull country. There was a nice garden, full of four-leaf clovers – neither Wystan nor Chester had ever found one. After a good breakfast of coffee and local bread, everyone worked until lunch which Chester cooked, excellently. After lunch, a siesta, then a walk; then tea in the garden; and at six, precisely, the strongest martinis I ever drank. Later a marvellous dinner, and after, records, and at nine, beddybyes. I taught them to drink *tisane* of elder-flowers, and was delighted to be told that the habit had 'taken'.

Wystan was incredibly generous with his time, and would talk on radio or television, would read his poetry and would lecture for a very small fee. But he was strangely stingy in small things. I only ever once asked him for a cigarette. 'If you smoke,' he chided, 'you must buy and bring your own.' And he objected to one's using more than a sliver of lavatory paper, or ever leaving anything on one's plate. He had very strict rules for himself, too. I once said how much I enjoyed waking in the night, because then I could read undisturbed, and he was horrified. 'Mother would not have approved my turning on the light' he said. 'When I wake, I lie in the dark until I fall asleep again.'

He had a great respect for women, putting Marianne Moore top of the list of women poets; 'she's darn good'. He also said Virginia Woolf was 'very great'. He thought women should take over politics, as then there would be far less cruelty than there is with men running the world, because all the weapons of war 'are phallic toys – essentially phallic – cannons and aeroplanes and all those things, and men need phallic toys and women do not. Now these toys are become too dangerous. Men's phallic toys are likely to bring the world to an end.'

I asked him, the very last time we met, if the idea of death worried him, and he replied:

> I don't think about death very much, because I can't imagine it. As the youngest child in the family and the youngest boy in my class at school, I always felt that I was the youngest everywhere, and it's been really only very recently that I've come to the conclusion that I'm not the youngest person present all the time. Now, though I'm in good health, I'm almost able to believe that I shall die.

He added that he'd been reviewing a book on suicide, which was very difficult for him 'because I simply can't imagine wanting to commit suicide under any circumstances. In the same way I can't possibly imagine going mad. It seems inconceivable. I don't think I could possibly go mad.'

'Writing,' he told me once, 'is our best means of breaking bread with the dead. And without that communication with the dead, human life is not possible and not worth living.' He took me to see the cemetery where he wished to be buried – and is. *Scripta manent.*

Basil Boothby
An unofficial visitor

*Basil Boothby first met Auden in China and was the British ambassador in Iceland when Auden
revisited it*

Auden and Isherwood stayed with me in the temporary capital of China, the Yang-Tse
Treaty port of Hankow where I was a member of the mixed consulate and embassy
staff. It was the summer of 1938. The Japanese had begun the conquest of China the
year before and Chiang-Kai-Shek's forces did not appear to be doing much to prevent
them finishing the job. However, the communists, at the end of the Long March, had
recently set up their north-western stronghold and were said to be doing better.
Thanks to a truce with the Government under pressure of the emergency, they were
actually free (after so many official campaigns to exterminate them) to circulate in this
wartime capital where they were represented by Chou-en-Lai himself.

This was the background to Faber's idea of sending out two of their most brilliant
young writers (at least Auden was already theirs) to write something to be called
Journey to a War, comprising poems, diary notes and reportage of the kind most
fashionable at that time. I think Auden himself saw the operation mainly as a report
to the militant left everywhere from this, the far-eastern front of a war which would
soon take place on a world scale (it had already begun in Spain) to check the right-wing
counter-revolutionary oppressors, of which Hitler, Franco and the Japanese were no
doubt the worst – albeit closely pressed by others nearer home. So interviewing Chou,
with whom I was on good terms, was one of their chief objectives, and there is a rather
good photograph of him in their book.

But this very serious side of their mission was only remembered in periods of duty.
We spent the rest of our time, at Auden's bidding, thinking of wildly amusing things
to talk about and do, and when they found out I did not mind being rather shyly
teased as an interesting Wykehamical specimen or lay-figure of establishment sol-
emnity (Auden used to say to me in later life: 'Don't forget you were brought up a
British Pharisee') or could learn without total *désarroi* that my heroine, Jane Austen,
was *really* only concerned with people's incomes, a sort of wildly hilarious fellowship
emerged and everything that happened seemed at once equally beautiful and absurd.
That I think was at least one of the ways in which Auden's genius made itself felt most
at that time when wonderful lyrical and comic powers were beginning to fuse with
deeper intellectual and mystical insights.

I didn't know much about the poetry movement of the thirties, but the counsellor of
the embassy, who was in semi-disgrace for predicting, in a manner dismissive of his
superiors' hopes, that the Japanese would occupy our temporary redoubt as soon as it
suited them, had already warned me that Auden's poetry was of the genuine explosive

kind, 'tremendous stuff' that made you 'sit up'. This was a view into which I enthusiastically entered on one of the first evenings of their stay when our ambassador, who
had come up from Japanese-occupied Shanghai, where for some esoteric reason the
main body of the embassy continued to lurk, and who was staying across the com-
pound with my immediate superior, strolled over for an after-dinner chat and was
greeted with an announcement by Christopher that Auden had written a marvellous
poem about a dead Chinese soldier:

Sir A. Clerk-Kerr: Let him read it to us.
Isherwood: He's gone to bed.
C-K: Go and tell him to come down and read his poem to the British Ambassador.

Whereupon with remarkable despatch Wystan was led in, blinking at the light and
looking more than usual like a big, mad, white rabbit. 'Far from the Heart of Culture.
. . .', he began, but Isherwood interrupted to say that the Ministry of Information
had taken exception to the next line as combining generals and lice in an undignified
way. We all laughed and I, one of the two survivors of the little group, will remember
those splendid verses until brain and memory suffer their expected change; rhetoric,
phrasing, sentiment, harmonized as Auden knew how to make them when he was in his
best form. If only Karl Marx had been listening, I thought, the whole ponderous
thesis on alienation, transferred and transformed from Hegel, could have given way
to the concept of the obscure soldier obscurely wishing the good of all mankind and
consenting to:

> Turn to dust in China that our Daughters
>   be free to love the earth and not again
> Disgraced before the dogs that where are waters,
> Mountains and houses may be also men.[1]

and if there was no visible, and orthodox urban proletariat, Chairman Mao, for one,
who had made his revolution with the country people, and is himself a nature-poet,
would not have cared.

When they left China, I wondered whether there was any hope of seeing either of
them again. Soon after their departure the Japanese duly fulfilled our counsellor's
prophecy (without a massacre this time) and permitted us to go down river and return
to our homes in good time for the hostilities, or as they were at first, phoney hostilities
with Hitler, to begin. But I still went on thinking about my extraordinary new
acquaintance and sometimes did odd things under his spell, like forcing my sister of
twenty-three to repeat after me with the right inflexions:

> Frantic the music of the violins
> To drown the song behind the guarded hill.

[1] In the search for greater austerity, which preoccupied the poet in later years, he substituted the
following instead:

> He joined the dust of China, that our daughters
> Might keep their upright carriage, not again
> Be shamed before the dogs, that, where are waters,
> Mountains and houses, may be also men.

Then we both, Auden and I, went to America: he to the most productive and creative period of his life, I to the boredom and anxiety of official duties, while Paris was falling, London burning and with feelings of despair which were miraculously lightened by the appearance of *New Year Letter*. When I read it I felt as if all my convictions about the political and moral life had found their right expression and the hardest problems of the psyche solved in less than two thousand lines of trim, sparkling iambic tetrameters. If the versification is Samuel Butler's and Goethe's rather than Dryden's, it is however to the 'master of the middle style', sitting prominently there (even flanked by a Frenchman or two in spite of the author's gallophobia) in the Court assembled to hear testimony relative to Auden's poetic vocation, that the tribute of this eccentric-traditional, didactic-lyrical, altogether firm and masculine poem seemed especially, I thought, to belong. But even Dryden could not have matched half those symbols and archetypes, some borrowed (with verse acknowledgements and quotations appended in wonderful footnotes, from Goethe, Groddeck, or St Augustine) but mostly of Auden's invention. When I wrote from Boston to express my praise and gratitude, he replied (from New York) with a ready sweetness and, I think, sincere pleasure; but I felt too insecure and too afraid of seeming a bore to take up his suggestion that we should meet. Soon after I was sent back to the Far East, where nobody seemed to be thinking about poetry. When I returned to England in 1944, from which home and friends seemed equally to have vanished, the simultaneous appearance of *The Sea and the Mirror* and *For the Time Being* oddly reproduced the experience of 1940. When I got married two years later my wife came to love so much the comic scene of Joseph overhearing unkind gossip about Mary, in what is apparently a New York bar:

> My shoes were shined,
> My pants were cleaned and pressed
> And I was hurrying to meet
> My own true love.

that she called our first child Joseph after Auden's rather than the evangelists' model. But the three of us didn't all meet until 1950 in New York, when we saw him sitting alone, not exactly in a bar, but in Luchow's restaurant. We shyly approached and immediately began a conversation which lasted the rest of the day, he in particular talking about opera and the marvellous compliment 'the greatest living musician' had paid him in asking him to do the libretto for a work to be called *The Rake's Progress*.

Then more than twelve years passed during which I thought more about his work than about him, but nevertheless wrote from each new post – Burma, London, Brussels – to let him know where we were and that our house was open to him. At last in 1964 when I was ambassador in Iceland, an Icelandic *savant* who had met him in New York and told him how warmly they (and we too) would welcome him, persuaded him that the time had come to revisit the mythopoeic land of his childhood, of his ancestors (as he maintained) and of that productive 1936 visit with Louis MacNeice. Of course he picked the American plane rather than the Icelandic one, on the grounds that it was more likely to deposit him at the Nato base in time for the splendid lunch the Government and learned men had prepared for him in the capital; of course it was the other one that was punctual, so, on the Government's suggestion, one of the great masters of internal flying on the island took me off in a tiny plane to pick Auden up and deposit us both at the right spot. He seemed happy and rather moved, and, without speaking in any very urbane or professional way, pleased everyone very much by saying he was on 'holy ground'. We all forgot the rather irreverent sallies, home truths about behaviour in buses, and some of the things people ate which had found their way into *Letters from Iceland*. He also seemed to like the atmosphere of our house and our readiness to fit in with habits which already tyrannized him, and even teased us (in order I suppose to alarm our professional conscience) by saying that the rest of his visit was going to be entirely 'cosy', private, and free of receptions, calls, lectures, and talk-ins, adding significantly the doctrine of the 'six lenient semble sieges' (from *About the House*) – meaning that six was a sufficient number for a civilized table. But in the end he did do very happily – and for his Icelandic hosts appreciatively – all the things which had been organized and abandoned to me by my American colleague. He had slipped off to explore another glacier, leaving instructions with his wife to cooperate with us in kindnesses to the American citizen most likely to achieve immortality in the department of English letters since Abraham Lincoln.

So we paid a delightful call on dear President Asgeir Asgeirsson, scholar and lover of our literature. He is now dead alas, as is Iceland's most renowned statesman of modern times, Bjarni Benediktsson, then Prime Minister, who came with a distinguished company to honour Wystan in our house; with him came a selection of the best students led by Donald Brander of the British Council and we had a real talk-in, even if only a few understood all the learned, amusing, and scandalous answers they got to their questions.[1] You could see what a good teacher he was, in a professional sense, by how soon they lost their initial diffidence and how quickly they began to laugh. From time to time thereafter friends made in 1939 would look in, in a tentative, tactfully Icelandic way, to see if he would like a chat about those days. Of one, Wystan said to my wife afterwards: 'Fancy him still being a communist,' and added that it was perhaps better that he should be staying at the British rather than the American embassy. He was very nice to my son, aged seven, too, particularly when the latter admitted literacy in respect of Tolkien and showed a readiness to be questioned about hobbits. After over-hearing Auden say (on my wife reading from a letter from my daughter, then in Rome, mentioning pinches administered by strangers in public places): 'Italian men have to make sure you know they've got a penis,' the said Harry announced later to his mother and a niece who was staying with us: 'I like that sort of conversation.' Other sorts of conversation, extending long after dawn over bottles of claret, included angry repetitions of French alexandrines with English stresses, making *Minos Juge aux Enfers tous les pâles humains* sound like 'The Assyrian came down. . . .' to show that 'Frogs' (except Valéry, to my surprise) didn't understand poetry. Another topic was the – subsequently notorious – repudiation of Yeats. 'Do

---

[1] Matthias Johannessen, editor of *Morgunbladid*, who supplied illustration No. 74 and wrote a moving and learned article at the time of Wystan's death, has pointed out his fidelity to his Icelandic vocation in choosing that part of the *Elder Edda* called *Völuspá* (translated by him and Paul Taylor) for the creation section of his 1970 commonplace book entitled *A Certain World*. This is indeed a compliment from a Christian poet who might have used *Genesis*.

you think he was telling the *truth* when he said he wanted to be a mechanical bird when he was dead?' – accompanied by furious, snorting, laughter, which made me think of Boswell's hero, that other strange Englishman from the Midlands.

After that he went off, relaxed and happy it seemed, to the lonely north-western farm he had visited with MacNeice, whose recent death was now often in his thoughts. The poem he wrote then, in excellent laconic haikus, gave a sort of report on his visit as a whole and celebrates *inter alia* a temporary victory over advancing neuroses of habit and appetite (somewhat less healthy than the mere 'darning and the eight-fifteen' of the post-Christmas reaction in *For the Time Being*). It first appeared in *Encounter* in July 1964 under the title *Iceland Revisited*. He sent us a manuscript of it with his 'thank-you' letter, in which he ascribed the easy way he had settled into our household, and the easy-going form his interviews had taken, to the constant presence of Fanny, our loving pug bitch. Admittedly Fanny was never off his lap, and figures in most of the official photographs of the visit. To her, he was able subsequently to show courtesy and consideration in return when we all visited him in Kirchstetten three summers later, and there was much fussing about what sort of food she would like or would be good for her. He worried also about Harry, whether he wasn't too bored and had been given the right books (Tolkien, I suppose) beside his bed.

We were never to see him so happy again, surrounded as he was then with the comforts of Chester Kallman's cooking, his parish church where we sang with him in the choir-loft, visits from English, American and Austrian friends, and especially the absurdities of Frau Emma, his housekeeper; she distinguished herself while we were there by making a great scene about Harry, then ten years old, being left to enter or even cross the garden alone when there were many plums on the trees and on the ground, for it was well known, was it not, that boys always stole fruit if unsupervised. Her death was one of the factors which darkened the last years of his life: '*Na Frau Emma*', as he said reproachfully in one of his last poems. We were never again – in Strasbourg, London, or Oxford – to see him even moderately happy and we knew he must be thinking like the man in his beloved Bach cantata:

> *Endlich wird mein Joch*
> *Wieder von mir weichen müssen.*

Auden by Anton Schumich, drawn in Vienna just before he died.

Golo Mann
A memoir

Golo Mann is the brother of Erika Mann, whom Auden married in order to help her obtain a British passport. This article appeared in the January 1974 issue of Encounter, *as a translation of an obituary in the* Süddeutsche Zeitung.

I cannot do justice to his work, because though I knew it well and loved it in some respects, I did not know it thoroughly enough. In any case, I am not competent to judge it or to assess its place in literature. Instead, I offer this bundle of personal memories.

I first heard his name in 1935 when he married my sister Erika, though he had never set eyes on her before the wedding. It was on his part a generous gesture to a German émigrée, to help her obtain a British passport. Auden's telegram agreeing to the marriage consisted of a single word: 'DELIGHTED'. A few months later he turned up at my parents' house at Küsnacht, on Lake Zürich, to indicate that he wished to take the relationship seriously. In fact, it developed into a kind of friendship. He was lanky and slovenly dressed, *'nicht gerade schön* (not exactly attractive)', as our housekeeper thought; his manner was appealingly awkward, but at the same time self-confident. If one studied him closer, he had the air of one who was used to being *primus inter pares*, one might even say a triumphant air, so long as this does not suggest anything exaggerated or theatrical. I took him to the airport, where he was to fly to Australia to cooperate in a propaganda film for the newly developing tourist trade. At that time he had already earned a reputation as a poet and a critic of distinction, and he continued in this dangerous métier for nearly forty years; always fresh, always original, and independent beyond description.

We came to know each other better in New York and in neighbouring Princeton in the first half of 1939. I have never talked to anyone whose conversation was more striking and provocative. Auden was a born teacher, which was his original calling in England, but a teacher of the old school. Of Goethe's conversation he wrote: 'What happens when one master of monologue meets another? After his meeting with Madame de Staël, Goethe reported, "We spent a very interesting hour. I couldn't get a word in. She talks well, but at great, very great, length". . . .' Auden went on to quote from Amalie von Helvig: 'In the meantime, a circle of ladies confronted our visitor [Madame de Staël] with the question, what kind of impression had our Apollo made upon her. She also reported that she couldn't get a word in. "But" (she is said to have added with a sigh) "when anyone talks so well, it's always a pleasure to listen." . . .'

I don't know whether Auden was thinking of himself here, but he might well have been. His conversation also was one-sided, and any remark one might try to interject was brushed aside with a 'Quite'. But I felt as Madame de Stael did, only without the sigh.

A few scraps of conversation in 1939 have remained in my memory. On religion: 'I take it for granted that when you write something you take the greatest possible trouble with it. Why? Success, fame, money? They are all very important. Yet they are not the real reason. What is the real reason?' – Later: 'In each of us, there is a bit of a Catholic and a bit of a Protestant; for truth is catholic, but the search for it is protestant.'

On fathers and sons: 'If the father is a novelist, the relationship is bound to be embarrassing, because he cannot help seeing the son as a character out of his novels.' On the principle of loyalty: 'If you can't keep faith, you are lost.' On lyric poets: 'They are not dependent, as people imagine, on feeling, inspiration, love, moonlight, despair; they are craftsmen who, like anybody else, earn honest money by working for the market. And that's all for the best; it imposes a discipline on them, without which their talent would come to nothing.'

He pronounced such words of wisdom with a certain dry didacticism, but also with humour, if they were amusing observations about daily life; but always *ex cathedra*, as if they were not subject to discussion.

I also think of his innumerable critical reviews as a form of monologue. Both in content and length, they are overgrown essays, though not in the sense of 'attempts'. Nor are they monologues in the classical sense of dialogues with oneself, but rather with the reader. Auden never argues with himself, never amends or modifies what he wishes to say. He puts his cards on the table; that is why I speak of his *ex cathedra* manner. Yet his style is never dictatorial; on the contrary it is intimate and friendly; relaxed is perhaps the best word for it. Nine out of ten of his pronouncements, taken at random, are so illuminating that to the reader it is as if the scales had fallen from his eyes.

He was the most intelligent man I have known, or rather, because 'intelligence' only suggests insight and understanding, the cleverest, with a cleverness which was essentially creative. He thought truths out for himself. Many of them could have been expanded into whole books. But he only presented them, in his own particular way, unsystematically. So there is no Auden 'philosophy'.

He did not always obey his own principle, that the poet is principally a craftsman, but most of the time he did. When, in January 1939, my youngest sister married the Italian literary scholar Giuseppe Antonio Borgese, the wedding guests found on their seats a printed poem, several pages long, '*Epithalamium, commemorating the marriage. . . .*' Not that Auden was particularly intimate with Signor Borgese, or with his bride. He simply seized the opportunity, like eighteenth-century poets who derived a part of their meagre incomes from such occasional pieces, or like clergymen from their ceremonial duties. Even in Auden's later volumes of verse, so-called 'commissioned texts', poems written to order and for a fee, have their appropriate place.

He liked to model himself on the eighteenth century. When we first met, he regarded Pope as his master, so far as he had a single one (in fact he had many; or none). In any case, this discipleship was the source of his long, philosophical, didactic poems, the

'Letters to . . . .' They were works which he himself took very seriously, but I think they were also intended as a proof that, in spite of everything, it was possible to write such works, or it was possible for him, even at the present time; that everything was possible to his genius and his strength of will. He was a master, a virtuoso, of poetic form, and he liked to show that he was.

I was a neighbour of his, in January 1939, at the time of the death of W. B. Yeats, whom he greatly admired. He immediately wrote two poems, *in memoriam*; the first extremely 'modern' with loose, scarcely recognizable rhythms. The second might have been written by Tennyson:

> Follow, poet, follow right
> To the bottom of the night
> In the deserts of the heart
> Let the healing fountain start. . . .

From Auden I derive my own definition of poetry: something which creates order and can be learned by heart. (I would not say that Auden was always faithful to the second condition. No one could possibly recite 'A Letter to Elizabeth Mayer' by heart.) A *Poeta Doctus*? His virtuoso mastery of all poetic forms and styles, his erudite references to mythology, sociology, psychology, his insatiable hunger for good books, for truth, for ideas, might make one think so. But I would deny that the description fits him. It conflicts too sharply with the charm and brilliance, the mischievous gaiety of so much of his writing. He said of Goethe that he found it difficult to express himself in prose, and easy only in poetry. Both came easily to Auden.

Of English poets, he loved Donne and Blake, also Pope; of the Latins, Horace; of German poets, Goethe (especially the *Westöstliche Divan*) and Hölderlin. He spoke the lines, '*Ich bin nichts mehr, ich lebe nicht mehr gerne!*' in a voice which only too clearly revealed his sense of the inexpressible grief which they convey – grief was indeed no stranger to him.

He had learned German in Berlin, before 1933, when the German capital exercised so strong an attraction on young Englishmen; he practised it later by translating (Goethe's *Italienische Reise*, in collaboration with his friend Elizabeth Mayer); and finally, in Austria, he made it his second language. He grasped every nuance of the language, as when, for instance, Qualtinger's 'Herr Karl' switches comically from Viennese dialect to a pretentious literary German. He claimed indeed to know the original of Herr Karl, the proprietor of a delicatessen shop in Vienna.

In 1940, I lived with him for a time in Brooklyn, in an old house, much reduced in the social scale, which he rented jointly with a New York writer named George Davis. Other lodgers settled in there. Since three of the inhabitants, Auden himself, Carson McCullers, and Benjamin Britten, later became very famous, I have often been asked about the household. It must surely, people say, have been a 'commune' of exceptional interest and distinction? To this I can only reply that a community of this kind often seems more significant to the hindsight of strangers than it did to those who shared in it.

As a matter of fact, when I think of the house in Brooklyn, the only figure I really

see is Auden – though in the role, not of a poet of genius, but of a stern head of a
family. He kept order in the house. There were two coloured servants, who cleaned
and cooked the meals – formal, heavy meals which were eaten in a gloomy basement
with plush-covered furniture. If anyone was late, Auden did not conceal his disapproval. Expenses were covered in accordance with a complicated system thought out
by Auden; all subscribed to the general domestic economy, and there were individual
prices for each meal. It was a serious question how many meals anyone had missed,
after due notification in advance. Once a week there was a 'bill-day', announced with
a certain satisfaction by Auden at breakfast time; afterwards he went from room to
room collecting payment. He ate enormously, and also drank a great deal, but only
wine – a cheap Chianti or something of that kind; never, in my experience of him at
the time, hard liquor.

No one was ever less of a Bohemian, though those who didn't know him might have
mistaken him for one. The cottage in lower Austria where he lived in summer from
the late 1950s onward was meagrely furnished. In the living room there was a large
rough-hewn table for writing on and a couple of chairs; no bookshelves; the floor
covered with piles of books and half-empty wine bottles. But this was only the outward appearance. He attached no value to the display of possessions, but much to a
strictly conducted rule of life. So long as I knew him, he never went to bed later than
eleven o'clock, so as to be fresh for work in the morning. If visitors were not aware of
his habit, he did not hesitate to impress it on them.

Benjamin Britten soon left Brooklyn and returned to England, presumably because
he did not wish to remain far away from his native country in time of war. Auden
remained. This did not endear him to his countrymen, soon to be his ex-countrymen.
When I showed him a hostile article in an English paper and said it required some
reply from him, he cut me short: 'There is no point.' It was another example of his
independence, self-confidence and pride. He knew that he would survive such a crisis,
best of all by taking no notice of it.

He was never rich, but after his first difficult period in America from 1938 to 1939,
he always earned enough to satisfy his needs. In business affairs he was a hard and
cunning bargainer. 'I always double,' he said, meaning that he always demanded
twice what he was offered. For the publishing profession he had no respect. 'They are
all criminals,' he said to me in German (*Sie sind alle Verbrecher*). He could be arrogant,
even contemptuous in his business dealings; believing, I think, that for one who practised so precarious a profession the best means of defence was attack.

He never wanted to write an autobiography, although there was no lack of material. A
writer, he thought, is a maker, not a doer, and only the latter has anything to tell
about his own life. It is well known that he began his career as a left-wing intellectual
and a militant anti-Fascist. His knowledge of Marx, Freud, Brecht; his visits to China
and to Spain at the time of the civil war; the poems written during the 1930s, are all
evidence of this. In 1938 to 1939, in America, he underwent a change. It was of a
religious nature. Perhaps his reading may have played a part in this, in particular
Reinhold Niebuhr's great work, *The Nature and Destiny of Man*, which he studied
and to which he devoted one of his most deeply considered pieces of criticism.

Fundamentally, however, Auden never allowed himself to be led by others; he picked out of books what he needed for himself and digested it to an extent which justified him, subjectively, in claiming it as his very own. At this period I heard him say one day: 'the English intellectuals who now cry to Heaven against the evil incarnated in Hitler have no Heaven to cry to; they have nothing to offer and their protests echo in empty space.'

From this he drew his own conclusions, which were the product both of reasoning and of his own very strong force of will. On Sundays he began to disappear for a couple of hours and returned with a look of happiness on his face. After a few weeks he confided in me the object of these mysterious excursions: the Episcopalian Church. And in the church he remained for thirty-three years. In Kirchstetten, an area where only a Catholic church exists, he went to Mass and on Corpus Christi marched in the procession, immediately behind the *Burgermeister*. The village treasured that; and he treasured the village. There is a book by William James called *The Will to Believe*; this was the case with Auden. I have no doubt that his decision was good for him, for his soul, for his way of life, for his work. It also made him even readier to help others, and with a readiness to help which was methodical, slightly severe, and protestant in spirit.

Consistent in all things, he revised his views of man, of society, of history in the light of his newly acquired faith. He remained, as before, politically aware. I have a letter from him in 1965 in which he discusses his ideas about the partition of Germany and related matters.

> Do you agree that what West Germany should do is to invest heavily in East Germany? So long as the difference in living standards between the two is as grotesque as it is now, Ulbricht *cannot* make concessions. Only a fairly popular régime can make them. And I did not meet a soul in East Berlin who respects *Der Spitzbart*. . . .

After the invasion of Czechoslovakia, he wrote a poem – 'August 1968' – which in a few lines conveys his violent sense of outrage. He no longer expected politics to provide any kind of salvation; disaster rather; and at the very best the avoidance of the worst disaster. What is known as 'history' now seemed to him a fundamentally irrational, cruel, hopelessly idiotic process. Instead of the spirit of universal love which is characteristic of the left, there came something which was close to global pessimism, modified by a deep sympathy for individual people.

There are two moving examples of this in his volume *City without Walls* (1969); the poem to his dead, unhappy neighbour in Kirchstetten, Joseph Weinheber, and the elegy to his housekeeper after her death.

> *Liebe Frau Emma,*
> *na, was hast Du denn gemacht?*
> You who always made
> such conscience of our comfort
> Oh, how could you go and die . . . .

Emma Eiermann and her brother Josef were German refugees from Czechoslovakia, and they took care of Auden's house and garden. Their misfortunes filled Auden with the deepest sympathy, and also with contempt for the working of 'history', for the way in which the Czechs had made these two totally innocent people pay for Hitler's crimes. The elegy is full of this feeling. When I returned to Kirchstetten after five years, and, alas, for the last time, they were both dead. The themes of the elegy are very characteristic of the later Auden: grief, gratitude, a loving understanding of a *coeur simple*, with all her idiosyncrasies and eccentricities; and also, which is something I have nothing against when it is of the right kind, an arch-conservative point of view.

> but catastrophe
> had failed to modernize you,
> Child of the Old World,
> in which to serve a master
> was never thóught ignoble.

Such women, he knew, have no successors.

How happy, or how lonely, Auden was at the end, I do not know. He had been a success for decades, had lived a life of independence in very beautiful places – California, Ischia, Austria. He had worked together with others, in his early years with Christopher Isherwood and later Chester Kallman – team work, that corresponded to his conception of the artist as craftsman. With a deep understanding of literature, poetry, psychology, theology, he had an equal love of music, which is a communal medium of expression particularly if one practises it as a librettist and song writer. This was one reason why he settled in Kirchstetten; he had to be near an excellent opera house.

He was fond of reading his poems aloud, not without a sense of the dramatic quality of the occasion. 'I am a ham,' he used to say. He was one who enjoyed making public appearances, who liked to entertain others. In short, he lived in an intricate web of human relationships. And yet, there was a touch of the solitary about him, especially towards the end: in the spontaneity of his conversation, so unconcerned with the listener, and also in his laughter.

But just as he had the will to believe, and the will to goodness, so also he had the will to happiness. In one of his last critical reviews, published a few months ago in New York, he digresses, as was his way, from its ostensible subject to another one, which was himself. He was, he said, a happy and a grateful man. He had been a worker and not a labourer. A worker is a man who enjoys what he does and is paid for it by society. A labourer is one who, in order to earn his living, has to perform work which he finds dull and uninteresting. He had had many friends, and still did: 'I have many friends whom I love dearly.' But there was the shadow of old age, always of old age. I quote from memory: 'I ask *le bon Dieu* to take me away when I am seventy. But I am afraid he won't. . . .'

Le bon Dieu was kinder than Auden hoped.

Ursula Niebuhr
Memories of the 1940s

Ursula Niebuhr, together with her theologian husband, Reinhold, was a close friend of Auden's

Wystan had already been living in the USA for a year or so when we first got to know him. When he was asked what he considered himself, English or American, Lincoln Kirstein tells us, Wystan would reply, 'I am a New Yorker.'

So he was when we first met, some time in 1940. Those were dark days for England. At the end of the year, President Roosevelt delivered his famous 'Arsenal for Democracy' fireside chat. The struggle between interventionists and isolationists went on, with many of the liberal and religious journals against intervention in the war, on the basis of various and differing ideological presuppositions. On 6 January 1941, President Roosevelt delivered his State of the Union Message to Congress on the Four Freedoms. These were the public events woven into my memories of those days, and were the background to what we were doing, to what Wystan and we were reading, and writing. Wystan, for example, on 4 January 1941 had a short review in the *Nation* of Reinhold's *Christianity and Power Politics*. The book was a collection of essays, most of which had come out in English or American journals, all of them critical of pacifism. The Nazi threat and the war, in the view of my husband, made the moral perfectionism of religious or secular pacifism not only politically irrelevant but ethically irresponsible, as well as being based on faulty theological and philosophical assumptions about human nature and history. Wystan's review was friendly, and a little critical on the theological side. He told us he was dissatisfied with what he had written as there was no chance in the space 'to do justice to the Dialectic'. The Dialectic was the validity of 'a sense of the unconditional'. In his review he asked whether or not Reinhold believed 'that the contemplative life was the highest and most exhausting of vocations, and that the church is saved by the saints.'

Reinhold and I were intrigued by this criticism, and not knowing him well at this time, had no idea how long he had been so theological.[1] The *Nation* had headed the review 'Tract for the Times', but Wystan had not dealt at all with 'the times'. We thought perhaps not being a US citizen, he may not have wanted to discuss the political implications of the book, which in the context of 'the times', were action and intervention.

Now, however, looking back, this theological stance of Wystan's seems to have been both definite and consistent at this time. He had given the Commencement Address the year before at Smith College, 17 June 1940, which was the week after the fall of Paris. He began by describing the war as 'the dreadful background of the

---

[1] We discovered later that both Wystan and Reinhold had contributed to a volume *Christianity and the Social Revolution*, published by Victor Gollancz in 1935.

thoughts of us all', and of 'the overwhelming desire to do something this minute to stop it', yet, 'to try to understand what has come upon us, and why – is indispensable'. His talk was called, 'Romantic or Free?' The statements and theses which were to become so characteristic are all there; particularly those analysing 'the paradoxical dialectic of freedom'. The label of 'romantic', he chose for all those who in one way or another reject 'this understanding of freedom'. The fate of such is the closed society. Conversely, the open society 'believes that logical necessity can be recognized by everybody and that in consequence, the truth is best arrived at by free controversy. But it will recognize that no thinking or voluntary behaviour is possible without making some absolute presuppositions, or acts of faith.' He described his own 'coming to the USA . . . as one of the most significant experiences of my life, . . . because owing to America's historical discontinuity, its mixed population, and the arrival of the industrial revolution while the geographical frontier was still open, I think I have learned here what I could have learned nowhere else: what the special demands and dangers of an open society are.' At the beginning of his address, he had said, 'I am quite frankly going to preach you a sermon.' At the end he reminded his hearers that sermons were supposed to begin with a text. 'I have kept mine to the end.' The text was from Rilke's *Words to a Young Poet*:

> The only courage that is demanded of us: [is] to have courage for the most extraordinary, the most singular, and the most inexplicable that we may encounter. . . . Only he or she who is ready for everything . . . will live the relation to another as something alive. . . . We must always hold to what is difficult, then that which now still seems to us the most hostile will become what we most trust and find most faithful. . . . Perhaps all the dragons of our lives are princesses who are only waiting to see us once beautiful and brave. Perhaps everything terrible is in its deepest being something helpless that wants help from us.

The characteristic style and authoritative mode of address are in this speech, as well as the framework in which his writing – prose and verse – would move.

A fortnight later (8 July 1940), he reviewed the *Wartime Letters* and *Fifty Selected Poems* of Rilke in the *New Republic*. He wrote sympathetically about Rilke's negative reaction to the First World War, 'Not to understand: yes, that was my entire occupation in these years'; and commented on these words of Rilke, 'To be conscious but to refuse to understand, is a positive act that calls for courage of a high order.' But he admitted that, 'It may at the time be difficult for the outsider . . . to distinguish it from selfish or cowardly indifference.' For him, Rilke was the writer to whom to turn, 'for strength to resist the treacherous temptations that approach us disguised as righteous duties.' Rilke had reminded that each of us 'shall plant a small hope that . . . we shall not forget that true revolution is "the conquering of abuses for the benefit of the deepest tradition".'

Meanwhile the war continued. In February 1941, Wendell Willkie, enthusiastically pro-British after his visit to England in the Blitz, testified before the Senate Foreign Relations Committee, and gave the pro-interventionist forces a great boost. Soon after, the Lend-Lease Bill passed both Houses of Congress. About this time, Reinhold and some of his colleagues and friends launched a little fortnightly, *Christianity and*

Crisis, to counter the isolation and political irresponsibility of the Protestant churches. Wystan approved of this venture, and offered to write for it.

In this historic context, Wystan was writing reviews, working on his poems, and reading Kierkegaard, of whom translations had been coming out on both sides of the Atlantic. He also was reading Tillich. We had lent him *The Interpretation of History*, also the mimeographed propositions for his Systematic Theology which were handed out to Tillich's classes. These in distilled and stripped form appealed to Wystan, and he found Tillich 'exciting'.

A review of Kafka's novels he wrote in February 1941, is very typical of what he was thinking and talking about at that time. Earlier he had said, in his rather magisterial manner, 'Of course, you can only understand Kafka if you understand that grace is arbitrary.' Someone who obviously did not know Latin, questioned the word 'arbitrary'. I hastened to translate it into the English word 'free'. Wystan, rather like a school master, gave his approval. 'Grace is free – Kafka tells us that we must have faith to recognize the necessary.' All this is spelt out in this review.

Many asked about his theological position. The reaction of some academic theologians and some of the clergy who read him at this time was intriguing. They were flattered that a well-known poet would read theology, but they were puzzled by his free use of theological categories. For them these were supposed to be kept in their proper place, in their pigeon-holes, or indexed in their files, in the same way that clothes that they wore to church on Sunday were kept for their proper use. But Wystan was taking them out, and scattering the terms – and was wearing Sunday clothes on weekdays.

One of this ilk asked me where Wystan 'stood' theologically. Afterwards, I told Wystan about this, somewhat facetiously, as I had been tempted to tell my solemn interlocutor that Wystan never stood anywhere, only sat. Wystan, however, became serious, and spelt it out for me exactly.

> I think my theological position is very much the same as Reinhold's, i.e. Augustinian, not Thomist. (I would allow a little more place, perhaps, for the *Via Negativa*.) Liturgically, I am Anglo-Catholic though not too spiky, I hope. As for forms of church organization, I don't know what to think. I am inclined to agree with de Rougemont that it will be back to the catacombs for all of us. As organizations, none of the churches look too hot, do they? But what organization ever does?

I remember he came to dinner one evening in the spring of 1941, bringing a couple of poems to give us. He thought Reinhold might use one or other in his new fortnightly, *Christianity and Crisis*. But Reinhold thought they were too 'sophisticated' and the average reader would not understand them. I wondered if that would matter as long as people liked them. I was a little embarrassed that Reinhold was not accepting the poems Wystan had brought us. Reinhold, however, told Wystan that American Protestants liked poems like Joyce Kilmer's 'Trees' – 'Only God can make a tree.' I became rather nasty and advised Wystan not to cast pearls before swine. Reinhold and Wystan, both being much nicer than I, thought this very funny and hungrily demanded dinner, which no doubt to suit the occasion was either ham or pork.

Wystan was then living at 7 Middagh Street in Brooklyn Heights. This was a cooperative household; Golo Mann then was living there; also George Davis, an editor of *Mademoiselle*. Benjamin Britten also had been there, and others came and went. Wystan was bursar or quartermaster, and rather enjoyed bossing the cook whom they employed.

One evening on Middagh Street I remember especially. We talked about all sorts of things and particularly Detroit. George Davis had come from there and Reinhold had lived and worked there for fifteen years as pastor of a church. It was the Detroit of Henry Ford, of the First World War and the twenties, and Reinhold accordingly had learned the facts of life about industrial production, and at first hand from his parishioners of the toll technological development took in terms of human and social values. Wystan was fascinated by the descriptions his friend George Davis and Reinhold gave of Henry Ford and of his Jekyll-and-Hyde personality. The technical genius who gave the world the Model T and the assembly line was presented by his public relations office as a great humanitarian, and largely was accepted as such, but to his subexecutives and to his workers, he was known as a cruel and exacting employer, who exhibited at times a definite streak of sadism.

When we left, Wystan insisted on seeing us to the subway. Before we got there, Wystan suddenly stopped, 'What about some coffee?' and marched us into a cafeteria near the St George Hotel, where we sat drinking very strong and rather bad coffee, discussing Kierkegaard. Wystan was absorbing Kierkegaard's three categories of existence: the aesthetic, the ethical and the religious.

In March 1941, the *Double Man* had come out, dedicated to his good friend Elizabeth Mayer. Later, this remarkable and charming lady collaborated with him on the translation of Goethe's *Italian Journey*. She and her husband, a physician from Germany, lived in Gramercy Park, and there obviously Wystan was very much at home.

New York at that time was very full of emigrés from Germany and France; the members of the Institute for Social Research from Frankfurt, Jacques Maritain, Jean Wahl, and the Swiss Denis de Rougemont and many others. Wystan wrote a review of de Rougemont's book *Love in the Western World* (in the English translation, *Passion and Society*) in the *Nation*.

De Rougemont's book looked at the history of romantic love – of passion – from its 'inception in the courtly love of Provence to contemporary personal and political forms'. '. . . At the root of the romantic conception of ideal sexual passion lies Manicheism, a dualistic heresy introduced into Europe from the East, which held matter to be the creation of the evil one and therefore incapable of salvation.' Thus 'all human institutions like marriage are corrupt, and perfection can be reached only by death, in which the limitations of matter are finally transcended and the soul is merged into the infinite nothingness of the logos.' All this finds expression in the Tristan legend. The love of Tristan and Isolde cannot find fulfilment, for it exists only in the economy of negation. Therefore death, rather than life together 'in honour preferring one another' has to be the fate of the lovers.

This legend [Wystan pointed out] in its turn creates its mirror image, the legend that . . . culminates in Mozart's Don Giovanni. . . . Tristan sees time as something evil to be passively endured; Don Juan sees time as something evil to be aggressively destroyed. The former is a suicide, the latter a murderer. . . . The two sides of the myth can combine only in a collective form, in warfare where every individual is at one and the same time the masochistic murderee and the sadistic murderer, or in the political relationship of the impassioned leader and the impassioned masses. Equally opposed to both isotopes of Eros stands the Christian doctrine of Agape [of unselfish love].

But what is the relation of Eros, of romantic or selfish love to *agape*, the word used in Christian thought to describe God's love for man, and also man's response to it? Was agape, (charity, *caritas*) so supernatural that it could be only the achievement of the saint? Such questions went beyond Wystan's review or indeed de Rougemont's book, but were the stuff and substance of much of our talks. C. S. Lewis in the *Allegory of Love* had instructed us in the literary history of courtly love. Anders Nygren, a Swedish theologian, had written three volumes on *Eros and Agape*. This Lutheran scholar emphasized the discontinuity between the two: ego-centric love and God's love, and criticized much of Christian theology, from St Augustine on, for letting the idea of self-love or Eros infiltrate the idea of agape. But a 'proper self-love', as described either by St Augustine or by Erick Fromm, made sense, and to some of us echoed the Hebrew commonsense in the Second Commandment, 'Love thy neighbour as thyself.'

About the same time as the review of de Rougemont's book, the *New Republic* published Wystan's review of the first volume of Reinhold's book, *The Nature and Destiny of Man*. Naturally what Wystan said was valuable to us, but even more interesting was what he found important. The book was a critique of secular and theological theories of human nature and history. Wystan however paid particular attention to the Christian doctrine of the Incarnation. He began by reminding us that 'it has taken Hitler to show us that liberalism is not self-supporting.' With 'so many of their absolute assumptions destroyed', our contemporaries should overcome their 'prudery' about theological terms and re-examine Christianity. He quoted Reinhold's words with approval, 'The issue of Biblical religion is not primarily the problem of how finite man can know God, but how sinful man is to be reconciled to God and how history is to overcome the tragic consequences of its false eternals.' He liked Reinhold's descriptions and discussions of man's freedom:

His essence is free self-determination, . . . man is a finite spirit lacking identity with the whole, but yet a spirit capable in some sense of envisaging the whole so that he easily commits the error of imagining himself the whole which he envisages . . . the sin is never the mere ignorance of his ignorance. It is always, partly, an effort to obscure his blindness by overestimation of the degree of his sight.

His comments betokened his interests, which later were to be expressed in his *Christmas Oratorio*. In the meantime, he borrowed from me many books on the New Testament, Bultmann, C. H. Dodd *et al*. As a student of the New Testament and of early Christian documents, I was sceptical about part of the so-called historical record. An event is always fact and interpretation, and sometimes the interpretation is more important than the fact. But this did not satisfy Wystan, who said of the Resurrection: 'It does make a difference if it really happened, doesn't it?'

The wartime summer of 1941 found Wystan teaching in the summer school at Olivet College, a denominational college in Michigan. He found it dull and he missed his friends in New York. 'For a combination of reasons, personal, artistic and climatic, I have felt very lonely and low here. The truth is, I do not like the provinces, particularly in the USA where they are provincial by so many thousand miles.' He had found that Reinhold was right about American Protestants liking poems such as Joyce Kilmer's 'Trees'. 'The Middle West seems to me an Eliot landscape, where the spiritual air is "thoroughly small and dry". If I stay here any longer I shall either take to the mysticism that Reinhold so disapproves of, or buy a library of pornographic books.'

That summer, Hitler invaded Russia. The bad news continued. Reinhold was involved in various interventionist affairs, and busy with a great deal of writing and speaking. I was with the children in the country working on lectures and reading. It seemed somehow so remote and irrelevant to be doing this, and I felt as if I was suspended in space while the rest of the world was acting and suffering. After listening to the news at night, I would read Proust for comic relief. I must have made some silly remark about this, for Wystan scolded me. 'I am very shocked by your undialectical remark about Proust. Do you know the Spanish proverb, "God writes straight with crooked lines"? As far as art is concerned, he has no option, because the straight ones leave no mark on the paper.' Then, immediately, to cheer me up, 'I would like you to read a poem about Henry James ['At the Grave of Henry James'] which owes much to Reinhold. It is in the last number of the *Partisan Review*.'

Of course we got hold of it, Reinhold looking with natural interest and egoism for traces of his 'influence'. This amused Wystan, who reminded us how often he and Reinhold had compared notes on the peculiar temptations in their respective callings. Reinhold had emphasized how prone was the Christian teacher or preacher to pride and exhibitionism. In the same moments as he would be committed to the work of the Lord, he could also stand outside himself and wonder if others were noticing or applauding his virtuous behaviour. The poem echoed this, particularly in the last two verses, and was going to appear again and again in Wystan's work.

> All will be judged. Master of nuance and scruple,
> Pray for me and for all writers living or dead;
>   Because there are many whose works
> Are in better taste than their lives; because there is no end
> To the vanity of our calling: make intercession
>   For the treason of all clerks.
>
> Because the darkness is never so distant,
> And there is never much time for the arrogant
>   Spirit to flutter its wings,
> Or the broken bone to rejoice, or the cruel to cry
> For Him whose property is always to have mercy, the author
>   And giver of all good things.

Wystan's range of interests and reading meant much and brought much to Reinhold. Reinhold some years later was asked by an interviewer from the *New York Times* about Wystan's influence on him. Reinhold spoke of Wystan's richness of imagination and learning, then chuckling added, 'He thinks of things that would never occur to me'. Wystan teased him about this remark, 'I am not sure how to take it. If it were Ursula I should know it was malicious! . . . If you want to be very nice, ask your publishers to send me a copy of your *Faith and History*.'

Whether in casual conversation or in action, Wystan always was kind and generous. His telephone calls; inquiries about the children – 'How are the measles?'; his concern about Reinhold's overworking; no one else had quite the same immediate understanding and sympathy. Marianne Moore and Elizabeth Mayer, those two wonderful older friends to whom Wystan showed such consideration, courtesy and devotion, both used to say of him, 'Dear Wystan, there is no one like him.'

He and I also shared very much the same sort of English and Edwardian childhood. We both had doctor fathers; devout mothers. As children, we had read some of the same books, such as Miller's *Red Sandstone*. Born the same year, we had been at Oxford at the same time, and although we had not known each other there, we knew some of the same people. And, Anglican liturgy had influenced us both. Wystan sometimes became very nostalgic for the nineteenth-century hymns of our childhood and would go to the piano and rapturously play and sing loudly from *Hymns Ancient and Modern*. Perhaps only those who had been at English boarding-schools of our period would find the hymn 'The Son of God goes forth to war . . . who follows in his train . . . the matron and the maid', or 'Can a mother forget the child she-bear (bare)' funny at all.

Reinhold found this nostalgia for our English and Anglican childhood both interesting and amusing. He asked Wystan once what of England did he miss most. 'Cold toast,' said Wystan. Although Reinhold did not share our joy in listening to records of English trains (Wystan had a passion for trains) or church bells, he and Wystan both loved to play ecclesiastical parts in family charades or as parlour performances. Wystan would be an English bishop preaching at a public school. He would blow out his cheeks and intone in a manner both vacuous and impressive to suit the uttered clichés. Reinhold used to enact a frontier American evangelist, and then both of them would portray the particular sins of religion: pride, sloth and self-righteousness.

Such performances were in demand not only for the birthday parties of our children but, naturally, were caviar for the theological and university students, who would come to our weekly evening 'at-homes'. One Christmas Day he came to dinner. We had to be very traditional for Wystan; there must be bread-sauce with the turkey, not American cranberry sauce, and lots of brandy for him to set ablaze on the plum pudding. Afterwards, he wanted us to listen to the present he had brought us. This was a record of Stainer's *Crucifixion*; a rather operatic rendition, aimed no doubt at a popular audience. Soon he was accompanying it with both voice and extra pianistic effects and stage directions – 'Let the old ladies get out their handkerchiefs; watch the vicar looking soulful'. Both of us were transported back to our youth, remembering the emotional release given by the Victorian music to the congregation and choir after Holy Week services and the three-hour service on Good Friday. While Wystan and I sang and listened, the rest of the family and other visitors had disappeared with Reinhold to the study. No doubt they thought to sing a Lenten oratorio on Christmas Day was a quaint old English custom.

In the autumn of 1942, with America in the war, Wystan, who earlier in the year had won a Guggenheim Fellowship, went to Swarthmore College where he taught for a couple of years. He seemed and sounded fairly happy there. The undergraduates liked him, and according to his colleagues, his lectures were 'wise, witty, original and stimulating'. Others told us that 'the undergraduates who took his lectures knew that they had had a tremendous experience'. Also, he was writing, working hard; by early 1944, he told us the Oratorio (*For the Time Being*) was finished, 'revised since you saw it' – and also *The Sea and the Mirror*, 'which is really about the Christian conception of Art'.

Often he and Reinhold would be reading and planning to review the same book. One such was C. N. Cochrane's *Christianity and Classical Culture : A Study of Thought and Action From Augustus to Augustine*. Both of them were impressed by the thesis and learning of the book. The author taught Classics at Toronto University, and had been much influenced by R. G. Collingwood with whom he had studied at Oxford. According to Collingwood in *An Essay on Metaphysics* (1939) the Christian Fathers of the early centuries had provided a valid metaphysic for the world of Graeco-Roman science and civilization which was moribund. Cochrane took over this thesis. He started by analysing the Augustan Empire, with its claim to 'eternity' as a final and definitive expression of classical order. The last chapters were, to quote Wystan's review, 'an exposition of the writings, in particular, his views on the doctrine of the Trinity, the State and Divine Providence in history.'

Wystan read the book many times and told us, 'I have just finished an article review of Cochrane's book after writing it four times. Trying to explain the doctrine of the Trinity to the readers of the *New Republic* is not easy.'

> [His] conviction of its importance to the understanding of the epoch with which it is concerned, but also of our own, has increased with each rereading. . . . Classical thought gives no positive value to freedom, and identifies the Divine with the necessary or the legal . . . classical idealism cannot therefore oppose tyranny on principle, it can only oppose a particular tyrant on the ground that his order is not the true order.

Opposed to this,

> the Christian doctrine of creation asserts, among other things, that there is nothing intrinsically evil in matter, the order of nature is inherent in its substance, individuality and motion have meaning, and history is not an unfortunate failure of necessity to master chance, but a dialectic of human choice.

From St Augustine's descriptions of the earthly and heavenly cities 'certain political conclusions' can be drawn:

> In so far as its members love themselves, a society is an earthly city in which order is maintained by force or fear of chaos, bound sooner or later to break down under the tension between freedom and law: in so far as they love God and their

neighbour as themselves, the same society becomes a heavenly city in which order appears the natural consequence of freedom. . . . There can, for the Christian, be no distinction between the personal and the political, for all his relationships are both; every marriage is a polis, every imperium a family; and he has to learn and forgive and sacrifice himself for his enemies as for his wife and children.

The second volume of Reinhold's Gifford Lectures, *The Nature and Destiny of Man*, came out in 1943. Wystan was reading it and planning to use it for his seminar at Swarthmore College. 'Does Reinhold ever have an hour to spare at Philadelphia on his way to or from Washington? I hope so, because I would like to come in from Swarthmore to see him.' Then:

It was such a pleasure to see Reinhold again, looking more of a benevolent eagle than ever. *The Destiny* is grand. . . . My seminar on Romanticism starts tomorrow. Poor things, they have no idea of what they have let themselves in for – Reinhold and Kierkegaard's *Concluding Unscientific Postscript*. Seminars last from 1.30 to six, so I have to provide refreshments. Quakers or no Quakers, I shall serve bread and cheese and beer at four o'clock.

One summer while he was at Swarthmore, Wystan first met Father H. A. Reinhold, a remarkable exile from Hitler's Germany. He had been an organizer of Catholic Seamen's Clubs there, and also a liturgical innovator whose writings later were to influence a whole generation of American Catholics. Wystan had read some of his articles in *Commonweal*, also, *Souls on Fire*, an anthology of mystical writing which Father Reinhold had edited and translated, and was anxious to meet him.

While Wystan was at Swarthmore, he sent me a note, 'Did you ever see a little book by Charles Williams, the *Forgiveness of Sins*, which was published in England about two years ago? I thought it very good indeed.' I had read it, indeed, and we often had talked about Charles Williams, his somewhat fantastic novels, his poetry and particularly, his theological writings. Wystan had met him before he had read any of his works, and had been enormously impressed.

Our meetings were few and on business, yet I count them among my most unforgettable and precious experiences. I have met great and good men in whose presence one was conscious of one's own littleness; Charles Williams' effect on me and on others with whom I have spoken was quite different: In his company one felt as intelligent and infinitely nicer than out of it one knew oneself to be. It wasn't simply that he was a sympathetic listener – he talked a lot and he talked well – but more than anyone else I have ever known, he gave himself completely to the company he was in . . . . When, later, I began to read his books, I realized why this was so; the basic theme which runs through all of them is a doctrine of exchange and substitution, the way of life by which, it was clear, he himself lived.[1]

In 1945, the American Academy of Arts and Letters gave Wystan the Award of Merit Medal and Prize. He was quite pleased about this, but even more pleased when

---

[1] Wystan wrote this as an Introduction to a paperback edition of the *Descent of the Dove*, the history of the Holy Spirit in the Church, which first had come out in 1939, in England, and afterwards was re-issued with Wystan's Introduction.

he was appointed to serve as an intelligence officer in the US Army with the rank of major, in Germany. Reinhold had been on some educational missions to Germany for the State Department, but Wystan was in uniform! So he made the most of his superiority, and showed us photos of himself.

The next year, Wystan accepted an invitation to teach at Bennington College for the spring term. When the term was over at the beginning of June, we fetched him to stay with us at our country cottage, about twenty-five miles from Bennington. There had been some sort of food strike at Bennington College. I cannot remember now for what reason, whether it was because the food was bad in that post-war year, or because liberal students and faculty wanted to have the kitchen helpers organized. But whatever the cause, apparently Wystan had resolved an impasse when at a meeting of the whole college, he had risen to ask, benignly but earnestly, 'When are we going to have some food to eat? I am sure we are all very hungry.' Still, his hunger remained. We fed him as royally as possible, but in the middle of the first night he was with us, Reinhold and I heard noises. Instantly, I got up – was one of the children wanting something? It was Wystan in the kitchen, opening the refrigerator, gazing rapturously at the roast beef. 'I just wanted to see if that beef was still there.' I am still chagrined after all these years that I was too sleepy to give him, there and then, a good slice of that beef.

Food was on his mind for another reason. Wystan's bread and butter letter to us on 19 June, spoke of his and Chester Kallman's plans for a dinner they were giving for T. S. Eliot. 'All in a dither about tonight. It is the first real dinner party I've given. The menu is:

> watercress soup (Chinese style),
> cold salmon (will the glazing go right?),
> Hollandaise sauce,
> new potatoes,
> kidney bean salad,
> zabaglione,
> Wisconsin blue cheese (a favourite of T.S.E.'s)

and as much Chilean white wine as we can stand. The rest is up to the Comforter.' He also sent books for Reinhold's birthday two days later:

I sent off the birthday presents yesterday ... the Henry James' *Prefaces* are the best stuff I know about the nature of the creative act. ... I got back to find an invitation from the Guild of Episcopal Scholars to address them in December on 'Religion and the Artist'. People seem to have an insatiable appetite for that kind of thing, and I find the word 'religion' very suspect, but I suppose I must do what I can.

Mr Eliot later wrote to us about Wystan.

I should like you to know what a comfort it has been to know that you take such an interest in Wystan Auden. Wystan is one of the younger poets of whom I have the highest hopes, and with whom I feel the closest sympathy. I saw him twice in

New York, but on neither occasion privately. I did not get the impression he was settled, and I feared he was wasting his gifts in 'adapting' *The Duchess of Malfi* for Elizabeth Bergner. I should be glad to have news of him occasionally from you. I think we shall have to be patient in waiting for the poetry, because I think his spiritual development has outstripped his technical development, while his technical virtuosity is such that it is able almost to deceive us (and himself) into thinking that it is adequate.

I had persuaded Wystan to lecture in the Department of the History of Religion at Barnard College, where I taught. He was willing to do this for the lordly sum of a thousand dollars for one term. He was lecturing at the New School for Social Research for the first term and would come to us in the following spring of 1947. He hoped that we would have a small group, as he had a class of over five hundred people, mostly older and very interested adults, in his evening classes at the New School. The subject for his lectures suggested itself; we did not have to think or talk about it. It was 'The Quest in Ancient and Modern Literature' and all his favourites were to be read: fairy tales, Kafka, *The Odyssey*, *The Arthurian Legend*, *Don Giovanni*, *The Aeniad*, *Alice in Wonderland*, *Don Quixote*, and *Faust*. The students, undergraduates from Barnard and Columbia Colleges, loved what they had to read, and him. I and a colleague took the tutorial hours, but Wystan insisted on reading all their term papers, much to the students' satisfaction. Soon many others from the university, faculty and graduates, were coming whenever possible to his lectures.

One afternoon before he started his lecture, he looked around in his short-sighted way, and held out his hand. I got up and provided him with some chalk, as he often had written words or names on the blackboard. 'No,' he said, with that wonderful smile, 'Smackers! What about the smackers?'[1] At that time, I had not the foggiest idea what smackers were, but my colleagues soon enlightened me. After the lecture I arranged for the bursar to send him his modest stipend at once.

Nine years later, in 1956, he came back to Barnard College to lecture again in my department. This was just after he had been elected to the Chair of Poetry at Oxford, and his lectures for us followed in the most part those he had given the year before on the BBC, *The Dyer's Hand*.

One day that term, the *New York Times* carried the news that Dorothy Day, the saintly Catholic friend of the poor and founder of the International Worker movement, was in trouble with her House of Hospitality, a hostel for derelicts and bums on the lower East Side. It did not comply with the fire laws, so, as the landlord of a fire-trap, she was ordered by the courts to evict her needy lodgers. Also she was fined $250 and ordered to appear in court.

The next morning, she was leaving the court, and passed a group of derelicts waiting for the hand-out of used clothing. The *New York Times* reported:

From their midst a man, who looked much like the rest, stepped out and pressed a piece of paper into her hand. 'I just read about your trouble,' the man said. 'I want to help out a little bit toward the fine. Here's two-fifty.' Miss Day, elated over having, as she thought, $2.50, thanked her benefactor and hurried on. In the sub-

---

[1] American slang word for dollars.

way on her way to Upper Manhattan Court, she looked at the cheque. It was for the full amount of the fine, $250. And it was signed by W. H. Auden. Miss Day was apologetic for not having recognized him. 'Poets do look a bit unpressed, don't they?' she said. Wystan Auden had read about Miss Day in the paper at breakfast and had rushed out to do what he thought ought to be done.

When next morning he arrived always very punctual for his nine o'clock lecture, he got a tremendous ovation from the students. We went back to my office afterwards to find a message waiting from the College President's office. The secretary had telephoned to wonder if Mr Auden would like his cheque immediately, especially after his generous gift. Wystan was still there, chatting with students and having a cup of coffee. I looked at him and said, 'Smackers always come in handy, don't they?' I doubt if he remembered the earlier occasion.

But to return to 1947, *The Age of Anxiety* came out in the early spring. Wystan did not want to talk about it. With the copy he gave us, he gave me a few extra lines. This is how it went on – after 'As they wait unawares for His world to come'.

> When creation shall give out another fragrance,
> Nicer in our nostrils a novel sweetness
> From cleansed creatures in real accord together
> As a feeling fabric all flushed and intact,
> Phenomena and numbers announcing in one
> Multitudinous oecumenical song
> Their grand giveness of gratitude and joy,
> Peaceful and plural, their positive truth an
> Authoritative This, and authentic Now
> Where in love and in laughter each lives himself
> For, united by His Word, cognition and power,
> System and Order, are a single glory,
> His pattern is complex and our places safe.[1]

I liked the lines, but what about them? Wystan would not tell me or talk about it anymore. I pasted the piece of paper on which they were written at the back of the book, and was puzzled. Always it was like this. Once a poem was published, he did not seem to want to talk about it any more; it was out, and that was that.

Reinhold and I were intrigued by his attitude. He always was so ready to talk about the process and job of creation. I used to ask him, should not the creator continue to be interested in his creations, in their continued existence and in their reception? He also showed a lordly disregard for all reviews and criticism. I suggested this was sinful pride. Reinhold envied his self-sufficiency, confessing he was insecure, and always most apprehensive about reviews. But all this had no effect on Wystan whatsoever. He would smile benignly and concede nothing.

Often we wondered whether we were too casual when he gave us his poems. After all, poetry should not be treated like a bunch of flowers – 'Aren't they beautiful?

---

[1] He had used these lines in 'Litany and Anthem for St Matthew's Day'.

Don't they smell nice?' We may sound like this when we first read them, but they stay with us; we live with them. They become dear friends to whom we turn, who tell us more whenever we listen. So, with Wystan we hoped our use of his poems showed our love and our thanks.

One day, the year before (1946), he had rung me up. What could I tell him about St Matthew? I started an academic summary of critical opinion on the first gospel. 'No, I mean the publican, the tax collector.' 'Oh dear, that identification is very dubious historically,' said I, in academic fashion. 'That doesn't matter,' said Wystan. He had been asked to write a litany for St Matthew's Day by a parson who had been up with him at Oxford who was now Vicar of St Matthew's Church in Northampton.

He had many friends who shared his theological interest. Since 1946, a small group of Catholics, Orthodox and Protestants had met occasionally but regularly in the evening. It was known as the Third Hour, and came into being through the interests and efforts of a remarkable lady, Helen Iswolsky, who taught Russian at Fordham University. The group met in the apartment of one or other of the members. In those days before it was fashionable to be ecumenical, it was ecumenical. I remember that Anne Fremantle, and Father William Lynch, S.J. and Kerensky were members when I first started going to their meetings.

In the summer of 1947, Wystan wanted to know all about the Church Offices, (Lauds, Prime, etc.) and their historical origins. I started to tell him. He wanted more and more; he needed the exact texts, not only their history. These I got hold of for him. In the rather incongruous milieu of Fire Island, a sand strand jutting out from Long Island, much frequented in the summertime by New York writers, he started on the sequence *Horae Canonicae*.

While working on these poems, he played both ends of the scale. He would ask searching questions about the development of worship, then suddenly would be entranced by some detail of ecclesiastical practice. No one else I knew who shared this world of reference had the eye or ear for the absurd or amusing, whether it was some learned footnote or liturgical rubric.

We talked about the motive for the Canonical Hours. After the Constantinian settlement in the fourth century, history was domesticated and time had to be sanctified. The Hours developed in the alternation of work and worship. The words of the Offices provided a kind of skeleton on which Wystan's imagination could work.

Suddenly, a query; 'Wouldn't it be nice to be a minor canon in a cathedral close?' In a way I agreed. I knew cathedral closes, and cathedrals (I had been married in one); the sounds, the organ echoing; the rooks cawing in the elms. 'But why a minor canon?' 'One wouldn't have to do very much work.'

Later, he was more ambitious and wanted to be a bishop. He wrote from Fire Island in 1947, 'Can't you and Reinhold come out here? Do please. . . . We had a carnival last week. I went as a bishop, mitre, cope and all. A friend went as a very rococo angel.' In 1970, talking to a group of doctors and medical students at the Down State Medical Centre in Brooklyn, he said, 'I like to think that if I hadn't been a poet, I might have become an Anglican bishop – politically liberal, I hope; theologically and liturgically conservative, I know.'

He was becoming theologically and liturgically more conservative. In spite of his friendship with Father Reinhold, he did not like liturgical innovation. His ear did not like the various English translations used. But even earlier, he had come to some definite conclusions both theological and ecclesiastical.

In 1950, he gave me a paper on vocations, lay and priestly. I sent it to a friend in England, then editor of *Theology*, where under the title of 'The Things That Are Caesar's', it came out the next year. Wystan was 'more pleased than I can say that I am to appear in *Theology* because nothing could so delight Mama who has, I hope by now, reached the sixth form in purgatory. I hope, though, she isn't boring her fellow penitents with the news.'

The article shows his Catholic view of the priesthood. 'The priest is in the world yet detached from the historical order.' He noted, 'after considerable controversy, the early Church wisely established the principle that the efficacy of the priest is independent of his moral character. The religious authority of the priest is an authority of office only; he is the medium *through* which men receive divine grace.'

The laity, according to Wystan, exercise 'responsibility for the natural and historical order. . . . The standards of efficacy, beauty and truth, by which . . . their activities . . . are measured, are valid irrespective of faith, but the Christian layman is conscious of exercising his natural gifts in the presence of God.'

When Graham Greene's *The Power and the Glory* came out, the figure of the priest illustrated Wystan's point of view. Reinhold, who was, after all, an ordained Protestant minister, did not agree. Preaching the Word and the witness of personal and social life were necessary and important. But for Wystan, these were lay functions; 'whenever and wherever the Church wields temporal power and exerts cultural influence, the priest discharges lay functions as well.'

Preaching, therefore, was a lay activity and a particular art form. Accordingly, it should be well done. He suggested that Reinhold's theological students might benefit by instruction from an Italian tenor. In more serious vein, he made some searching comments after hearing Reinhold preach. The sermon was somewhat on the order of a university sermon, and Reinhold was not as 'existentialist' as usually he was. Afterwards, we analysed it, and Wystan wrote to me;

Your comment was quite correct that it sounded like a review of *The Nature and Destiny of Man*, and for that, the occasion was wrong. Looking around at my fellow congregation, I felt the effect was to make them smug. *We* are not like Dreiser (How many of them have seen as clearly as Dreiser just how dreadful life is? If they haven't, they haven't earned the right to say he is wrong). *We* are not like Aquinas (How many have used their reason enough to criticize him?). We know we see through a glass darkly, we know that hereafter we shall see face to face, we are good honest biblical Protestants. . . . It seems to me a sermon must attempt one of three things, to teach and explain doctrine, to call the sinner to repentance, or to refresh those that are heavy laden, and the preaching to a church congregation now is very different from preaching in Union Square. Kierkegaard as usual put his finger on the sore spot when he said that the task of the preacher is to preach Christ the contemporary offence to Christians. We who profess ourselves Christians must not be allowed to forget how much justice there is in Nietzsche's assertion that as a whole we are a nastier lot than the pagans. (One has after all to be pretty nasty to admit that one is in need of Grace.)

The year after *Nones* came out, which Wystan dedicated to Reinhold and me, Reinhold had his first stroke. Wystan intuitively understood the affront that such an illness was to a man's *amour propre*. As Reinhold gradually got better, Wystan humorously and seriously suggested various ways for Reinhold to express both his frustrations and his writer's instincts. Wystan and Reinhold had been influenced by Martin Buber, and his dialogic principle of the 'I and thou'. Wystan had been talking and writing about the different selves contained in our own particular self. He illustrated this by giving us a dialogue very like the one published later in his article, 'Balaam and the Ass'.

> If a large lady, carelessly, but not intentionally, treads on my corns in the subway, what goes on in my mind can be expressed dramatically as follows:
> Self: (in whom the physical sensation of pain has become the mental passion of anger) Care for my anger! Do something about it.
> Cognitive Ego: You are angry because of the pain caused by this large lady who carelessly but not intentionally has trodden on your corn. If you decide to relieve your feelings, you can give her a sharp kick on the ankle without being noticed.
> Self: Kick her.
> Super Ego: Unintentional wrongs must not be avenged; ladies must not be kicked. Control your anger!
> Lady: I beg your pardon! I hope I didn't hurt you.
> Self: Kick her.
> Super Ego: Smile! Say 'Not at all, madam'.[1]

Reinhold liked this dialogue, and, to cut a long story short, Reinhold started thinking about and then writing what was to become the book, *The Self and the Dramas of History*.

Wystan sent me a birthday letter in August 1947. He wished me well on reaching his age:

> I don't think I am over-anxious about the future, though I do quail a bit sometimes before the probability that it will be lonely. When I see you surrounded by family and its problems, I alternate between self-congratulation and bitter envy. I shall probably die in a hotel to the great annoyance of the management, but I suppose when it comes to the point, one won't care so much.

[1] *Thought*. XXIX, No. 113 (Summer 1954).

Maurice Mandelbaum
Swarthmore

Maurice Mandelbaum was teaching at Swarthmore during the war at the same time as Auden

W. H. Auden taught at Swarthmore College from the autumn of 1942 through the spring of 1945. During the second of those years he occupied the third floor of the house in which I lived with my wife and children. During one or one and a half years he and I taught sections of English composition to students who were in a naval unit stationed at the college for academic work before being assigned to Officer Candidate School or sent to camps that prepared them for immediate active duty. For some months, Auden also taught spoken English to a contingent of officers of the Chinese navy who, for some reason, had been sent to Swarthmore. There is, I think, some doubt as to how well he and any of these officers ever understood one another.

Many stories concerning Auden's residence in Swarthmore circulate among former students and faculty, and most are in some measure true. There is a compilation of the best authenticated of them in an article by Professor Monroe K. Spears, now at Rice University. Professor Spears spent a year as visiting professor at Swarthmore, and did as much archival research on Auden as was possible; in addition, he gathered oral and written communications from Auden's friends. His account appeared in the *Swarthmore College Bulletin* of March 1962. While the details of some of the stories had changed in the twenty-year interval, they had not grown appreciably, nor had they been greatly embellished. The aspect of Professor Spears's account that proved most surprising to me related to the intensity with which Auden had participated in the life of the student body. I had forgotten that he had written articles for the weekly student paper, had given public addresses, and had helped direct a performance of *The Ascent of F6*; I had not forgotten the memorable occasion on which he had organized a comic programme of 'bad taste' for presentation to the whole student body. Bad music was played, bad verse recited, general chaos reigned, and Auden himself introduced each number in a different, and often arbitrarily invented language. Auden was also invited by the graduating class to present a final, formal address to the class; it was entitled 'The World of the Flesh and the Devil', and Professor Spears gives a brief account of it.

Auden was a conspicuous public figure at Swarthmore, but was nonetheless able to maintain a degree of independence rare in so small and ingrown a community. It was a community which he did not wholly like, as is evident in his poem, 'A Healthy Spot'. The germ of the poem lay in lines five to eight:

> Just what is wrong, then, that living among them,
> One is constantly struck by the number of

> Happy marriages and unhappy people?
> They attend all the lectures on Post-War problems. . . .

These lines reproduce, almost verbatim, a remark made to my wife and me as we sat one afternoon having coffee in a booth in the drugstore. Some days later he showed us the poem – it was not usual, I might say, for him to show us unpublished work. The chief exceptions were 'In Sickness and in Health' and portions of 'The Sea and the Mirror' which he was writing while he lived with us. He did have friends in Swarthmore. Chief among them were Wolfgang Köhler and his wife. My wife and I also saw him regularly from about the middle of his first year in Swarthmore. Another couple close to Auden were the Wolfgang Stolpers; Auden was also a friend of the rector of the Episcopal Church in Swarthmore. He, however, must have had a host of other friends, either in Swarthmore or in Bryn Mawr, where he was also teaching during this period. I infer their existence from the fact that Auden never ate either lunches or dinners at home, and while he usually ate luncheon alone I recall that he was almost always invited out for dinner.

His schedule, as I knew it when he lived in our house, was to rise relatively early – I should say well before seven – and come padding down from his third floor to our kitchen to make himself a pot of coffee; he would work without interruption, except for trips to replenish the coffee, until well after our lunch time – perhaps until two. He would then go to the centre of the village to buy his lunch, usually at the Dew Drop Inn, a tiny restaurant, and we would often not see him again until late evening. (His classes usually met, I believe, in the afternoon; if he had had any morning classes – as may have been the case – his usual routine, as I remember it, would have been different on those days.) His morning work hours were wholly devoted to his writing, and he made a point of adhering rigidly to that schedule. He insisted that one had to write with regularity, whether or not anything would issue from the effort. On Sundays this routine was routinely broken: he would attend church, going to the early service to avoid a sermon. He would then spend much of the morning reading the Sunday *New York Times* with us, and talking; he would then leave us and visit others.

Mention of the Sunday newspaper leads me to recognize how little the war seems to have impinged on our conversation, in spite of the shadow of its presence in our close contacts with Wolfgang Köhler, who was self-exiled from Germany, and with many German refugees who visited him; in spite, also, of Auden's ties with England. Furthermore, he and I were at the time teaching composition to future combatants, already in uniform. It is now difficult for me to understand why I do not know more of how the war may have impinged on Auden's attitudes, or on his life during those years in Swarthmore. I may have avoided the subject because of my own lack of war service; I think it more likely that we avoided it because by this time Auden's attitudes, in spite of the war, were basically apolitical (as I believe what he wrote during this period shows). In fact, these two possibilities combine. At about the time the draft was instituted a friend had nominated me for intelligence work connected with cryptography, but my application was turned down because I was too young: I was being saved for the draft. When, because of my eyes, I was rejected for military service, I applied for an interview with a historian who had come to Swarthmore to recruit for the Office of Strategic Services. It was Auden who dissuaded me from entering that service. Whether it was because he felt antipathy toward what he regarded as a sham war service, or whether he foresaw the likelihood of my wife's suffering a breakdown (which she did, not long after), I do not know. What he did was to persuade me that our joint teaching, and my teaching philosophy to the civilians still in residence at the college, was a course which was not only innocent but proper. Perhaps if I had talked with Köhler about the matter I would now better understand Auden's view, but I do not recall that I did; in this matter Auden was my guide. Once I had accepted his advice, I do not believe that the subject ever again arose between us.

There was, however, another point at which the war and the Nazis entered our conversations, and here we each might have had Köhler's experience in mind. (When James Franck, the physicist, was dismissed from his professorship by the Nazis, because he was non-Aryan, Köhler had published a letter of protest in the *Deutsche allgemeine Zeitung* and had waited at home, with friends, all that night, expecting to be arrested.) At some point Auden, in all seriousness, talked about whom one could trust if, or when, fascism came to the USA. It turned out that, with a few exceptions, each of us was more inclined to trust non-academics than academics. I am afraid that before long the seriousness left the game, and we started playing it with malice against some of our colleagues, inventing the excuses that each would give for betraying us.

Auden was fertile in inventing such games, not all of which were equally malicious. One evening when he, my wife and I, and other friends were in our living room, Auden suddenly cited lines from his *New Year Letter*:

> That each for better or for worse
> Must carry round with him through life,
> A judge, a landscape, and a wife. . . .

and he asked each of us to say what his own particular landscape was. It was a revealing game. Auden's landscape, I might add, was in the Cotswolds.

To speak of the games that Auden played brings to mind some of his pedagogical devices. At Swarthmore he taught a variety of courses, including one on 'Romanticism from Rousseau to Hitler' and one on Elizabethan poets. It may have been in the latter course, or in another poetry course, that he mimeographed poems with which his students would not be familiar, leaving out words and requiring the students to fill in the blanks. Some of the omissions were designed to test grasp of the rhyme scheme and an ability to supply an appropriate rhyming word; most, however, were missing adjectives, adverbs, or verbs, designed to test the student's sensitivity to the poetic context of the excised word. In the English composition course that we taught jointly, a more playful side of Auden's pedagogical technique showed itself. We believed we should teach the members of the Navy unit to write simple prose, to understand and be able to recount what they had read, to remember even complicated sets of orders, and to be alert and patient observers. Among the devices we used, most of which Auden invented, I recall the following: to write a detailed and coherent account of what the student had done from the time he got up to the time he arrived at class; to memorize a complicated set of instructions; to learn to be able to recall the details of a mock battle between opposing forces fighting on the Swarthmore campus, including the disposition of the troops at any specified hour (maps of the campus were provided); to spend several hours in Trotter Hall, one of the most frequently and radically remodelled buildings on the campus, and to reconstruct from such clues as stairways, partitions, windows, light switches, visible electrical conduits, and fixtures, some of the remodelling which that building had undergone. (Auden and I had the advantage of being able to examine a series of blueprints in the office of the Superintendent of Buildings and Grounds, in order to verify and supplement the observations we had made during the course of two or three afternoons.) If such pedagogical exercises suggest a combination of imaginative whimsy and rigid demands, they have, I think, conveyed an accurate impression. In his educational theory, Auden was entirely anti-progressive. I still remember some of his defences of types of corporal punishment, such as that of the master who would raise a delinquent student from his seat by yanking on the short hair at the side of the temple. (As the beneficiary of John Dewey's progressive school at the University of Chicago, I was always horrified by this; it may be that Auden took special pleasure in that fact.) Since I never saw Auden with students, I do not know to what extent his theoretical views were reflected in his actual behaviour: I should be surprised if he had been distant, or insensitive, or even severe.

My recollections of Auden at Swarthmore of course include some occasions on which we had discussions which bordered on philosophical topics; however, not only were such talks comparatively rare but we never confronted each other in argument, or in defences of our antipodal positions. I am confident that the same could be said with respect to the intellectual relations between Auden and Köhler in whatever discussions they had of philosophy or psychology. Of Auden's academic friends in Swarthmore I am fairly certain that only the economist Wolfgang Stolper, who had strong interests in Barth and in Jaspers, tended to share Auden's orientation and concerns. To be sure, Auden and I often discussed philosophy obliquely, in terms of historical figures who served as personae through whom each of us could put forward his own views. For a time we even considered writing a series of essays together on some aesthetic themes, in differing styles and from our different points of view. After initial explorations we found that we could not even agree on the themes, and seeing that nothing good could possibly come of the project, we quickly dropped it. Undismayed, Auden tried to widen my horizons in another way, by introducing me to Kierkegaard, but that too was a failure: philosophy proved to be no meeting ground for us.

Some ten years later Auden lectured at Dartmouth College, when I was on the faculty there; he stayed at our house for two or three days, and we had an easier time in discussing philosophy. It was at about the time he produced his volume of selections from Kierkegaard. It seemed to me that not only had his interest in Kierkegaard grown, but that his commitment to a Kierkegaardian position had deepened. Also, perhaps, that his interest in Freud had lessened. As to Kierkegaard, one can of course find parallels between Auden's individualism, his contempt for conformity, standardization, and 'progress', and the same themes in Kierkegaard. The character of their theological position was, I believe, even more similar. In both respects Kierkegaard had surely exerted a direct and lasting influence on Auden. Nevertheless, it seems to me misleading to bring Auden too close to Kierkegaard, since each was a highly personal thinker and in their essential traits of character they differed fundamentally. To be sure, I knew Auden well during only a short span of his life, and saw him rarely thereafter. Yet, during that time I learned of the generosity of spirit which was his. Generosity of spirit seems to me to be one of the most striking attributes of his reviews and his criticism; it was also present in all of the views he expressed privately to me concerning other poets. One need merely think of this generosity of spirit to see the gulf which separates him from Kierkegaard, and to recognize at the same time an affinity between him and his friend Reinhold Niebuhr. Pride of self, as Niebuhr held, is our constant temptation. Its presence makes true friendship impossible. It was through those of his friendships which I best knew – with the Niebuhrs, with Marianne Moore, with the Köhlers, and with Elizabeth and William Mayer – that I think I had greatest insight into Auden's character. And for his loyalty and generosity to me during a difficult time, I am deeply grateful.

James Stern
The indispensable presence

James Stern was with Auden in Germany in 1945

Even if I were qualified to write of the poet I would choose the friend. And by friend I mean the human being to whom one could fearlessly say anything.

Looking back over the past three and a half decades, almost all of our married life, we see him everywhere: in New York and Brooklyn, in Amenia and on the Main Line, in the shack we shared on Fire Island, in Bavaria and Berlin, in Oxford, in London. And here, in 'Wiltshire's witching countryside' – where we celebrated his last Christmas.

The emphasis on the 'we' is deliberate, for Tania and I had the good fortune to share the friendship in about equal proportions. Preferring to live with his own sex, yet hankering after the atmosphere of a family, of what he called a 'nest', he gravitated increasingly towards married couples – not always with the happiest results: 'Why,' came a cry from Ischia in 1949, 'Why do most of the ladies I meet go mad?' Fortunately Tania was an exception. Indeed, as a teacher of gymnastics she was to experience a side of him denied to most of his friends, including myself. Beyond this and the sense of solidarity common to self-imposed exiles, another bond drew us instinctively together: we spoke German – a fact which inspired endless discussion, translation, collaboration, not to mention hilarity, and led to Wystan and myself being sent to Germany in the spring of 1945. And there I experienced a side of him denied, perhaps, to some of his friends, including Tania.

How to describe, in a few pages, his uniqueness? What he meant to us? What we have lost? I think we both feel, as never before, that part of ourselves has gone. For he was more than a friend, more than a personality: to us he was an indispensable presence. To many he was an intellect, an oracle. To us, above all, he was fun. He was so alive. So gay. And his heart was large.

In exile, alone and lonely, in grief and the gloom of war, in deep depression (whether his or ours), under personal attack ('Letters from home are beginning to take a sharper tone about my absence. And my bunion hurts!'), his curiosity, his fundamental optimism, his boundless sense of the absurd, never deserted him. His departures were a sadness, and his arrivals more eagerly anticipated, more welcomed, I think, than those of any other man we have known.

To most people, I suppose, he was above all the born teacher, the leader, the one who knew the answers. Ask Wystan, he'll know. He usually did, often said so. Even at what age he would die. Wystan, really! 'Oh, but I do. I shall live to be eighty-three.' Like Goethe? 'Was he eighty-three? Grunt.' And what will you die of? 'Blood-poisoning.' Not heart? 'Heart? Strong as a horse!' Drugs? Drink? 'My dear, I'm as tough as an old tree. Head like iron.'

At sixty-five he was still boasting of never having had a hangover. And alas I had reasons to believe him. A dawn-riser, however late to bed, he would talk too loud too early. With that naturally vociferous, carrying voice he could fill a hall, dominate a crowd, out-talk Tania. His presence could not be ignored – even by the deaf. Wystan, I have just reckoned that you demolish at least fifteen thousand cigarettes a year. 'Ah, but I don't inhale!' Wystan, that butt's burning our one good table! 'Oh. Sorry.' Pause. 'Why is it that people who aren't rich have valuable furniture?'

Little wonder that his 'untidyness' became notorious. The speed at which he could wreck a room was barely credible, certainly dangerous. On one occasion, a day after he had moved into our flat in New York, I had to return to pick up a manuscript. It's a fact that if it hadn't been for the pictures on the walls I wouldn't have known where I was. Frustrated burglars could not have created greater chaos: they would hardly have covered the floor with books and clothes, all the furniture with papers, and filled every receptacle, including a flower vase, with the remains of cigarettes. God, Wystan, what a mess! 'My dear, I do love this apartment, but I can't understand why it doesn't have more *ash*trays!'

Yet whenever I had uttered a critical remark, I would immediately regret it: he was so imaginatively indulgent of one's own weaknesses. He could express in a sentence that combination of affection, authority and encouragement which he knew the child for years had craved in vain. From upstate New York: 'You owe it to us all to get on with what you're good at. If I hear another word about you not being able to write that story, I'll come thundering down disguised as your father, and beat you up!'

Strange to think that it was he who could not understand how anyone can write a novel. 'It is something I just cannot imagine myself doing,' he once told me. And I tried to explain that unlike him I am a simple soul, that I found much contemporary poetry, including his, just too diffy. 'When I write,' I said, 'it never occurs to me to stop to *think* what a character in a story would say or do.' Wystan just stared at me. Then grunted. I still feel pretty sure he didn't believe me.

Like others of his generation who began feeding on a diet of Freud and Groddeck not so long after they had been weaned, Wystan had snap answers to most questions. And convenient pigeonholes for people. How do you like Tom? 'All right. But, oh, so anal!' Emily? 'Schizo to her toenails!' Harry? 'That old manic! Grunt.' Indeed, life, I used to think, became not unlike one continuous crossword puzzle.

As the years passed, those near him often remarked that he had grown too didactic, over-compulsive in his habits, that the pedagogue had become something of a tyrant. Although such comments came no doubt from those who did not appreciate his sense of humour, who took him (as he often complained) too seriously, the grumbles certainly contained some truth. No host or hostess would deny that as a guest he was demanding, maddeningly punctual, impossibly impatient, the more so as he grew older. Like my soldier father, he lived by the clock. Wystan, are you hungry? Tania would ask. 'Well, my dear, it's four minutes to one. You are surely not suggesting that lunch is going to be *late*?' Like most of us, what he did not 'fancy' – parsnips, fresh air, spaghetti, daylight – was automatically bad for him. And of course there must be an acceptable reason for everything. Wystan, it has stopped raining, shall we go for a walk? The look of horror: 'A *walk*? What on earth *for*?' As for his fellowmen, should some acquaintance fall from favour, that person promptly lost all his virtues and soon had ceased to exist. Nor did success altogether dissipate jealousy. Forced to admit that the poetry of a British contemporary was good, he would quickly if half-mockingly 'put a curse on him'. At least one such poet very soon expired.

When he did make a blunder, the following week it had 'never happened'. A social *faux pas*, on the other hand, could become a classic story. He and I used to have a race as to which of us would be the first to lose all his teeth. I forget who won, but it was a near thing. He had just acquired his first set from our mutual friend, Chester Kallman's father, when – at a Boston tea-party given in his honour by a group of elderly ladies – the hostess asked him to extinguish the flame under the silver kettle. Wystan, now forty-five and far from thin, filled his lungs to capacity. And blew! 'My dear, the *din*! My uppers went crashing into my neighbour's empty teacup!' On a much later occasion (he must have been sixty), while delivering a sermon from a Scottish pulpit, the uppers cracked, broke in two. 'You know, I could hear the clacking inside my head, feel the sweat running down my chin! In terror I glanced at my watch: ten minutes to go!' After the service he asked his local host what on earth he had sounded like. 'What d'you think he said? That he hadn't noticed any difference!'

When and where, people sometimes ask, did we first meet Wystan Auden? In 1937, when he was on his way to or from the civil war in Spain. The place, ironically, was the Café Flore in Paris, where we had an apartment on the Quai de l'Horloge. A northerner of almost albino pigmentation, already bitten by the Germanic bug and the *boîtes* of Berlin, Wystan adamantly refused to see any good in the French. Above all he professed to dislike the language (which he never learned to speak). Even in middle age, having had 'a lovely time' in the capital, he felt the need to add: 'I still feel Paris is not my city. . . .' France to him, like England to some American writers we have known, remained an *idée fixe*, one of those ineradicable prejudices we found advisable in his presence to avoid.

Among friends at French cafés one did not read a book. He did. Needless to say, all five or six of us had drinks. He didn't. He had a coffee. And should someone suggest a drink, he would shake his head and grunt. Pale, smooth-skinned, full-lipped, with a large brown mole on each cheek, he sat there, bent over, oblivious, absorbed. For one who found concentration difficult, it was an envy-making sight. But most vivid in my memory are the hands, the fingers – the fattish, fleshy, unfeeling fingers. Each nail bitten down to the quick. I realize only now how long and often I used to find myself staring at those nails, wondering how they came to be like that, for never was I aware of him biting them!

Next time we met was in the electrifying atmosphere of pre-war New York – where wine in Wystan's diet, we noticed, had already displaced coffee. Here before long, in the streets, in our bed-sitter on East Sixty-Eighth Street, we were greeting one another in the language of our friends, the refugees:

Allo! Wie geht's dir? [Hullo! How are you?]
Was machst du? [What are you doing?]
Pause. *Wie HEISST du?* [What's your NAME?]

In the German language Wystan had acquired a remarkable vocabulary and fluency. However, neither actor nor linguist, he spoke German rather as he spoke American English. For years his musical ear heard nothing odd when he talked of, say, 'dăncing in the ahfternoon'. Of all the Anglo-Saxons I knew who lived and worked in the United States, Wystan in my opinion was and remained the most unalterably English, the most unlikely expatriate. I would even suggest that the conflict of allegiance in a man with his heart and conscience during that catastrophic epoch was sufficient to cause those ravages in the now famous face.

And yet at the time when I was closest to him (in both senses of that word) and he was little short of forty, hardly a wrinkle of strain had begun to show on that face. During these months we were continually together, under circumstances about which I was to write a book but of which Wystan in the years to come could very rarely be persuaded to speak. He did, however, while awaiting my arrival, write to Tania in May 1945:

> SOMEWHERE IN GERMANY
>
> The town outside which we live was ninety-two per cent destroyed in thirty minutes. You can't imagine what that looks like unless you see it with your own eyes. We are billeted in the house of a Nazi who committed suicide and also poisoned his wife, children and grandchildren. . . . The work is very interesting but I'm near crying sometimes. . . . Good Rhine wine costs thirty-five cents a bottle and the weather is wonderful. The people, though, are sad beyond belief.

The main purpose of this letter, I should add, was to ask Tania, whom Wystan had entrusted with power of attorney, to send a cheque for a hundred dollars to the sick wife of 'one of our sergeants' (a refugee who was in Dachau). A characteristic Wystan gesture.

The suppressed name of the town was Darmstadt. And it was there that I caught up with him. When I say that we were continually together I mean that we not only ate and travelled together, we shared a jeep and often a room. I am not sure which I (or he!) found the more difficult. Wystan by now never went to bed with less than one full bottle of the local wine, with the not surprising result that he invariably had to get up in the middle of the night. Since we seldom remained in the same town (or room) for more than a few days, it is again not surprising that he never knew where he was in the dark. If he switched on the light he woke me up. If he didn't I ran the risk, indeed the near certainty, of an even more rude awakening. What I think is surprising and, I feel, does credit to a couple of pretty difficult men, is that in all those weeks we never once had a row, although I twice provoked and expected an explosion. Once intentionally. A family boast is of our skill behind the wheel of a car. To say that Wystan did not share this talent is a gross understatement. I was secretly terrified each time I got into the seat beside him. Secretly, for I have found that for a passenger to express nervousness to a driver is to ask for trouble. And it is a measure of Wystan's ingrained superiority that it never occurred to him to offer me the wheel. One morning in Nürnberg at the prospect of a long and complicated journey to interview a Nazi brewer, I couldn't stand it any longer. I simply got into the driver's seat ahead of him, waited until he was seated beside me, mentally closed my eyes and ears, held my breath, and moved off into the ruins. 'And without,' I heard him muttering between his teeth, 'without so much as a *by your leave.* . . .' However, he did not explode. And I breathed not a word. Just drove on. And the subject was never mentioned again.

At the thought of the other occasion when I expected an explosion my heart still sinks. One morning on the Starnberger See, where we had to work *en masse* in a vast room and sleep *en masse* in dormitories, I rose very early in order to finish in peace the writing of a long interview of the previous day. I had hardly settled down at the typewriter when I felt the unmistakable sensation that I was not alone. I glanced up, and there in the furthermost corner, beyond rows of empty desks and chairs, with his back to me but his head turned, sat Wystan – his face a study of anguish fighting with fury. I was already out of the room, I think, before realizing fully that I had disturbed him in prayer.

Never have I been reminded of that moment with greater poignancy than when, shortly before his last visit to us here in Wiltshire, I read his beautiful appreciation of the poet Walter De la Mare. Here is the Writer writing:

> To be well-bred means to have respect for the solitude of others, whether they be mere acquaintances or, and this is much more difficult, persons we love. . . .

Lincoln Kirstein
Siegfriedslage

Lincoln Kirstein, the founder of the New York Ballet, first knew Auden when he came to New York

Beyond the Isar, – *Reichsdrückmeisterei*;
Drück? Dreck. Vast warehouse bulked with
    Nazi fill
Of drug, gun, uniform – feckless supply.
In leagues of corridor, abandoned room,
We've set High Headquarters, 'midst
    sloven chill –
Our *ersatz* vict'ry and rankling gloom.

My bureau, a dust-sifted shoe-box cell
Usurps the top floor of which stair is shot.
I serve my Sergeant, Filthy Flaherty. He'll
Tell the World his canned Cagney Irishry;
Bathes once a month, need it or not;
Buzzed up at coffee-break and spat at me:

'Man. Get a load of this. Waiting below,
A wild man's parked, and he allows as he
Wants *you*. He must be nuts, but pronto:
Git. See for yourself. Gawd, it's just a
    farce –
Some simulated Major, VIP
Who does not know his silly English arse
From one damned hole in our accurséd sod;
Hies here to Headquarters a lousy mess, –
In *carpet*-slippers, yet! Before Gawd,
He lacks his HELMET LINER, and is clad
In uniform which Patton must suppress.'

Dunstan, driving from Kempten, else I'm
    mad, –
It's *you*, heaped high in Quixote jeep with
    loose
Bedding, valay-packs; manned by nordic
    cook,
Wehrmacht driver, yesterday's PWS, –

Enemy personnel, but how the hell,
Released to you? It beats for keeps, The
    Book.
Yet here you are, crummy and very well
To haul me off to supper, talk the night.

Sergeant is useless, never'd let me go;
I skip right o'er his head, which is not
    right,
Straight to my Captain, piteous pleading
    thus:
'Sir, an old friend awaits me here below:
May I go with him? Filthy'll make his fuss,
But I'll be back by dawn; inspection stand.'

My Captain snickers: 'Soldier, is this Ass?'
I play deep hurt: 'Don't, sir,
    misunderstand.
It's (simulated) Major Morden, sir;
His invitation prompts a formal pass –
Of prose and verse th'ingenious author.
Here, his momentous present mission's for
Interrogating Pastor Wiemöller, –
Sage U-Boot Kapitän of the Erst Worldwar;
Whom Hitler jailed, or did he? It's obscure.
But Dunstan Morden will prompt,
    uncover.'
'Permission granted. Back by dawn, – but
    sure.'

His jeep was comfy, like a busted sack:
Pot, kettle, mattress, a fat case of books,
Floor-lamps, victrola, Wagner's profile
    plaque,
Discs, a crate of wine, God knows all
    what –

Salvage or pillage. The teenage cook's
Worried about his steaks, a cute kid, but
The fierce chauffeur will kill us if he can,
Cuts every corner, never honks his horn
And barrels wrongside down the autobahn;
Finally achieves a silk Bavarian lake
For a four-colour travel-poster born,
Schloss miniature, pasteboard cut-out fake
Domesticating Rheingold's local name,
Hight SIEGFRIEDSLAGE, mean
    memorial
To hero Siegfried of operatic fame,
Sieglinde's tenor, Mime's fosterson.

Upstairs, a dormitory; windows all;
Unrolled neat bedding for ten men, each
    one
An international-type specialist:
Dutch, English, Dane, plus two
    Americans –
Morden, with chum Tim Burns, complete
    the list
Tho' Tim is Afro-Irish in addition –
Intellectuals cosmopolitan
Sworn to high secrecy on topflight mission.
What they're now up to here, one may not
    say:
(Investigating the repentant kraut?
Did he mind bombing more by night or day?
From RAF or from a US plane?)
Has this some use? File and forget? No
    doubt
Archives are avid; still, it's to *my* gain,
For by this site I learned th'essential score,
Nervous prognosis of hist'ry ahead.

A poet sketched the full orchestral score,
Sight-read symphonic fate precipitate;
Defined some main determinings in man's
Hate which 'no man can ever estimate'.
Prussians have a sense of status only;
They must be over us all – or under.
Equals are no compeers for these lonely
Infants who've one word: GROSS – for
    great, big, grand,
Extraordinary, huge. Their blunder
Is semantic. 'To rule' they understand

As enforced order by gross control.
They rest undefeated; this gimcrack peace
Is but a breather for us both, each soul
The same. Unwar, never a victory,
Bequeathed to all our epoch – slight
    surcease:
'Organized hatred. *That* is unity.'[1]

Twenty years on – absolved, rich,
    competent
To kill again, but next time on 'our' side;
Russia an ally who shan't relent
Her quasi-oriental tricks of tension
So all the luck we wait on here – denied
Or distilled to the dreariest dimension
Of mindless spirals in biomorphic daft
Jounce of organs' or organisms' junctures,
As free as pistons in a confined shaft;
Captious hide-and-seek of whimsical guns,
Cops and robbers whose gamesome
    punctures
Waste random blackmail on risky runs.

I get depressed. One often gets depressed
When pliant minds for whom the human
    aim
Spells complex logic logically expressed,
Are rendered sanguine by the basest acts,
Discounting tragic or ironic claim,
End up near truth with just the lyric facts,
Yet past complaint or wisecrack cynical
Reducing analysis to partial
Documents of the jejune clinical.
A poet made uncommon commonsense.

I change the subject. Aren't there some
    martial
Arts safe from ordinary murder? Hence
Asked the silly question – as one must,
Concerning our 'war-writers'. 'What think
    you
Of Soanso?' whose combat verse was just
Out, Pulitzer-prized, compassionate, fine,
Deeply experienced, sincere; so true
It made me weep. I wished it had been mine.

'Thin stuff,' he snapped. I knew it then:
    thin stuff,

1 John Jay Chapman, *Lines On the Death of Bismarck*, 1. 22.

'Poetry,' he said, ''s not in the pity.
It's in the words. What words are wide
    enough?'
Yet if one's greedy in our craft or art,
Shrewd, apt, ambitious – here's a recipe
To fix some blood-types for a wounded
    heart,
Resecting style, or better, grafting tones
Eavesdropped in anguish o'er field-
    telephones,
Wise walky-talking through our murky
    mess,
Rococo bingo, gangbang or deathdance,
A microscopic keyhole on distress –
Merciless, wilful, exquisite, grim, frank,
As in some masterpiece ironwrought
By that tough butterfly, Ronald Firbank
From whose 'Flower Beneath the Foot'
    recall
The texts they taught: 'What Every Soldier
    Ought
To know'; the Hon. Mrs Victor Smythe's
    'All
Men Are Animals'; field-manuals' skit.
No epics more. Grand style our wars are
    not.
Teasing is all. Let's skip the heartfelt bit.

He's restless now. Gossip is done tonight.
Kümmel. Then hit the sack, for *punkt* on
    eight
Morden rates Wiemöller in his light bite.

Near dawn I drag his driver deep from
    sleep
Too soon, but scared I'll make inspection
    late;
In chill midsummer mist grope towards his
    jeep.
Coffeeless, furious, he whirls me fast
Towards Headquarters, through growing
    light, on time.
Dazed, do I meditate through forests passed:
History's long hurtle, my precious part
In decades left me and the health in rhyme;
How one believes, nay, *must* believe in ART.

Heavy the burden; indeed so onerous,
I needs must to my Sergeant spill it all.
Better: my Captain. He'll alert our Brass:
'Listen! d'you know what This is all About,
Really – *about*?' Cassandra's howls apall:
OUR PRESENT VICTORY'S BUT
    OUR FUTURE ROUT.

No dice. Who'd listen? No use, and, who
    cares?
With us, stout England, the enfeebled
    French
Shall shrink our risks to what dubious
    shares
Of salvage as th'Imminent Will intends.
Stubborn enseamed inertia shall entrench
Its sturdy virus – blind, complacent, send
Its livid chain through our complacency. . . .

POSTSCRIPT: WYSTAN AT WAR

It's no secret that Wystan knew war. His sonnet sequence from China in *Journey to a War* (1939) may not seem as heroic as the lines prompted by Spain's civil war, but they are more compact, photographic and vivid. However, it may not be widely known that he served, equipped with the (simulated) rank of Major, in the United States Army, from before the taking of Munich to late in the autumn of 1945. I was then attached to Headquarters, Third US Army, having accompanied General Patton's command from the Normandy landings as jeep-driver, courier, interpreter, and finally in Germany, one of an Arts and Monuments unit.

I first got wind of Wystan in early June near Coburg; he seemed always to have just left wherever I'd been directed to search, leaving behind him a brushfire of incredulous curiosity. Who in hell was this guy? He wore sort of an American uniform and spoke like a Britisher, while it was standard operating procedure that Patton permitted no limeys in Third Army territory. Hence Wystan was rumoured to be on some sort of clandestine mission which was never revealed. When we finally met, under circumstances here described, he did not talk much about why he was in Germany, less perhaps from military discretion than over-all irritation at endemic stupidities and inconveniences in our current situation. Patton would be dismissed for enthusiastic employment of ex-Nazis in administering Bavaria back to democracy. In this, the great commander expressed a governing American superstition that neo-Nazis and anti-Nazis were more or less like Republicans and Democrats. Wystan took this as less naïve than criminal.

The piece here reprinted formed about half of a narrative contrasting the behaviour of old American and young Soviet officers I was then encountering. It was intended for *Rhymes of a Pfc.*, a book first published in 1964 which Wystan noticed in *The New York Review of Books*. This notice is included in *Forewords and Afterwords*, his collected reviews and prefaces. I omitted *Siegfriedslage* from *Rhymes* because I knew he was touchy about any invasion of his personal life, and equally because it was too long and diffuse. However, as here cut, it subsequently appeared twice, once in *Shenandoah*, the Washington and Lee University review in a tribute to his sixtieth birthday in 1967, and again in the *Festscrift* issued by Random House, his American publishers for his 1972 birthday. Since it was never mentioned, I assumed it neither pleased nor displeased him.

I worked with Wystan and Chester Kallman various times in theatre, as well as on a TV production of Mozart's *Magic Flute*, the Metropolitan Opera's production of Stravinsky's *The Rake's Progress* and the New York City Ballet's *Seven Deadly Sins* of Brecht and Weill (all three with George Balanchine) as well as on the medieval *Play of Daniel* (with Noah Greenberg). There were several other projects which did not develop. With Chester always at his side, Wystan was on a peak of professionalism. He knew just what he wanted, how to get it with the least wasted motion; no hysteria or temper tantrums, the use of which are fair theatrical method, if not the most practical. His behaviour in the army, from what I could observe, was similar. The whole business may have been a bloody bore but he made his usual arcane distinctions as to what was 'boring but not a bore', in contrast to what was 'boring *and* a bore'. Also, within it, a not entirely uninteresting job was to be done, the more ungainly aspects of which might offer material for future use. As far as I know, he never wrote about the Second World War except for an anonymous or collective War Department document which one imagines lies filed and forgotten awaiting some academic dissertationist, the likes of which he so disdained.

Watching him among the military, I was, as always, deeply impressed by a presupposed effortless expertise in attaching to his person the exact support required to make him comfortable, keep him amused and, one suspects, better informed on levels less tainted than those officially appointed. In the artistico-theatrical arena, he'd long been accustomed to command. In the army, he behaved exactly as an off-beat intelligence officer is supposed to behave. I first fancied he cast himself as such in a token or symbolic rôle, to be played to the hilt. Soon, however, I realized that this was merely what I, myself, was doing - 'acting-like' a soldier, or attempting to disguise my self, while always feeling like an amateur civilian. Wystan, on the other hand, exactly incorporated Intelligence – in a personification rather than an impersonation. I watched him in theatre and opera-house in which, by the time I knew him best, he had increasingly less interest, although always understanding perfectly what intelligent service was to be rendered. In the requisition of libretti, words for music, one was always astonished at the vast skill he brought to severely restricted limits of script or scenario. Part of his medical heritage was a respect for the measure in science and the science in metric. He was a most versatile craftsman, the craft including organization, participation, accommodation, deployment and refinement, all of which, in theatre, add up to 'creation', although this was a term, relative to the inventive process he disliked.

He will always be known as a pranksome verbal artificer and master jeweller in the Vulgate. Many contributing to this book knew him as a collaborator of genius in several fields only tangentially to do with the ordering of words. In the army, for example, his security was such that his outlandish or outrageous personal accent or appearance was firmly offset by a transparent intellectual and moral authority, in that historically and hence politically, he knew exactly where he and we were at. Few others of us did. In American terms he might have been called business-like, although his was like nobody else's 'busy-ness'. To anyone who might have had some notion of his big secular reputation, his immediate exercise of command in the army was mysterious, and in a mad way, magical. How dare he behave like that? How manage to get away with it? For old friends like myself, rather than new contacts whom he seems quickly to have convinced, it was like watching a straight-faced comedian, performing in level seriousness, a characterization entirely the reverse of what should have been an appropriate norm. Why did his superiors put up with it? Why did they not fault his comfy, ragged, unpaired carpet-slippers, the omission of helmet-liner, the appalling lack of proper dress – or address? Possibly, because as far as superiority went, he believed everyone either exactly as informed or curious as himself – or rather more – as students awaiting instruction. He constated with brevity, acted with urgency and made generalizations later useful to appropriate. Paradoxically, from the eccentric atmosphere emanated a fresh objective utterance which quite defused the fantastic. His presence was comforting, almost endearing; he was at once so cheerful, so harm-less, so bright and so right. The scale was large; generosity of spirit was such that there was no trace of condescension in the particular perspective by which he domesticated, miniaturized or brought down to an irreducible earthiness, the most unlikely, if precise, analyses of current fact and fiction.

Those younger *litterateurs* who are now put off by his late assumption of a 'comfy' persona, his over-all declension into domesticity in recent verse, may discover therein a similar wealth of uncommon commonsense and a specific wisdom of sensibility. With the virtuoso's reversal and contempt for self-repetition and idiosyncratic form-ulae, he sought, as a cleanser of rhetoric, a relaxed tone which, to me, is more impressive than much earlier lapidary, gnomic, or indeed more 'literary' diction. His late conversational idiom is no less mannerly or even mannered, but it is more subtle, less private in its presumption of familial intimacy; more sober, grave, in modest awe of the huge range of experience and phenomena which reduces so much poetic practice to thin discourse. In uniform, as well as in that civil dress which became more and more recklessly untidy as time passed, and which, to be sure, was the unofficial combat-kit worn in his undeclared but constant skirmishing against the young, his elders and Manhattan at large, there was always his supremacy which one sought, feared, sometimes waited anxiously for, often adored and usually followed. Who was ever like him, for correction, direction, fair judgement, command?

It has been given to few English poets to be equally loaded in their lyrical, didactic, dramatic and monitory voices through an overt strategy of mental ammunition and imaginative material. He understood tables of organization very well. He paid his respects to the professional military man with hilarious exaggeration in the lines concerning George 'the bachelor's baby' in *For the Time Being*. As for war itself, certainly the *Sonnets from China*, as these now appear in *Collected Shorter Poems : 1927–1957*, tell more about soldiers and soldiering than most verse written between 1919 and 1969. What other oracle would have uttered:

> Think in this year what pleased the dancers best,
> When Austria died, when China was forsaken,
> Shanghai in flames and Teruel re-taken.
>
> France put her case before the world: *Partout*
> *Il y a de la joie*. America addressed
> Mankind: *Do you love me as I love you?*

Nicolas Nabokov

Excerpts from memories

Nicolas Nabokov composed the opera Love's Labour's Lost, *for which Auden and Chester Kallman provided the libretto*

Wystan Auden slid into my life thunderlessly in the late autumn or winter of 1943. I met him through Isaiah Berlin, who turned up in Washington earlier in 1943 as a wartime secretary of the British Embassy. Isaiah Berlin and I had met on a bright summer day at Kay Halle's flat in Washington and had become close friends.

I still hear through memory's wilderness the first sounds of Wystan's nasal, noisy voice, his clumsy laughter, his assertive way of telling not quite exportable (English parsondom's) jokes and can recapture my astonishment at seeing the dirt of his fingernails, his sartorial neglect (in childhood Russia I imagined all Englishmen as romantic, but *soignés* Lord Byrons, or Beaux Brummels) but also being startled by his quick mind, his staggering erudition, the ebullient sense of humour and his dogmatically funny prejudices, such as: All French are 'frogs', Germans 'Krauts', most Russians 'inscrutable' and 'shifty mystics' ('not really reliable, my dear') and that 'drink should not be served before sundown' (which in winter meant fairly early) and 'gin is good while whisky bad for you'.

With persons like Wystan relations either click at once or they never do. Mine did. We started seeing each other not very often but at least three or four times before he left for Europe in the early spring of 1945. Once or twice we met in Washington, another time he came to visit me in Annapolis, at what he called 'the Adlerian Great Books Mill'. I also stopped once on my way to New York at his college in Pennsylvania.

I remember particularly that visit, partly because I was impressed by the commodious, even grand looking flat Wystan was lodged in – high ceilinged, drapes, a working fireplace and a study – and partly because it was one of the few times in life I got thoroughly and completely unblissfully drunk on gallons of Gallo's Californian burgundy.

There were other people around at Wystan's flat that weekend, some for lunch, others for dinner.

Among Wystan's dinner guests was a Frenchman, whom he introduced as being 'perfectly tame, my dear' – meaning sufficiently Americanized to be acceptable to Wystan's anti-French bias.

Wystan – like a proper Anglican homosexual – intensely disliked 'that dreary immoralist' as he called André Gide. During dinner he got into a scrape with the Frenchman about Gide's *Si le grain ne meurt*.

In a passage of this largely autobiographical book, Gide describes, how after a night of love-making with an Arab boy, he took the boy out to the desert's sand-dunes where they continued '*nos ébats amoureux*' until long after sunrise.

'Nonsense! Preposterous!!' shouted Wystan. 'He's a conceited liar!! How could he have an orgasm after a night of love-making. I bet he couldn't even produce an erection!' And Wystan doubled up into loud, high-pitched laughter.

The evening was long. There was little to eat and much too much to drink and – as I said – I got miserably drunk. I vomited copiously into a john and collapsed on a sofa in Wystan's living-room. I was in poor shape next morning when Wystan took me to the local railroad station. On the way in the taxi he chided me in the crankiest tone of his voice: 'You shouldn't drink that much, Nicky.... Russians never know their measure.... It isn't good for your health ... and, God, were you drunk! ...'

THE FRIENDSHIP

First (Winter 1944–5)

... Auden appears in Isaiah's living-room in Washington in an American military uniform. He looks snappy and incongruous. He is laughing loudly, very pleased with himself.

'What does this mean?' I ask, perplexed by the unexpected masquerade. Auden explains that he has joined an American Government wartime outfit. 'I'm in the Morale Division of the US Strategic Bombing Survey, commonly known as USSBS. I'm an "Usbuster"', and he roars with laughter. He is to be shipped overseas, perhaps in a few days, he explains. 'In fact I've come to say good-bye, Isaiah. I'm glad Nicky is here. . . . I can say good-bye to both of you.'

I ask the freshman Usbusster how does one get into his outfit. I've been trying for over a year to join the Allied Armed Forces overseas in some sort of capacity, but to no avail. 'You just call them on the telephone,' says Auden, 'and then go and apply for a job. Here, I'll give you the phone number,' and he produces a crumpled piece of a yellow pad. 'Call this number at the Pentagon and ask to speak to Miss Katz, or to. . . .' and he recites a row of Jewish names all beginning with the letter K. 'As a matter of fact they're looking for people like you . . . people with many languages. . . .'

Miss Katz gave me an appointment and received me as if I were an old friend. She introduced me to a Mr Kohn. Mr Kohn interviewed me at length and took me to the office of Mr Kalksteen. Mr Kalksteen cross-checked Mr Kohn's questions and added a few of his own concerning matters of health. Both gentlemen exhibited a massive accent rrrolling' the 'r's like a machine gun. I went back to Baltimore (I had switched from St John's College in Annapolis to the Peabody Conservatory in Baltimore during the 1944–5 academic year), having signed and countersigned a dozen of applications and other US Govenment forms.

Then for two months there was silence. I concluded that the Pentagon had forgotten about me and my applications.

One bright day in April I was called out of my music-history class at the Peabody Conservatory. 'You have a call from Washington, from the Pentagon', I was told. Miss Katz was on the other end of the wire: 'Remember me, Mr Nabokov?' she asked in a coy, Mae West-ish tone of voice. She gave me an appointment for the next day and advised me to take with me a change of clothes and my 'toiletry'.

A few days later, pumped full of vaccines, I was flying in a 'secret' direction aboard a DC4. I was tied to a bucket seat and surrounded by twenty-five odd males in Army fatigues, like myself.

Second: (Hamburg, June 1945)

Our largely German-Kosher Usbusstian *Moralisches Autfitt* was loaded upon four jeeps and two lorries – for some unknown reason called *half-tracks* by the US Army. We were being transferred from Hamburg to Bad Homburg near Frankfurt, where the German headquarters of USSBS were.

That famous spa used to be referred to by disgruntled GI's as 'bad Hamburg' probably because of its meagre supply of 'frat' or more commonly 'piece of tail'.

It was an ice-cold June evening and we had *sehr viel* mileage to cover before we'd get to that girl-less, or whoreless, Spa. It was a hell of a journey. Purely arctic – and 'no drink'. My T4 driver, Himmelstoss, was quite *ausser sich*. 'Vai do we haff to drife *durch die Nacht*, I ask you,' he exclaimed, 'I'm *ganz eingefroren*.'

We reached the Kurhaus Hotel of 'bad' Homburg at about three in the morning in a state of frozen pork. We were told that the Kurhaus Hotel was the place we would be billeted in. 'But of kors die fucking Army' had disposed of it otherwise. The Hotel was packed. Indeed all the hotels of Bad Homburg were packed by previous arrivals. The USSBS and the Psychological Warfare outfits had invaded the little town before us. We were offered to spend the rest of the morning in the dining and the ball rooms.

'Is there coffee around?'

'No.'

'Whisky? Gin?'

'No'. . . and the 'no's' were firm, definitive, unarguable.

The sight of the ball- and dining-rooms was forbidding. Obviously a huge brawl had taken place there a few hours earlier. The floor was strewn with all kinds of debris: empty beer and pop cans, gin and whisky bottles, broken glasses, filthy paper napkins and moist cigarette and cigar butts. All of it swimming in puddles of murky liquids (vomit and wine not excluded). The air stank like a pigsty.

I did not waver an instant. I wiped clean the bar, spread my sleeping bag upon it, crawled into it and conforming to the bar's shape, turning into a huge green L-shaped caterpillar I dropped into oblivion, despite the frozen condition of my limbs.

The next thing I knew was a face leaning over me and saying at the top of its voice: 'For God's sake! What are *you* doing here in this place?' Auden was clean-shaven, freshly washed and on the lookout for breakfast, furious that the dining-room had *not* been tidied up and was instead invaded by corpses in sleeping bags.

Towards noon everything and everybody got sorted out, billeted, washed and fed. I was given a room that I shared with disgruntled Himmelstoss and another USSBS driver. Auden was on the same floor with a colonel and a mid-western professor.

The weather turned fair, sunny and warm. Lilacs were in full bloom and the little spa did not look 'bad' at all, but pleasant, untouched by the war and neat, yet unfortunately invaded by a pack of noisy Americans.

We had nothing to do except to wait to get paid and attend debriefing sessions led by Ken Galbraith and other 'inventors' of the USSBS operation. Auden said that at those sessions 'a lot of mid-witted folk talked mid-minded trash in bogus socio-political jargon with a most obscene German accent. All of this is *waste*, my dear. . . . But it had better remain that way . . . it is none of *our* concern.'

The USSBS was being disbanded. Its leadership was hurrying home to well-up-holstered jobs. Auden had handed in his report and was going back to America via England, where he was to visit his family.

'This *Morale* title still makes me squirm', he remarked, 'it is illiterate and absurd. How can one learn anything about morals, when one's actions are beyond any kind of morality? *Morale* with an 'e' at the end is psycho-sociological nonsense. What they want to say, but don't say, is how many people we killed and how many buildings we destroyed by that wicked bombing. . . .'

Most of the daytime at Bad Homburg Auden and I spent taking long walks in the pine-woods that surrounded the little middle-German town. Or else we sat on the terrace of the hotel having drinks and trying to avoid our gregarious Usbusstian colleagues. 'Most of them,' explained Auden, 'are crashing bores, my dear. They have *no*, or *wrong*, ideas about everything and belong to the world that neither you or I can possibly like or condone.'

What did we talk about during those walks, or sitting on the hotel's terrace? Or rather, what do I remember now of these talks? I know that we talked a lot about the war and its consequences. Auden, like so many of us, was shocked at the spectacle of desolation of German cities and the total disarray which we found Germans to be in.

The Fifties

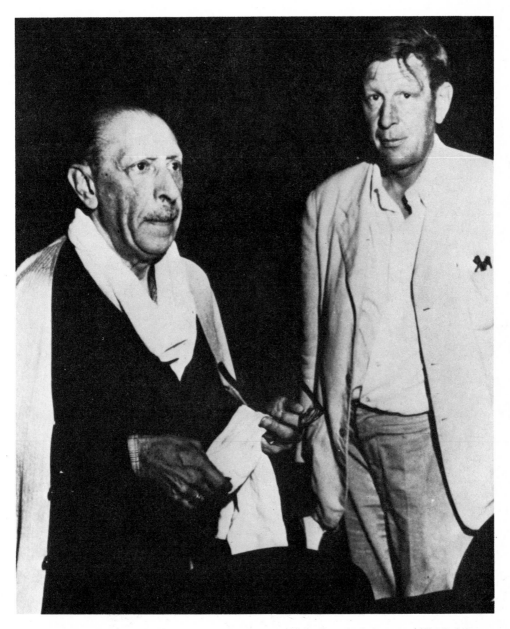

40 Igor Stravinsky and W. H. Auden during rehearsals for Stravinsky's opera, *The Rake's Progress*, for which Auden and Chester Kallman supplied the libretto.

41, 42 Two scenes from a production of *The Rake's Progress* at the Edinburgh Festival in 1953.

43 Auden was fond of
pets. BELOW In Ischia with
his pet spaniel.
44 RIGHT With Ursula
Niebuhr and her poodle
Winnie, which was
baptized 'Alexandra' by
T. S. Eliot and
unbaptized by Auden and
Ursula Niebuhr.

45 LEFT Auden in 1956 after a lecture at Barnard College.

46 BELOW Ischia in the fifties, where Auden rented a villa each year.

W. H. AUDEN

THE
OLD
MAN'S
ROAD

VOYAGES
NEW YORK 1956

W. H. AUDEN

THE
OLD
MAN'S
ROAD

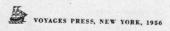 VOYAGES PRESS, NEW YORK, 1956

47 ABOVE The title pages of the (*left*) 'limited signed edition' of fifty copies and the (*right*) 'regular edition' of a small collection of Auden's poems, issued by a small independent publisher and later collected in *Homage to Clio*.

NONES

W. H. AUDEN

RANDOM HOUSE · NEW YORK

48 LEFT The title page of *Nones*, published in 1951 and Auden's first collection of shorter poems after the war.

W. H. AUDEN

GOOD-BYE
TO THE MEZZOGIORNO

poesia inedita
e versione italiana
di Carlo Izzo

ALL'INSEGNA DEL PESCE D'ORO
MILANO · MCMLVIII

49, 50 LEFT and BELOW Title page and first part of
an Italian edition of Auden's '*Goodbye to the
Mezzogiorno*', dedicated to and translated by Carlo
Izzo. This poem, written in 1957, when Auden
left Ischia, marks a turning point in his life and
possibly his style.

GOOD-BYE TO THE MEZZOGIORNO
(For Carlo Izzo)

Out of a gothic North, the pallid children
Of a potato, beer-or-whiskey
Guilt culture, we behave like our fathers and come
Southward into a sunburnt otherwhere

Of vineyards, baroque, la bella figura,
These feminine townships where men
Are males and siblings untrained in a ruthless
Verbal in-fighting as it is taught

In protestant rectories upon drizzling
Sunday afternoons, no more as unbathed
Barbarians out for gold, nor as profiteers
Hot for Old Masters, but for plunder,

Nevertheless: — some believing amore
Is better down south and much cheaper
(Which is doubtful), some persuaded exposure
To strong sunlight is lethal to germs

(Which is patently false) and others, like me,
In middle-age, hoping to twig from
What we are not what we might be next, a question
The South never seems to raise. Perhaps

A tongue in which Nestor and Apemantus,
Don Ottavio and Don Giovanni make
Equally beautiful sounds is unequipped
To frame it, or perhaps, in this heat

It is nonsense: the myth of an Open Road,
Which runs past the orchard gate and beckons
Three brothers in turn to step out over the hills
And far away, is an invention

6

ADDIO AL MEZZOGIORNO

Usciti da un gotico nord, pallidi figli
  D'una civiltà di patate e birra-o-whisky
E di colpa, ci comportiamo come i nostri padri e scendiamo
  Nel sud verso un riarso altrove

Di vigneti, barocco, *la bella figura,*
  Queste femminili città dove gli uomini
Sono maschi e tutti fratello e sorella, ignari della spietata
  Intima lotta verbale che s'insegna

Nei rettorati protestanti durante i piovigginosi
  Pomeriggi domenicali, non più come lerci
Barbari in caccia d'oro, né come mercanti
  Smaniosi di Vecchi Maestri, ma pur sempre

Avidi di saccheggio: convinti, alcuni, che si faccia all'*amore*
  Meglio nel sud e molto più a buon mercato
(Il che è dubbio), persuasi, altri, che il venire esposti
  A un sole violento sia micidiale per i germi

(Il che è chiaramente balordo), e altri, come me,
  Nella mezza età, mossi dalla speranza di scovare da
Ciò che non siamo quel che potremo essere in séguito, domanda
  Che il sud sembra non porsi mai. Forse

Una lingua nella quale Nestore e Apemanto,
  Don Ottavio e Don Giovanni dànno
Suoni egualmente belli, non è attrezzata
  Per formularla, e forse in questa calura

Non ha senso: il mito d'una Strada Aperta
  Che passa davanti al cancello dell'orto e invita
Tre fratelli ad andare uno dopo l'altro oltre i colli
  E via lontano, è invenzione

7

51 The National Book Awards ceremony in New York, July 1956. John F. Kennedy (then Senator) chats to three of the prize winners. *Left to right* Auden (for *The Shield of Achilles*), Kennedy, John O'Hara and Herbert Kubly.

'I know that they had *asked* for it,' he would say, 'but still, this kind of total destruction is beyond reasoning. . . . It seems like madness! Don't you feel that way, my dear? It is absolutely ghastly.'

He did not like those 'obtuse Krauts', as he called Germans at this time of life, 'but still, Nicky, is it justified to reply to *their* mass-murder by *our* mass-murder? It seems terrifying to me, don't you agree? And I cannot help but ask myself, "Was there no other way?"'

He would drop into silence for a while and add in a quieter tone: 'Well . . . I've done my do . . . and I'm glad to leave. . . . It is, all of it, a sorry mess. . . .'

We talked about the extermination camps we had seen in the course of our inspection tours . . . the horror of them . . . especially what Auden referred to as 'the horror of their meticulously systematic organization'. 'I knew that the *Krauts* could be cruel. . . . But none of us could have imagined that they could go that far. . . . They applied to it the same pedantic organizational skills a piano-tuner does when he tunes a virtuoso's concert grand', and Auden would stare in front of him shaking his head.

But we also talked about music and poetry and read, or recited to each other verses, he in English, I in German and Russian.

He asked me questions about Stravinsky. Like me, he did not like as much Stravinsky's so-called Russian period as he did *Oedipus Rex* and the *Symphony of Psalms*. 'That Russian stuff, Nicky, is folksy haberdashery, haberdashery, not much different, except in degree of quality to those Hungarian bores – Kodaly and Bartok.' And he asked whether I had heard Stravinsky's opera *The Song of the Nightingale* and how did it sound. 'Did it make sense?'

He thought that ballet was a 'very, very minor art', despite what 'Lincoln Kirstein thinks about it', but that 'I suppose, within the limits of ballet, Balanchine is its only jinny, at least he strikes me as if he were the only one to make something musically sensible out of ballet choreography'.

But as he soon proved, he was a true lover and potential connoisseur of opera. And I say potential because the real knowledge of opera came to Wystan Auden through Chester Kallman in the years to come (in fact in that future collaborating team, Chester played, I am sure, the determining role).

He had two projects he wanted to tackle 'sometime soon', he said: one was to make a '*pertinent* and *palatable* translation into English of Goethe's *Italienische Reise*; the second to write a longish essay on Kierkegaard'. (Ultimately he did both, a decade later.)

To Auden, Goethe's travel book was a masterpiece of 'observation and imaginative description'. It stood at the fount of the Romantic movement, more so, he believed than Werther's *Leider*, or Rousseau's 'crashing bore, *Emile*'.

'And then my dear,' he would say excitedly, 'Goethe's prose style is admirable. It is still pre-Hegelian, unencumbered by all those prefixes and post-fixes and page-long verb forms.'

I knew nothing about Kierkegaard and was intrigued, when Auden said that Kierkegaard was the only nineteenth-century thinker next to Nietzsche worth talking about – 'He's the inventor of existentialist philosophy, but he remained, as is proper, a Christian existentialist', explained Auden. It all seemed a mystery to me until several years later in New York Auden presented me with a plump volume of *Either Or* and read parts of it aloud to me. Only then, but still faintly, did I understand what Auden had meant by calling Kierkegaard a Christian existentialist.

Auden's stay at Bad H. was coming to a close. The USSBS was packing up and disbanding its various component parts.

The sun had disappeared again and a grey mist enveloped our hotel from morning to night. We sat indoors reading, doing crossword puzzles and, after sundown, drinking.

One evening, long past dinner hours Auden and I were sitting in a deserted room adjacent to the bar. For some reason the bar was closed and therefore its surroundings deserted. There was only one other couple in another corner of the room, a British officer and his American WAC girlfriend.

We had brought down our own provision of drink from our rooms. Auden gin, I bourbon whisky. I found a bucket of melting ice and we were set for the night. Auden was supposed to leave the next day. Suddenly, looking straight at me Auden asked: 'And what are your plans, Nicky? . . . Are you being de-mobbed like me and returning back to America or are you staying here, in Germany, with all that American brass?'

In a way I had been expecting Auden's question. Had he not asked it, I would have induced him to do so. I needed his advice. I was in a quandary. I knew that his advice would be sound and compassionate, but also strictly impartial. It would, I thought, help me make up my own mind.

Although I had known Auden for over two years, I had never spent any length of time in his company. The eight or ten days at Bad H. were like a boat trip; we were together every day and had nothing else to do but to enjoy being together. To me it was a blessing, not only because I discovered Auden as a person and re-discovered him as an extraordinary mind and as a great poet, but because he helped me solve, what to me at that time appeared like a riddle.

I had just gone through a traumatic experience in North Germany. An experience that in more ways than one affected my future life, and which, though it may seem 'old hat' now, was new at the time.

It had to do with two evils, with nazism *and* with communism. But it also had to do with a third one, a far more terrible one, namely with the Western Allies (and mainly America) playing into the hands of Russian communism by committing the *sin* of sending back to the Soviet Union millions of people either willingly, or unwillingly imported from there by the Nazis.

I soon discovered that *nothing* had changed in the communist empire and that, what was going on in my former fatherland was a hell, as vast if not much vaster than the one we had just laid bare to public inspection, right here, in Germany. I felt pangs of conscience and a kind of helpless misery at not being able to do something about it, to help Americans and especially the American military leadership to realize the tragic plight of these hundreds of thousands of Russian, Ukranian and other DPs gleaned from Soviet Russia, being now shipped by *us*, like cattle into slavery and almost *certain* destruction. 'How can one stop this insane policy?' was the thought that went through my head all the time, day and night. Shouldn't I stay in Germany, in Berlin, and help in whatever way I could?

I explained my dilemma to Auden speaking in a low monotone in order not to be overheard by the love-couple in the other corner of the room. I told him, why our encounter in that illusionist's spa was to me providential, so profoundly helpful and asked his advice.

Auden looked serene gazing in front of him into space. The love couple had started gathering its coats and hats and was leaving. Auden waited until they had gone. Then, very gently and quietly, in that embarrassed, timid way he sometimes had, he said:

'Well . . . Nicky . . . couldn't we wait until tomorrow? Could I answer your question at breakfast? . . . I'm leaving the hotel at seven. Let's have coffee say at six-thirty. Is that okay?'

Next morning Auden was in the breakfast room before me. I could not fall asleep for a long, long time. Himmelstoss and his companion snored like a chorus of cossacks and my head buzzed with unanswered riddles.

Auden looked disgruntled. 'You're eight minutes late', he said and plunged back into a crossword puzzle he had been working at. We sat in silence sipping tepid, transparent coffee.

Then Auden looked at his watch again and remarked: 'I'm supposed to be off in six minutes, but I don't see the bus, do you?'

No, the bus wasn't there. *'Noch nicht da'*, said the German waiter, *'odder* officers are *vaiting* in the *lounch'*.

'Now about your question Nicky. . . .' Auden's voice was matter of fact, impersonal. 'My answer to it is neither "yes" nor "no", or rather neither stay nor go . . . it is *entirely* your own business. I'm sorry Nicky, you've *got* to make up your own mind. No one can, or should make it up for you. It would be improper and wrong. . . .' and suddenly he smiled broadly. 'But if you do go to Berlin I may perhaps come and see you there. May I?' He got up, picked up his gear and started dragging it to the lounge through a labyrinth of chairs and tables. The bus had arrived and was loading Usbussters in fatigues each one with his huge sausagy duffle bag. The light was grey and misty, but there was a faint June scent of lilacs and bird cherry in the air.

'As for the substance of your question,' said Auden before he mounted the bus, 'it is indeed horrid and monstrous! It is barbarous to send people back to a hell without even asking them for their consent! But then, what humans do to each other is usually messy . . . and a *sin* against God's laws.' He stepped into the bus and waved at me from inside. He pulled down a window and hailed me: 'Nicky, whatever you do, keep well . . . and drop me a line.'

Third

From 1947 onward, when I returned from Berlin to New York, Auden and I started seeing each other much more frequently. Both of us now lived in New York. Visions of him surround me, as it were from all sides, first in New York, then under other skies and in other climes, all of them pell-mell, with no respect for chronology.

Auden in his small, dark flat below Chelsea (NYC), before the appearance of Chester K. The flat is pervaded by a permanent stink of cat piss. He is seated on the edge of a couch and is reading Kierkegaard, but so indistinctly that I can barely understand the words.

Auden at the poets and writers 'to do' I organized in Paris in 1952 for the Congress for Cultural Freedom. He is in front of a lectern with a mike giving his address. It is, all of it about the evil ways of our lives, the need for repentance and also the need 'to venerate our dead'. Faulkner on my left whispers whiskyly 'That's mighty fine.' Madariaga on my right shrugs his shoulders and mutters – '*qu'est-ce que cela vient faire dans affaires*'.

Auden asking me what he should wear at the Stravinskys. 'I have a dinner jacket, but it's become tight around the belly.' He also wants to know must he kiss just Mrs Stravinsky's hand, or both *his* and *her* hands, when he greets them. 'What is the proper Russian custom, Nicky, you must know?' It is early 1948. He is on his way to the Stravinskys to discuss *The Rake's Progress*.

Auden in Berlin 1963–4. Intractable, difficult, cranky. Two domestics have carried in Darius Milhaud (he can't walk) to a luncheon party I am giving for him at the occasion of the post-war premiere of Milhaud's opera *Oresteia*. 'You're twenty minutes late, Nicky,' he croaks from the other end of the dining-room to the general surprise of the twenty-odd Berliner notables. '*Quelles manières*', whispers Madeleine Milhaud getting seated on my right.

Auden and Japan. 'Why don't you, Wystan?' I ask, trying to persuade Auden to go to Japan on a lecture tour for the Congress for Cultural Freedom. 'Yes, why don't you?' chimes in Chester. 'Oh no no! by no means, my dear!' exclaims Auden. 'Why should I? It is so far away . . . and then you have to eat all that raw fish, drink tepid rice-wine and live in cardboard houses. . . . And someone told me that the toilet seats are much too small for my bottom. . . . Besides I can't distinguish one Japanese from another. . . . Let Stephen go, he likes that sort of thing.'

Auden at the Prime's house in New Delhi: (Auden speaking). 'We had to sit on the floor, my dear and were given lukewarm tea. . . . A female in costume, with donkey-bells around her ankles danced, jerking and jiggling her head, making eyes at everyone and fanning out her fingers. Preposterous nonsense! And imagine, all that boredom and not a drop of drink! I got up and told the Prime that it "wasn't my cup of tea" and that I'd like to go back to my hotel. . . . His daughter, a glum-looking young lady took me to the door and sent me back packing.'

Auden . . . Auden . . . Auden . . . getting older, crankier, lonelier, cracking the same jokes. . . . Repeating himself ('Had I chosen the orders I would now be a bishop': five times in two days) . . . finding life absurd . . . wanting to get out of it. . . . Yet still working as hard as ever and remaining endowed with the same great mind, the same gift, the same fathomless knowledge.

Robert Craft
The poet and the rake

Robert Craft, Stravinsky's biographer and assistant, came to know Auden while work was in progress for the production of Stravinsky's opera The Rake's Progress, *the libretto of which was written by Auden and Chester Kallman*

As soon as Wystan Auden accepted Igor Stravinsky's invitation to stay at his home in Hollywood, the composer and his wife began to search for a clue to the most important fact for them to know about the poet: his height. Would he be too tall to sleep on the couch in the den? Finding no hint in his writings, the future hosts turned to a photograph for possible prosopographical leads, and reached the conclusion that probably he would not fit. This was confirmed when he crossed the doorstep, at which point Stravinsky was obliged to improvise – something he would never do in music – by extending the 'bed' with a chair and pillows to accommodate his guest's legs and feet.

During the following week the two men shaped the content, plot, form and characters of *The Rake's Progress*. On two evenings the Stravinskys entertained friends, and on two others the hosts and their guest attended performances of *The House of Bernarda Alba* and *Così fan tutti*, the latter in the parish hall of a Hollywood church. As for Southern California's natural and architectural wonders, the poet shrank at the very mention of them and refused even to glance in the direction of the Pacific. In fact he ventured from the house only one other time, to visit a doctor to whom he complained of deafness, and who miraculously restored the hearing faculty by extricating some formidable accumulations of earwax. Like the World, the opera scenario was created in Six Days. On the Seventh the makers separated, only then realizing how extremely fond of each other they had become.

Inspired by his vision of the drama, Stravinsky composed the prelude to the Graveyard scene. Back in New York, Auden also set to work, but with the collaboration of his friend Chester Kallman, whose participation had not been broached in Hollywood. Auden did not reveal this partnership until it was a *fait accompli*, and the first act of the libretto had been sent to Stravinsky. The composer was greatly disturbed, both because he had not been consulted and because it was Auden alone whom he wanted. But he said nothing and twelve days later received the manuscript of Act Two, on which Auden's and Kallman's names were again billed as equals. The final act was delivered by Auden in person – in Washington DC, where Stravinsky was conducting – no doubt to smooth over this question of dual authorship. In any event, the poet sought to reassure the composer that 'Mr Kallman is a better librettist than I am', that 'the scenes which Mr Kallman wrote are at least as good as mine', and that 'Mr Kallman's talents have not been more widely recognized only because of his friendship with me.' Stravinsky's magnanimous answer was that he looked forward to meeting Mr Kallman in New York.

The dinner in the restaurant of the Hotel Raleigh that night (31 March 1948) was memorable mainly as a study in contrasts: in culture, temperament, and mind – as well as appearance, for the shabby, dandruff-speckled, and slightly peculiar-smelling poet (attributes easily offset by his purity of spirit and intellectual punctiliousness) could not have been more unlike the neat, sartorially perfect, and faintly eau-de-cologned composer. At table, too, while the poet demolished his lamb chops, potatoes, and sprouts, as if eating were a chore to be accomplished as quickly as possible, and gulped Stravinsky's carefully-chosen Château Margaux oblivious to its qualities, the composer fussed over his food, and sniffed, sipped and savoured the wine.

These habits appear to illustrate an essential difference between the two men. With Auden the senses seemed to be of negligible importance, whereas with Stravinsky the affective faculties were virtual instruments of thought. Powerful observer though Auden was, he displayed little interest in the visual sense, being purblind to painting, for example, and even to 'poetic' nature, for he was more concerned with the virtues of gardening than with the beauty of flowers. And whatever the acuteness of his aural sense, the idea of music appealed to him more than music itself, music with words – opera and Anglican hymns – more than Haydn quartets. That the music of Auden's poetry is not its strongest feature, therefore, should hardly surprise us. A conceptualizer in quest of intellectual order, he was a social, moral, and spiritual diagnostician above all.

To return to the contrasts between poet and composer; though both were religious men, and equally keen on dogmas, ritual, faith in the redemptive death, the poet had evidently arrived at his beliefs through theology, the composer through 'mystical experience' (however diligently he may have applied himself to the *Grammar of Assent*). Theology, at any rate, was a frequent topic in Auden's conversation with Stravinsky – and an exasperating one, except when the poet digressed on Biblical symbolisms (e.g. the moon as the Old Testament, the sun as the New), and on the argument of *sui generis* (that 'man's image is God-like because the image of every man is unique'). But Auden preferred to theorize about such subjects as angels being 'pure intellect', and to postulate that 'If two rectangles, with common points between them, can be described on a face, that face is an angel's' – which sounds like a put-on but could have been scholastic exercitation.

The conversation in the Washington restaurant began with a reference to an announcement of a forthcoming performance of Stravinsky's *Oedipus Rex*, with the entire text, not just the Narrator's part, in a new translation by e. e. cummings. Auden was prepared to vouch for cummings's awareness of the composer's intentions and was certain that only the speeches would be in English – an especially welcome comment since it indicated that Auden himself was acquainted with the opus. Thereafter the talk about music quickly turned to the Wagner and Strauss operas that he most admired but that were far from Stravinsky's present interest and, in the case of Strauss, familiarity. Incidentally, Auden did not subscribe to Strauss's estimation of himself as an epigone of Wagner: 'Wagner is a giant without issue,' the poet said.

Begging indulgence for her English, Mrs Stravinsky asked the poet how to improve it. He advised her to 'Take a new word and use it in ten different sentences.' (She chose 'fastidious' and with no implicit criticism of her mentor went on: 'My *husband* is very fastidious.') Auden's articulation of English, and his accent, were obstacles for the Stravinskys. Aware of this, he offered supplementary bits in German (*unbequemt*) and French, thereby adding to the Stravinskys' confusion since his pronunciation of these languages was a still further impediment; he was obliged to write '*au fond*' on the tablecloth, for example, before the Stravinskys could understand what he was saying. (When I first heard Auden lecture, at Barnard College in the spring of 1946, he was continually interrupted by requests to spell out what he had said on the black-board – which provoked *sotto voce* but clearly-enunciated derogations of the intelligence of the audience.) His vocabulary was odd, too, not in rare or classical-root words but in such British expressions as 'fribble'. The problem of comprehending his speech was still further aggravated in later years by the installation of loose-fitting dentures.

Answering a question about his travel plans, Auden said, 'I like to fly and am not afraid of crashing. It is simply a matter of whether one's time is up. My time will be up when I am eighty-eight.' (This writer heard him reiterate that statement and the number so often as to wonder whether the seer was finally betrayed not by his destiny but by his too intelligent understanding of the future.)

Suddenly Stravinsky switched from 'Ow-den' to the poet's first name, and was enthusiastically met on the same basis with 'EE-gawr', a cultural *faux pas* – the use of the given name without the patronymic being inadmissible to Russians – which the composer overlooked. Still another cultural difference was exposed at departure when Auden, his body wobbling from one of his pumping handshakes, charged for the door, only to be detained there by the Stravinskys' Russian-style hugs and kisses.

At last, on 5 April, in New York, the composer met Chester Kallman and was immediately won by his intelligence and sense of humour. Furthermore, Kallman was not only easier to understand than Auden, but the younger man could also bring out the older man's sometimes dormant affability – as well as subdue his tempers, which the poet himself usually proclaimed with 'I am very cross today.' No criticism is implied in the observation that the Stravinskys were happier with Auden when Chester Kallman was present. Between Washington and New York Stravinsky had read the opera's final act and hence could give his blessing to the partnership, telling the librettists how delighted he was with *their* work.

Auden went to Europe for the summer, Stravinsky to his Hollywood studio to compose the first act. Coming east again in the winter for concerts he expected to play the completed scenes for Auden on the very morning of arrival in New York (3 February 1949). At 6.55 a.m. Auden met the train in Pennsylvania Station – this time inclining toward the Stravinskys, the better to receive their Russian embracing – to explain that he had jury duty and to ask that the audition be postponed until evening. In their hotel suite at dinner time he was elated at 'having hung the jury and obstructed injustice in the trial of a taxi-driver who would have been a victim of the prejudice of car owners.' Then, questioning Auden about legal processes, the Stravinskys appalled him by revealing that they had never voted, whereupon he lectured them sternly on their civic responsibilities.

The poet was less voluble after hearing the first act of the opera, but he asked the composer to 'change the soprano's final note to a high C, and to take fewer pains in the future in making every word audible; in the interests of verbal distinctness, Stravinsky tended to alternate the voices in duets and trios, rather than to blend them. As for the 'C', the composer thought the word was unsuitable for the upper octave, which led Auden, with the help of some 'uh-uh-uh'-ing and 'now-let's-see'-ing, to write a new last line on the spot. Auden stood behind Stravinsky as he played, trying to follow the music over his shoulder and unaware of how irritated the composer was by this, as he was by several violations of his strict rule of silence.

At the end of the same month Stravinsky conducted a concert in Town Hall and invited Auden to read a group of his poems on the programme. Unlike his normally untidy, unwashed, uncombed, and unpressed appearance, the poet arrived at concert time looking uncomfortably well-groomed. His restlessness and impatience were intensified by stage-fright, and since the event was a matinée, and therefore pre-martini hour, his chain-smoking accelerated. Leading with his chin, and moving awkwardly, he read 'In Praise of Limestone', 'The Duet', and 'Music is International'. His voice spluttered and occasionally barked, thus adding to the impression he some-times gave of an extremely gentle hound. Yet by sheer force of intellect he was always in total command of the audience. He acknowledged the warm applause with a surprised grin, a spastic bow, and a rapid exit such as he made at dinner parties upon discovering that it was past his bedtime.

Auden went to Europe again that summer (1949), while Stravinsky again returned to his studio. But the second act was longer and the libretto more complex. In November the composer asked the poet to come to California to help solve some problems, but he was too busy teaching, and it was Stravinsky, therefore, who eventually came to New York. The two men conferred together several times in the composer's rooms at the Lombardy Hotel, Stravinsky by this time visualizing every detail of the dramatic action. How long, for example, would it take to wheel the bread machine on stage? Auden, responding swiftly, and as if he had had a great deal of experience with baby carriages, jumped to his feet, extended his arms and crossed the room pushing an imaginary vehicle of that sort, while Stravinsky held his stopwatch like a starter at a track meet. But this somnambulistic exercise could not have had much validity since no one knew the dimensions of the stage on which the opera was to be performed and as a result the music here is generally found to be too short.

Stravinsky wanted an American premiere, preferably in a small New York theatre, where, he believed, the opera might survive a brief 'run', a notion that seized him after seeing *The Consul* (of all things). Lincoln Kirstein helped to approach potential backers, the most promising of whom, until Stravinsky refused to play the score for any non-musician, was Huntington Hartford. Then, since Billy Rose's opinion was sought, if not his money, he was hidden in a group of Stravinsky's musician friends, for whom the composer had promised to play the score – like Odysseus among Poly-phemus's sheep. It was inferable from Mr Rose's countenance after a few minutes that Tom Rakewell could expect a crueller fate in the commercial theatre than in Bedlam.

The Venetian premiere was arranged by Nicolas Nabokov after a year-long struggle against the pococurantism of Italian culture officials. As soon as he heard about the contract, Auden asked for this writer's help.

7 Cornelia St.
N.Y.C. 16
16/2/51

Dear Bob,

It's wonderful news about Venice. But there are one or two matters which – strictly *entre nous* – Chester and I would like to know about.

It seems to us that, if there is, as I understand, a *large* sum of money being paid for the première rights, we are entitled to ten per cent thereof. What do you think?

As the contract is not being negotiated through Boosey Bean,[1] we are completely in the dark as to the facts.

Could you use your discretion, and if circumstances are propitious, mention the matter to *Il Maestro?*

Hope Cuba is fun.

Love,
Wystan

The sum was twenty thousand dollars, but part of it was Stravinsky's conducting fee, and the amount that the librettists eventually received is not known to me.

The preliminary rehearsals took place in Milan, where Stravinsky and Auden were constantly together and closer than at any other time in their lives. Stravinsky lived in the Duomo Hotel, but the librettists, having neglected to make reservations, were obliged at first to reside in a *bordello*, where, they said, 'the girls were very understanding, but the rooms could be rented only by the hour and so were terribly expensive.' Auden came to rehearsals in a white linen suit, polka-dotted in front with Chianti stains. He was assigned to two jobs, coaching the chorus's English, no word of which could be understood, and advising the '*maestro della scena*'. He ignored the second, since he disapproved of everything in the staging: 'It could hardly be worse if the director were Erwin Piscator and the singers were climbing and descending ladders.' Nor did Auden like the sets, particularly a Neapolitan-ice-cream-coloured 'London', but he objected only to the one of Truelove's home in the country: 'With a house as grand as that,' he told Signor Ratto the designer, who had probably not read the libretto, 'the Rake would be better off marrying the daughter right away and foregoing his "Progress".'

The outstanding event during the sojourn in Milan was a dinner that the librettists gave for the Stravinskys. After it they all attended a performance of Giordano's *Fedora*, which was very disappointing in comparison to Chester Kallman's hilarious preview of it. At such times Auden relinquished the stage, except to contribute scraps of background information or to alert the Stravinskys to imminent highpoints. He was proud and happy. But, then, Wystan Auden's devotion to Chester Kallman was the most important fact of the poet's personal life, as well as the real subject of the libretto (the fidelity of true love); it transcends the confession of Auden's most popular lyric. More touching still, when Chester Kallman was unable to attend the second performance of the opera in Venice, Wystan Auden quietly left the theatre

---

[1] Betty Bean, of Boosey and Hawkes.

before the end, not wishing to risk having to bow alone and to receive credit due to his friend.

Kallman was indispensable to Auden in at least one considerable area of his work: the older poet could never have written librettos without his younger colleague. What is more, in everything that Auden wrote, he relied on Kallman's critical judgement. No less important, Chester Kallman, though hardly an adherent of bourgeois behaviour himself, succeeded in imposing some of his Brooklyn common sense on his partner. Kallman was also the domesticator – if only to a degree – for he was so mild a tamer that the animal was never entirely housebroken. Finally, and appearances often to the contrary, the two poets took care of each other. Kallman always knew, despite Auden's protective friends, that no matter how 'lost' his colleague might seem to be, he was actually capable of finding his way home, of handling his business affairs, and of attending to his physical needs.

Auden and Stravinsky remained close friends to the ends of their lives. But other memoirs will describe the 1950s and 1960s – hopefully including an account of the mayhem of an Auden birthday party, or one of Kallman's, for he and Mrs Stravinsky celebrated theirs together on the same date. It remains to be said, and regretted, that two further collaborations, as well as an additional scene for the third act of a revised version of *The Rake*, came to nothing. A second libretto, whose protagonists were to be 'Rossini (the man of stomach), Berlioz (the man of heart), and Mendelssohn (the man of sensibility)', did not develop much beyond the talking stage. But the text of *Delia*, the masque specially designed for Stravinsky, *is* complete, awaiting a composer with some of the gifts of a Stravinsky or of a Mozart.

POSTSCRIPT

Here is a view of the poet and the composer at one of their last meetings, and two final glimpses of the poet alone:

18 December 1969. The Essex House. Balanchine, Lincoln Kirstein and Auden for dinner. Auden rather ornery and not on his best mettle. His uppermost concern nowadays seems to be in keeping to the split-second timing of his daily routine. He replies to Stravinsky's 'How are you?' with, 'Well, I'm on time anyway.' For the poet's sake dinner has to be served at exactly seven o'clock, and therefore it must be as carefully planned as a bank robbery. But Auden even gets tight on schedule, and to the extent that that, so far as he is concerned, Stravinsky's Château Margaux could be acetified Manischewitz. Still in this condition he makes a totally unrelated, to say nothing of *outré*, exclamation: 'Everybody knows that Russians are mad,' which might be described as emotion recollected in alcohol – except that the recollecting is ahead of time, this particular emotion being tomorrow's. Towards the end of the evening, while V. A. S. looks on in horror, he opens three closets before finding the urgently needed one. But the refractory mood gives way to one of deep affection for Stravinsky, who becomes the object of a tender speech in German.

After the poet leaves, his hosts speculate as to the reasons why his standard of living failed to keep pace with his income, why he lives in the same hovel that he did twenty years ago, and why he is still wearing some of the same clothes. Are the dark glasses, the tattered coat, the frayed bedroom slippers that he uses for winter social outings a

protective disguise for the 'greatest living poet'? Not according to his own interpretation of the psychology of clothes, anyway ('they enable one to see oneself as an
object'). Whatever the answer, if he had had a tin cup in his hand, it would have
been filled with coins shortly after he reached the street, especially since he sang so
merrily on the way out.

11 January 1972. New York. Wystan and Chester for dinner, the first time we have
seen them together since Chester moved to Europe, or either of them since Stravinsky's
death. Conversation is like old times: Wagner, life in Niederosterreich, fellow
poets. The librettists disagree on the merits of *Crow*, Wystan defending the language
of the book and insisting that it contains 'quite good things'. Some of the talk is *from*
old times, in fact, Wystan repeating his hoary anecdote about dinner at the Eliots in
the early 1930s: 'I told Mrs T. S. E. that I was glad to be there and she said: "Well
Tom's not glad".' When Wystan announces that his bedtime hour has struck, Chester
admonishes him saying that *he* is not ready to leave, whereupon the reproved one
becomes petulant.

21 February 1972. We go to Wystan's birthday party and combination farewell dinner
and last supper at the Coffee House on West Forty-Fifth Street. A mob scene during
cocktails, but at the actual cenacle the host is seated at a table that is slightly elevated
and, no less appropriately, Arthurianly round. When glasses are tapped for silence
some telegrams are read in a not-very-pious hush, and a toast is proposed. But no
sooner has the speaker begun with 'I don't know what genius is . . .' than he is interrupted by an indignant 'Well who does?' from, of all people, Auden himself.

   To answer the question, which was ignored: *we* do, and always did when we were
in the presence of Wystan Hugh Auden, though it was for much more than this
reason alone that we loved him.

Louis Kronenberger
A friendship revisited

Louis Kronenberger was Auden's co-editor in his Book of Aphorisms

Of Wystan as a poet, as I have elsewhere remarked, I could speak with great personal
enthusiasm but with no professional authority, and it seems most fitting for me to
write about him as a friend. Actually his great gift of friendship is in itself something
to commemorate. The friendships can go back to early schooldays – he had a school
photograph taken when he was perhaps eight years old, which he would happily
produce for you, pointing out a small boy several rows above him as Christopher
Isherwood.

   By such chronology I can't claim to have known Wystan particularly long. We first met during the 1940s in New York, where we both lived: a friend we had in common, Nigel Dennis, had asked me to a party where Wystan would be, and had told Wystan that I'd be delighted if he would edit a volume in a series of Great Letter Writers of which I was general editor. I had barely got to the party when, with a word from Nigel as to who I was, Wystan with a great smile came right up to me, already talking as he came: 'Hello!' he said, with an outstretched hand, 'I'd love to do a book for your Letters series, and the letters I want to do are Sydney Smith's.' I can't recall just what unimpeachable adjectives he showered on Smith while I in turn expressed unconditional approval. Neither can I recall what we further talked about, but my mounting admiration as we talked, together with my jubilation over Sydney Smith, sent me home very happy.[1]

Nor can I quite recall just how we got to know each other better. When Wystan reappears in my memory it is his taking me to dinner in a Greenwich Village restaurant, and thereafter his every so often dining with my wife and me, or we with him. I remember him at our place on one particular night when a friend had brought along William Faulkner: in the course of much pleasant talk Faulkner mentioned the opera house in Oxford, Mississippi, and Wystan asked what just that meant in so small a town. 'Oh,' said Faulkner, 'it's where *anything* goes on after half-past seven at night.'

As Wystan and I got to know each other better there was much pleasant talk between the two of us, and from his side something beyond that; it was fascinating to have him take hold of a subject and set it brilliantly before you. We never talked of his own work for very long: he had great assurance of a kind, but was remarkably free from that vanity in writers – and by no means least in poets – of wanting not only to be lengthily praised for what they write, but to be held sacred for what they are. Wystan's response to praise was a pleased grunt, with a second grunt to end matters – people weren't to be allowed more than two portions of praise any more than two portions of roast beef. Set against Wystan's grunt was his extremely prompt explosive laugh on catching the point of a joke or an anecdote.

His promptness of reaction generally – his quickness in reply, his what seemed like instantaneous judgement – struck me as one of his most outstanding and dazzling qualities. I never saw him at work, but the great amount of writing he consistently turned out – including fine critical pieces which demanded a great deal of preliminary reading – argues how rapidly he worked. Saxe Commins, who was Wystan's editor at Random House, once told me that when Wystan's *Collected Poems* was first issued, he felt the book should have some sort of prefatory note from Wystan and said so to him. Whereupon Wystan immediately sat down, and never stopping or slowing down, brought forth the beautifully organized and worded prefatory note that all his admirers are familiar with.

He was criticized for writing too much and, by implication, too fast, often by professors who didn't write too well: surely it was a professor who conceived the fable of the hare and the tortoise. But with Wystan such speed seems to me altogether in character. His was a disciplined speed – he was a man who moved fast in almost every way. Out of the blue he would affectionately phone you long-distance, give his reason

[1] Wystan never edited Smith's letters because before he got to work on them a very good edition appeared in England.

for phoning in little more than a sentence, rattle off or inquire about something, and hang up. Wherever he went crossword puzzles seemed to go with him, to be pounced on and solved in no time – the puzzles mostly from English publications and involving foreign words, nonce words, alternate spellings, recondite puns, defiant anagrams and obsolete Welsh proper names. The same ingratiating speed operated with him as both guest and host: as guest when he got up to go, he went; as host, when you got up to go, he jumped up with you. It was the same, I'm sure, when he got up in the morning to work. Once at a friend's house he gave us his directive for working: get up very early and get going at once, in fact, work first and wash afterwards.

If long on speed, he quite lacked swank or side: the absence of both arose from temperament as well as character. I once asked him why, having when young been taken up by rather grand members of society, he drifted away from them. His answer rang as true as it was terse: 'I enjoyed it very much for a while and then I'd had enough of it.' What, his great talent aside, seemed most remarkable about him was how decidedly he knew what he wanted, or liked, or disliked, or found boring; indeed it was because he was so sure-footed that he could think and act so fast. It was impressive to see someone incapable of shilly-shallying or of bemoaning the road not taken. Yet, though there was no self-importance about him, neither was there easygoing assent or indulgent acquiescence.

He showed almost no interest in possessions, or in living at all splashily, or even in what might be called upper-Bohemian comfort. For some twenty years he lived in a down-at-heel apartment building in a step-from-the-Bowery part of town. But he was himself no real Bohemian: if rumpled-looking in appearance, he lived no gypsy life within; it was orderly, not to say regulated. To me there seemed to be just enough furniture for his needs, food for his sustenance, and clothes for staving off pneumonia. The only time he ever bawled me out was for having too many clothes: one suit – well, yes, a second one should the first get soaked in a downpour – was sufficient.

Yet for all his individuality and sturdy adherence to what might be called his ten commandments, he had a remarkable faculty, partly by ignoring other people's ways, for adjusting to things. However English he seemed at times, he was predominantly cosmopolitan, very much at home in America and equally so, I discovered, in London and Oxford and at his house in Austria. To be sure, much of what I thought of as his Englishness rested on habits, injunctions and values acquired very early in life. His own personal sense of what's done or is not done smacked much more of the nursery and the schoolroom than of later, worldlier origins. As for people, he seldom wasted time dissecting or passing judgement on them; someone, to him, was either a gent or not a gent – this a judgement in terms of character, not class.

Let me set down a few of the rather expressive bits and pieces that I recall, from various places, about Wystan. At Oxford on our getting up from dinner at Christ Church he told me that in moving to the Common Room one must on no account talk to one's host and must also not refuse to take snuff. (I found taking it quite enjoyable, though after feeling quite set up from sneezing briskly each time, I gathered that not to sneeze was thought more aristocratic.) In London, when my wife and I were starting off on a motor trip, Wystan particularly stressed our going, even though it was considerably out of the way, to Ashby-de-la-Zouche 'for the best martini in England'.

Visiting him in Austria I had my first experience of driving with Wystan at the wheel – driving madly, *natürlich*, at top speed, and I must say, very masterfully as well. In Boston I had a long distance call from him and in telling me what was new he said he had just been asked to give some famous lectures for a tremendous fee. 'That's great!' I said. 'It would be awfully nice,' he answered, 'but nothing occurred to me that I wanted to lecture on, so all I could do was say no.'

Whether in London, in Austria, or at Oxford he was a very enjoyable host, and in New York particularly so. There for a great many years he gave himself a birthday party, sending out formal – and fruitful – invitations, to 'A Birthday Party' with, printed at the foot of the invitations, 'Carriages at one'. The parties, where the only drink was champagne, became a good deal of a tradition: the guests feeling like fellow-members of a club, the presents piling up near the front door, the champagne bottles piling up behind the improvised bar; the host very radiant and ambulatory, the guests very radiant and audible, and I have no doubt that the carriages – unheard because of muffled horses' hooves – arrived promptly at one.

No less pleasant were the dinners Wystan gave my wife and me at the St Mark's Place flat that he shared with Chester Kallman, a remarkably inventive and fine cook. There the T. S. Eliots might be our fellow guests; on other occasions appeared a fellow resident whose kinfolk Eliot had honoured. At dinner, with all the warmth and good talk the food and wine provided, we were often amused by the presence of Wystan's and Chester's large cat who toured the dinner table, offering the soup tureen his tail or the casserole his paw. He never conversed, or ate, with us but was an invariable source of interest.

As opposed to Wystan's lack of interest in possessions and his illiberality towards himself, towards others his generosity, whether in opening his purse or in furthering people's careers, inevitably became very well known. It might be for persons or causes in need; with writers it was often to praise them, or recommend their work to publishers, or give publishers quotes for their books, or favourably review them. Mine is a very real debt to Wystan: for one thing, he had me invited to give lectures at Oxford; for another, when he was compiling his commonplace book, *A Certain World*, he had me invited to compile one also. (After reading mine when it appeared, and speaking well of it, he added: 'You haven't much interest in nature, have you?' I couldn't deny it.) Wystan was also uncommonly generous with his time in reading the work of writers, particularly young ones, and in talking to them. At Oxford I saw him at eleven o'clock in the morning – it might have been true of any morning – having a cup of coffee in a sort of basement cafeteria and with the greatest good nature answering various stray students' questions and reading various better known students' poems. Earlier with him, the child had been father to the man: in telling me about Wystan's undergraduate days Nevill Coghill, who had been his Oxford tutor, spoke of the rather curious student themes he got from his other tutees; when Coghill would raise an eyebrow, the students would retort: '*Wystan* says it's all right' – a dictum from which there could be no appeal.

Wystan was very enjoyable to work with, even on the floor. When he and I did the Viking – and Faber – *Book of Aphorisms*, we worked separately from the outset, which let us assert our tastes and crochets and which also saved us from conferences. (Wystan's great preference for German culture and literature and mine, by comparison, for French greatly facilitated a fair amount of our reading.) We finally, however, had to get together to put things together, and early one afternoon Wystan arrived at my house with a big bag full of aphorisms to amalgamate with mine. All the aphorisms were by agreement on three by five inch file cards, and the total was overwhelming. Having decided to sort them into categories, which would be carried over into the book – humanity, society, religion, history, the sexes, the arts, and so on – we found the only feasible place for sorting them out was the floor of my study. The ensuing three hours, if photographed or filmed, might have revealed two late-middle-aged and obviously crack-brained men sprawled out on the floor and engaged in a very punitive or pathological game of slapjack: *slap, slap, slap*, as the piles of cards grew taller and often tumbled on to one another; *slap, slap, slap*, in the midst of which my wife entered to announce that Edmund Wilson had just phoned asking whether he could come up for a drink, and when asked would he come later – 'Wystan and Louis are stretched out on the floor sorting their aphorisms' – he insisted that actually we must be stretched out on the floor dead drunk.

After my wife and I moved to Boston in 1963 we saw Wystan much less, only on occasional jaunts to New York; but in the six or seven years before he died he was a very welcome and unobtrusive Boston house-guest of ours who, to divert himself, could always turn to the crossword puzzles he had brought along, or to inspecting and sometimes exploring the books on our shelves. The first time he stayed with us we realized, late in the visit, that with the best of intentions we had gone in for very misguided hospitality. He had come for a few days and the sofa bed that was the best sleeping accommodation we could offer him seemed to us – for so large a guest and such a length of time – rather uninviting. (When, to work on *The Rake's Progress*, Wystan first came to stay with the Stravinskys, they too worried about the studio couch that was their only extra bed and described his Procrustean appearance in it.) Hence, except for the first night, I booked a room for him at a club of mine close by, where if he chose he could also have breakfast. Each morning he would arrive at our flat very early and unfed; on the last morning a fierce, old-fashioned Boston blizzard also arrived, preventing his flying to Washington. When he asked if he might stay another night and was urged to, he then asked: 'I don't have to go to that place again, do I?' The intonation had enough of the small boy about it to be very touching, but it also bespoke Wystan's conception of hospitality – something linked much closer with friendship than with transformable furniture.

Linked with each visit was a poetry reading he gave at Boston College and each time he spoke very successfully to a crowded auditorium, looking neatly if not very fashionably dressed and wearing the carpet slippers that his suffering feet made necessary. During his visits he and I talked, as usual to no great extent, about poetry, whether his – especially a new book of his – or other people's, or poetry itself. He seldom spoke of anything he had written. As a poet, his one claim to primacy was his knowledge and command of English prosody. Much of our talk was of poets long ago; Skelton, whom he had written an essay on, or Campion or George Herbert, or an emerging poet he liked of whom I knew little. But most often we shut up shop early.

On his last visit to us, in the spring of 1972 – soon after a splendid celebration, given by Random House in New York, of his sixty-fifth birthday – he gave his usual Boston College reading. This, it seemed to me, brought his largest audience and most responsive one. Over the years, if I may digress for a moment, Wystan had noticeably improved in reading or reciting his poems. I remember introducing him in the 1950s at the National Institute of Arts and Letters when, as he read his poems, a slightly mumbled and not always audible speech, aggravated by his indomitable English accent, made for a disappointing performance. As time went on he overcame this, seeming better with each Boston College reading; indeed he happily confessed that he had become a 'ham'. He could never lay claim to showmanship, but he scored in a different way from his engaging personality.

His final visit to us was for the customary few days and adhered enough to routine to be termed a ritual. On one of the nights we would have a small dinner party for him. Every day he would get up very early to have lots of black coffee and nothing else for breakfast. During the morning he went to work on his crossword puzzles or investigated the book shelves, taking down three or four books (one of them, I remember, was Thoreau's *Collected Poems*); had dry vermouth at lunch; had coffee at four o'clock; had martinis at six o'clock; loved soup for dinner and was always given it; relished what the English call the joint and refused what they call the pudding; drank wine steadily from dinner until he took to his sofa bed; spread on top of the bedclothes his overcoat and two or three coats of mine, and spent the night under them.

But though the routine was successful as always, about the visit something seemed lacking. Wystan was his usual courteous and unobtrusive self, and the bread-and-butter letter to my wife was as warm as all the others had been. But while he was with us he seemed much less communicative than normally, which is why I have omitted from the routine the talks the three of us had always had – jolly sessions given to anecdotes, to jokes, to unmalicious gossip, to trading childhood experiences and amusements. This time Wystan lacked his usual animation and often showed no interest. He did not look well, but hadn't at other times with no loss of vivacity. This was the last time we saw him. From Oxford months later we heard that he was by no means his old self: there was no mention of illness, but even among friends at enjoyable dinner parties he almost never spoke. I don't know what caused the change; I do know that he had looked forward to spending his last years at Oxford, housed at Christ Church as one might suppose Forster had been at King's. Concern about him during the year or so before he died has helped in its way to diminish the poignancy of his death. His life and work remain: I shall think of him, miss him, honour him as he unforgettably was.

Auden by Cecil Beaton

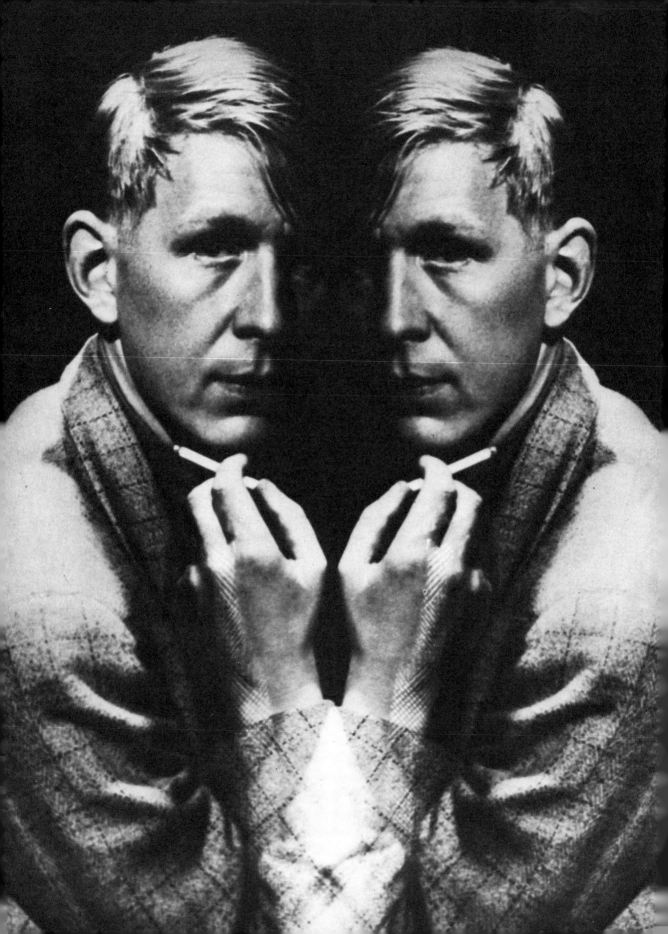

52, 53, 54 Cecil Beaton photographed Auden on three occasions. The first occasion was in 1930, the year Auden began teaching at Larchfield Academy, Helensburgh.

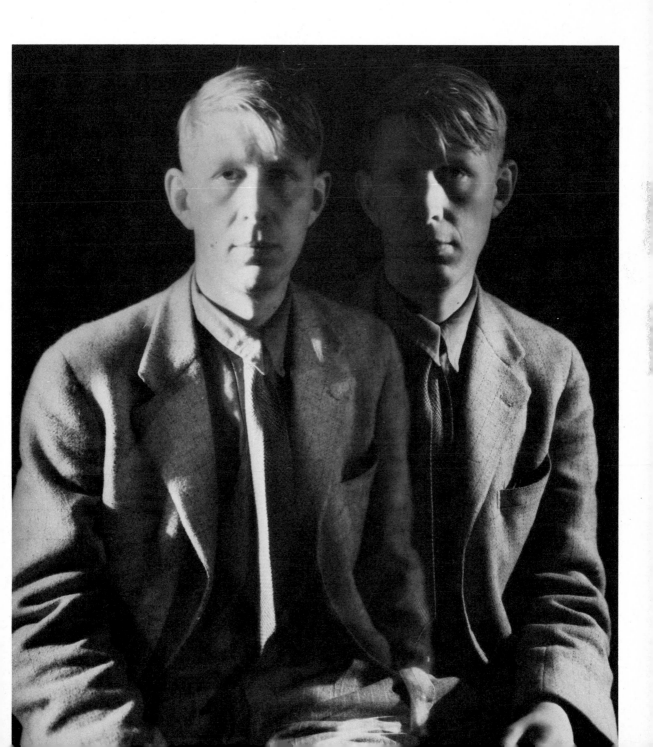

55, 56, 57, 58 The last of the 1930s sequence.

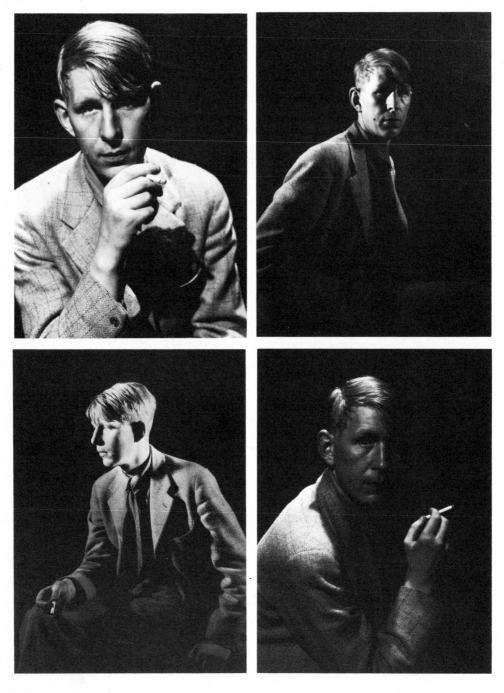

59 The next occasion when Sir Cecil photographed Auden was in 1954, in America.

60, 61 BELOW LEFT and RIGHT Auden in
1954. 62 RIGHT From the last sequence of
pictures Sir Cecil took, in 1968.

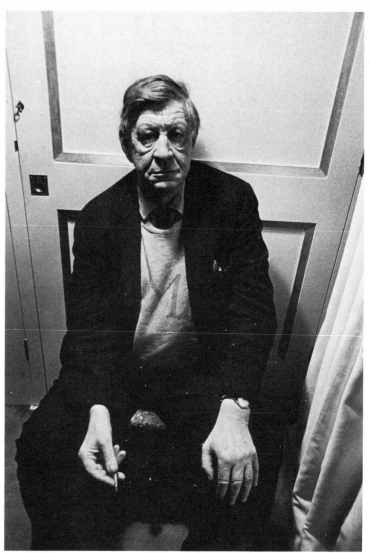

63 In 1968, with Dionysus.

64 OVERLEAF In 1968, wearing his Tolkien sweater.

Sketches and Portraits

65 ABOVE A drawing by David Hockney, 1968.

66 RIGHT A drawing by Maurice
Feild of Auden in the 1930s, when
Auden was a fellow-teacher at the
Downs School, Colwall.
67 FAR RIGHT A pencil drawing by
Anthony Rossiter, 1970.
68 BELOW 'Lullaby' by Henry
Moore. 'Lay your sleeping head, my
love,/Human on my faithless arm. . . .
Both this and 69 OPPOSITE 'Sketches
of Auden' are from a de luxe edition
of Auden's poems, with illustrations
by Henry Moore, published by the
Petersburg Press.

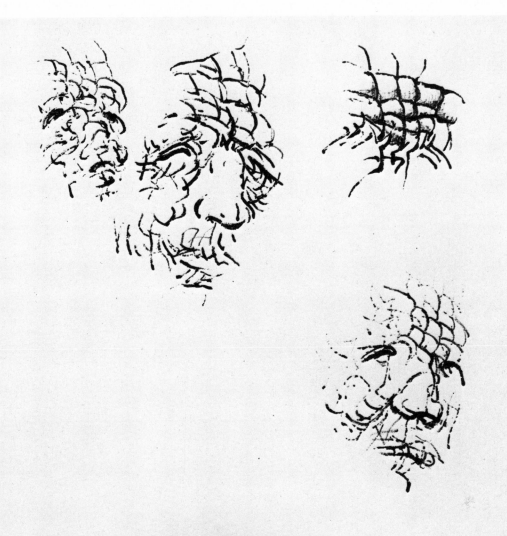

Wystan Auden
Sept 30th /73..

when I heard of Auden's death I was finishing
one of the illustrations for his book — I had
been with him in Vienna only the week before
& his presence came back vividly. The monumental
ruggedness of his face, its deep furrows like
plough marks crossing a field. I tried to put this
on paper, to fix his memory for myself:

Henry Moore

71 A portrait by Sir William Coldstream, 1937.

Orlan Fox
Friday nights

Orlan Fox became a close friend of Auden's in the poet's later years

Wystan often claimed that the personal *he* was not worth writing about because he was 'not a man of action'. But isn't our 'trans-Atlantic Goethe' worthy of note, I once chided. He smiled, but would not answer. Yet, as Bill Gray, another American friend of Wystan, recently reminded me, he was not averse to the memoirs of close friends. I think it important to record that, distinguished poet or not, the man was fun to know, that he had a deep sense of carnival.

New York – Friday Night: In retrospect I feel that anything I write about Wystan ought to have a dateline. Sometime in the mid-sixties, over table at his apartment on St Mark's Place, he shyly suggested that we routinely have dinner every Friday night at his place. Quite honoured of course, I agreed and religiously after that we almost always dined alone on Fridays when he was in residence in New York.

I assumed at the time that Tuesdays were H.A., Saturdays, I.S., Sundays, L.K., because it was characteristic of him so to structure his calendar. I had long since recognized that Wystan was shy, deeply shy, and he was at his best with friends *tête-a-tête*. In fact, except at parties and on other public occasions, he rarely introduced them.

Therefore, I felt the invitation meant that I, after years of being a friend, was now becoming 'family', which meant relaxed private conversation, sometimes serious, sometimes gossipy. It meant sharing complaints and unembarrassed silence. And, yes, it meant the luxury of being boring or repetitious. Friday nights, to both of us, were sacred.

Certainly, Wystan had other friends in New York who qualified as 'family'. I think of Lincoln Kirstein, in particular. Sadly, however, on leaving New York, Wystan announced to the press that he was going to Christ Church because he could be dead a week in the city before anyone found his body. So there were no set 'Tuesdays' or 'Saturdays' or 'Sundays'. Fridays were indeed special.

The regimen sounds like a train schedule. You buy the food, I'll furnish the booze. You cook one Friday, I the next. Yes, the format of the evening was predictable, but not the content.

The evenings reflected his heavily structured day. He rose at a certain time, drank coffee and read or did the crossword until a certain hour, worked, had an aperitif before lunch, dined, worked, had tea, more work, and then cocktails and the relaxation of the evening. He never wrote at night – 'Only the "Hitlers of the world" work at night; no honest artist does.'

I might add that the observation I made that he was shy is punctuated in my memory by three occasions. The first I have described. Much later, near the end of his residence in New York, he shyly asked if I would share quarters with him. I politely declined. Now I regret it, since he then determined to settle in Christ Church for its community and camaraderie. But at the time, I explained that I was settled in my own apartment with a pretty definite life style of my own. It was understood that I could never conform to his regimented day. He sympathized, but I now realize it was a cry for help, for companionship. The subject was never mentioned again. Then, over a Friday dinner, he abruptly asked would I mind if he dedicated *Epistle To A Godson* to me. It was gentleman-to-gentleman request, which moved me deeply. I said I would be honoured. 'Thank you,' he replied, 'I'm sure your mother will be pleased.'

Wystan had a loathing for photographs. 'The camera always lies,' he would say. 'It just ain't art.' Yet, I remember two snapshots of him that he was fond of. One was of Wystan and his brothers with his mother in centre; and the other, taken late in life showed him sitting on a bench at scholar's table at Christ Church, his legs dangling, looking very much like a 'precocious schoolboy'.

Actually, when he showed me the picture I remarked on this. He gave me the bright approving look I remember from the first time I met him when I said something intelligent about Prior, whom I'd been reading in college. When I saw the photographs accompanying the appreciation in a certain prestigious British newspaper following his death, I was quite disturbed. Certainly the series of photos showed the physical deterioration, but they could not portray Wystan, as he portrayed himself in his last book:

Each year brings new problems of Form and Content
new foes to tug with: at Twenty I tried to
vex my elders, past Sixty it's the young whom
    I hope to bother.

To me, at least, his life, and his work, have a sensible continuity. I think of all the Quest poems throughout the body of his work that are common but differentiated by age. I contrast the early love poems with the voice of a man describing the comforts of a settled household, the angst of ageing and finally the dread of impending death. But I won't pursue this kind of parlour Freudian analysis of the man and his work. I'll leave it to the scholars to explicate the poems and draw what conclusions they may.

On this subject, I recall when he was working on a new definitive *Collected Shorter Poems, 1927–1957* to be published by Faber, he exclaimed, 'God, how careless I used to be. I feel as if I'm just beginning to learn my craft. The revisions will be a gift to any Ph.D aspirant.' Incidentally, the poem he most regretted writing is 'September 1, 1939'. 'It was not honest,' he explained. His favourite, I believe, was 'In Praise of Limestone.'

At this point all Friday conversations over a period of time have become fused, as if they were of one evening. Therefore, I offer the following abbreviated – and random – notes:

On Poetry

Because I am not a poet, he would sometimes comment on the works of the living. (He confided he disliked talking 'shop' with other contemporary writers.) Few, in English, he admired. Sometimes, with a wink and a wrinkle of his nose, he would say of some writer, 'He won't do', or 'He's smelly' – meaning he's solipsistically playing in his own faeces. And he deeply deplored the confusion of poetry with propaganda and polemics.

I often had the feeling that Wystan believed, in later years, he had no peer among living poets.

'I am proud of my friends and of my knowledge of metre,' he would often say. He also liked to brag that he had written successfully in every known metre – 'But, people don't notice that.' Once, I asked him if he'd ever written a cinquain. 'What on earth is that?' he exclaimed. Having just come across the form in Babette Deutsche's *Poetry Handbook*, I explained it. He merely grunted (and, to my knowledge, never wrote one).

Of poetry and prose he admired he had a prodigious memory. I suspect that this sprang from his English schoolboy training, the memorization of lines, and he never quit. Once, over a martini, he quoted what seemed to be a page from Henry James' *American Scene*.

On Sex

Many years ago, he announced, 'Oh that. Well, at my age, I've put on the widow's cap.' He would cut short my narrative of some insignificant or commonplace sexual adventure, but would listen, with attention, to an anecdote that was either anatomically or psychologically interesting. At the same time he would complain about novelists who insisted on describing *the act*: 'for there are really so few things a male and female can do in bed.'

Perhaps I should say, at least as I knew him, sex to Wystan was essentially peripheral to love. And he loved profoundly. No one could have written,

> Lay your sleeping head, my love,
> Human on my faithless arm . . .

without that experience. David Luke once told me anything should be forgiven a man who composed those lines.

I heartily agree. He was proud of his love poems, and he would sometimes tell me about the person and the circumstances of the composition of the poem. Those to whom they were addressed will, of course, recognize themselves.

Wystan, as the obituaries noted, was the husband of the late Erika Mann. He married her at Christopher Isherwood's urging in order to give her a British passport. The marriage was never consummated. According to him, she was responsible for rescuing the manuscript of *Joseph and His Brothers* from the Mann household. 'I can't say we're friends,' he would say, 'but she did us that service.'

On Personal Relationships

While I can only speak from my own experience, the relationship between the two of us was extremely complex. At first, when I came to know him, there was definitely a father-son relationship. He advised what books I should read. At dinner parties, as the youngest, I opened the wine and served the table as he carved.

Then as we got to know each other, there was the older brother-younger brother situation. He would give advice such as, 'Sorry you're depressed. The only remedy I know is lots of hot baths and crosswords.'

As we became real pals and the Friday nights were instituted, we became brother-brother. We might exchange jokes. One I remember he liked to tell was about Christ and the woman taken in adultery: Christ says, 'Let him who is without sin throw the first stone.' The words are hardly out of his mouth before a stone whizzes past his ear. He whirls around. *'Mother!'* Or he might confide: 'I'm writing a poem in hexameters about insects. Am rather pleased.'

He could be mother scolding the son over thirty years his junior – 'Don't slouch in your seat; gentlemen sit upright.' And, curiously, when I came out of the kitchen serving food, there could be Wystan eagerly anticipating the nourishment and care of mother. He always sat on a volume of the OED, as if he were a child too short for table.

Then we could have our private schoolgirl jokes, such as 'Any news?' and 'Au reservoir', taken from E. F. Benson's *Lucia* books.

And we could be conspiratorial schoolboys. Once, when he was asking how work was going, I complained I had to write a salute to an officer in my company who was retiring after fifty years of service. After a few enquiries about the man's character, he dashed off a toast that was approved with praise by my superiors and gold-lettered into a farewell scroll. It was just for fun, and remained our secret until quite recently when I confided it to our very literate chief executive. The chairman was delighted.

On Religion:

A number of Christian sects promptly organized memorial services at the announcement of his death, including the Catholics – through the Catholic Workers, no doubt, headed by that remarkable woman, Dorothy Day (whom Wystan himself called a true saint because she had the guts to help the 'undeserving' poor). Wystan was an Anglican. Yet, he began to attend Greek Orthodox services in later years to hear the mass in an ancient language. This was after his local Episcopalian church had gone 'mod' to accommodate the 'Jesus freaks' of the East Village where he lived.

In the company of other friends of Wystan, I attended the memorial mass at St John The Divine, seat of the Episcopal bishopric of New York. It was celebrated by the former Bishop of New York, who knew Wystan personally. I was so numbed by the occasion that I failed to recognize Bill Meredith who approached me after the service – and Bill had been one of several friends and associates who read a number of Wystan's poems during the ceremony. There was one moment in the mass when I could not contain my tears – while the boys' choir sang an anthem composed by Wystan with music by Benjamin Britten:

> O lift your little pinkie, and touch the evening sky.
> Love's all over the mountains where the beautiful go to die.

Wystan professed high church, and he was a lion in his theology. On that subject, I offer a few anecdotes, which though they may suggest 'low' were in perfect continuity with his character.

He loved to sing, and would often comment that a great voice was the greatest gift to man. He himself could just carry a tune and liked to bellow good Anglican hymns. Some years ago, I obtained a hymnal from my mother, who's a devout Christian. On many occasions we would sip martinis over our favourites. He had a singing voice like a sonic boom. No matter if the neighbours had complained – which they never did – we howled away in complete joy.

Another remembrance; he was on a lecture tour. It happened I was in St Louis on a business trip on the occasion of his sixty-fourth birthday. We arranged to rendezvous at the rather seedy Jefferson Hotel over the weekend. Adjoining rooms. I brought tons of British-style crosswords and a bottle of champagne. He whizzed through the crosswords, sipped the wine with pleasure over birthday dinner in his rooms, and, at my suggestion, happily attended the Sunday service at the St Louis Episcopal Cathedral on Sunday morning.

His singing voice echoed through the structure. Embarrassed, yes I was. Then, I decided not to be. Heads turned, of course. Finally, the Father climbed into his pulpit, suspiciously eyeing us. He was awful, very orthodox but completely inept when he tried to quote modern poets. Wystan grunted, and turned to me in a stage whisper: 'Knows nothing about theology – or poetry.' Then I was embarrassed. I had my fingers crossed that he wouldn't try to quote WHA; mercifully, he didn't.

And a sad memory; I was not present at the funeral service at Kirchstetten in Austria. However, in the past, when I visited him there, I accompanied him to the local Catholic church. As protestants, we were perched in the balcony of the chapel. We would have been placed there in any case, along with the schoolteacher, doctor, and other distinguished citizens or guests. Below were the villagers. Wystan, in his excellent German, still bellowed the hymns. We listened to the service politely, and with the valediction, scooted off to the local tavern for beer and sausage. I think it's marvellous that he chose to be buried in Kirchstetten. The villagers adored their Herr Professor. In the end, it was the only community in which he was really comfortable. When they renamed the lane to his house *Audenstrasse*, officially, he expressed embarrassment; privately, he told me he was pleased.

On Music

I'm haunted by the opening lines of 'The Garrison':

> Martini time: time to draw the curtains and
> choose a composer we should like to hear. . . .

Of course, he was referring to the arrangement in his house in Austria. But it struck me as so true of our evenings. I don't know how many serious works he introduced me to, but he certainly taught me how to listen.

Wystan's taste wasn't strictly highbrow. He adored the witty lyrics of Cole Porter, for example. He considered *Kiss Me Kate* better theatre than *The Taming of the Shrew*. And he thought Frank Loesser's *Guys and Dolls* a masterpiece. A favourite camp of his was to sing, with a squeaky, gutter Brooklyn accent:

> Take back your minks,
> Take back your pearls [poils],

> What makes you think
> I am just one of them girls [dem goils].

At the same time he considered the works of certain ballad singers and rock groups the loutish charivari of semi-literate nannies trying to appease restless children.

In the early sixties when Chester Kallman still lived in New York, he and Wystan were commissioned to do the script and lyrics for a musical comedy version of *Don Quixote*. I saw some of the songs they composed. Funny, they were, and absolutely brilliant. But the work was too good, and the producer paid them off and found someone else who would suit Broadway. *Man of La Mancha* was the result.

His collection of records of serious music was heavy on opera. *Lucia di Lammermoor* is the acid test for anyone who thinks he likes opera, he would say. Or: 'No gentleman can fail to admire Bellini.' Once, while listening to a patter from Donizetti, he remarked, 'They remind me of mice quarrelling over a piece of cheese.'

Then, of course, there's his own contribution to musical literature. I think the Auden-Kallman librettos stand beside the works of Da Ponte and Hofmannstal in their greatness. It's a pity that they haven't been collected into a single volume.

One should be careful in calling them Auden librettos. Once, when I was raving about the 'brothel scene' in *The Rake's Progress*, he firmly corrected me: 'You should thank Chester for that. He conceived and wrote it.'

The Professor

He liked to play the role and was totally accessible to anyone who seriously wanted advice about writing. To the young poet: 'Learn everything there is to know about metre.' To the aspiring novelist: 'Read Austen for her style; Dickens for his characterization; Hardy for his structure, and Firbank for his comic invention.'

He always insisted on keeping his telephone number in the Manhattan directory. He would see most anyone over tea who called him up for an appointment. Certainly, he cut tea short when the guest began asking what he meant in certain poems.

Letters from strangers not accompanied by self-addressed stamped envelopes were immediately tossed away. I remember one exception, a fan letter from a prisoner at Attica who had discovered his poetry in an anthology. The correspondence lasted a couple of years, until Wystan's move to Christ Church. One Friday evening, Wystan greeted me excitedly waving a letter. He announced with pride, 'He's *now* reading Kafka.'

His Citizenship

Although he often gave various joking motives for becoming an American citizen, the true reason was that he wished to escape the clubbish, stifling intellectual atmosphere of the late thirties in London. Not that the us could lay much claim on him – 'I'm really a New Yorker,' he would say.

He liked to tell about his interview with an immigration officer when he applied for us citizenship. Question: 'Your profession?' Answer: 'Poet.' Next question: 'Can you write?' Wystan answered yes with a straight face, but he told me later, 'I've always regretted not saying, 'No, it just comes to me.'

His US citizenship cost him dearly – possibly the Nobel Prize, possibly a knighthood, and possibly the poet laureateship. But can one say what kind of poet, or man, he would have become had he remained a British subject?

His Hobbies

None in the conventional sense. By the time I knew him, travel had become a bore. He almost never took vacations. There are two exceptions I can remember: a pilgrimage to Hammerfest, Norway, which, on his schoolboy map, was the northern-most town in the world; the other to Jerusalem, three years after the Six Day War. In rereading the letters from him, it's obvious he preferred Hammerfest.

Planes abroad, first class always, were a convenience where one might meet, to his surprise, someone like Boris Karloff, which he once did. When on a US domestic flight for a reading, he took an analeptic swig and wondered where on earth he was landing.

Mysteries, in the mode of Agatha Christie, he liked. But his principal method of relaxation was the crossword. 'The *New York Times*' one is a scandal,' he often complained. 'The puzzle master doesn't know arse from. . . .' I introduced him to the *New York*, which claims its puzzle is 'The World's Most Challenging'. It's taken from the London *Sunday Times*'s puzzle, but apparently heavily edited for Americans. Wystan could do it over three sips of his martini. Not surprisingly, he was always pleased with people who could come up with a good answer to the anagram of WYSTANHUGHAUDEN. His favourite was 'Hug a shady wet nun'. 'Did you know that TSELIOT is an anagram for "litotes"?', he liked to ask.

His Eccentricities

Everyone who knew him has remarked on the house slippers he wore in public. Well, he did suffer painfully of corns. But he admitted to me that he deliberately chose the tackiest style – 'At my age,' he said, 'I'm allowed to seem a little dotty.'

A standard Christmas or birthday present from me was bubble bath, which he adored. I usually had to go to the children's section at Woolworth's to find a soap that would really give a good froth. One hilarious occasion, when after a latish dinner party, Wystan went off to his customary bath, his guests, hosted by Chester Kallman, continued with drink and chatter; Wystan suddenly emerged from the bathroom stark naked, bubbles afloat. He stalked with great dignity across the den, turned, sniffed disapproval at the continuance of celebration, and went off to bed. We all went into peals of laughter, but he had made his point, and the party broke up soon afterwards. Such disapproving auntish posturing earned him the epithet, invented by Chester, of 'Miss Master'.

About money he was absolutely old-fashioned. He would usually announce what his income was for the year once he'd done his taxes. I must say I never pressed him for this information, but he was proud of what a poet could earn. One night I was staggered when he told me he had a stupendous sum of dollars in his bank account; 'You never know when you might need it,' he explained. I did a little arithmetic and pointed out that by putting the money in a savings account, he could easily pay the expense of his annual trip to Europe with the interest. Sometime later, on my advice, he put a parcel of his account into a mutual fund.

And there was always the mischievous schoolboy in Wystan. I'm told that, surrounded by an honouring dyke of dons at a certain Oxford college last winter, he declared, 'Of course, everyone pees in his bath.'

His Letters

'Dear Wystan, many thanks for your letter. I'm very disturbed by the news that the new doctor in the village has diagnosed a heart condition – "whatever that means" as you say. . . .' This was the beginning of my last letter to him. He never replied, which he usually did by return mail. Instead, there was the cold news on radio and TV of his death.

That he asked that all of his letters to friends and other correspondence be destroyed was consistent with his character. I don't think for a moment he thought that 'family' would cash in on his letters. I believe it was his way of saying to the public that one should read his works to discover W. H. Auden, the poet, the man who had been gifted with a great talent; his peccadilloes are not important to his work. In fact, while recently rereading the great stack of correspondence I've saved over the years, I had the distinct impression of the conversations we had enjoyed. His correspondence was conversational, exactly in his voice, and it was topical, sometimes anecdotal, sometimes of a serious nature. I'm afraid his request has had an adverse effect: I have been approached by people who want to know what's so 'juicy' about the Auden letters. Nothing, I insist. Yet, I shall honour his request only to a degree. They shall never be shown in public, nor published, but I refuse to destroy them. I shall save them for some quiet evening, make it a Friday night, when I'll pull them out and converse with a dear friend.

With his estate's permission I quote a poem entitled 'A Contrast' that he typed on the overleaf of his last letter to me, dated 31 August 1973.

> How broad-minded were Nature and My Parents
> in appointing to My Personal City
> exactly the sort of Censor I would have
>   Myself elected,
>
> Who bans from recall any painful image:
> foul behaviour, whether by Myself or Others;
> days of dejection, breakages, poor cooking
>   are suppressed promptly.
>
> I do wish, though, They had assigned me a less hostile
> Public Prosecutor, Who in the early morning
> cross-questions me with unrelenting venom
>   about My future –

'How will You ever pay Your taxes?' 'Where will You
find a cab?' 'Won't Your speech be a flop?' – and greets my
answers with sarcastic silence. Well, well, I
    must grin and bear it.

Of course, he knew he was ill, possibly dying. He often told me that he wished to live
to the canonical age of seventy. Well, Wystan, dear Wystan, it wasn't to be. Yet,
considering his immense output of work, one would guess he outlived us all.

Hannah Arendt
Remembering Wystan H. Auden[1]

Hannah Arendt, a political philosopher whose writings have won her many international awards,
knew Auden well

I met Auden late in life at an age when the easy knowledgeable intimacy of friendships
concluded in one's youth can no longer be attained, because not enough life is left, or
expected to be left, to share with each other. Thus we were very good friends but not
intimate friends. Moreover, there was a certain reserve in him that would discourage
familiarity, not that I tried it ever; I rather gladly respected it as the necessary secre-
tiveness of the great poet, who must have taught himself early not to talk in prose,
loosely and at random, of certain things which he knew how to say much more
adequately in the condensed concentration of poetry. Reticence may be the *déformation
professionnelle* of the poet.

    In his case this seemed all the more likely as much of his work in utter simplicity
arose out of the spoken word, out of certain idioms of everyday language – like

    Lay your sleeping head, my love,
    Human on my faithless arm.

This kind of perfection is very rare; we find it in some of the greatest of Goethe's
poems and it must be true for most of Pushkin's work, because the hallmark of them
is that they are untranslatable. The moment they are wrenched from their original
abode they disappear in a cloud of banality. Here all depends on the 'fluent gestures'
in 'elevating facts from the prosaic to the poetic' (which Clive James rightly stressed
in his essay on Auden in *Commentary*, December 1973). Where such fluency is
achieved we are magically convinced that everyday speech is latently poetic and,
taught by the poets, our ears open up to the true mysteries of language. It was the very
untranslatability of one of Auden's poems that, many years ago, convinced me of his

[1] Copyright © 1974 by Hannah Arendt

greatness. Three German translators had tried their luck and mercilessly killed one of my favourite poems: 'If I Could Tell You' (in the *Collected Shorter Poems 1927–1957*) which arises naturally from two colloquial idioms, 'time will tell' and 'I told you so':

> Time will say nothing but I told you so,
> Time only knows the price we have to pay;
> If I could tell you I would let you know.
>
> If we should weep when clowns put on their show,
> If we should stumble when musicians play,
> Time will say nothing but I told you so. . . .
>
> The winds must come from somewhere when they blow,
> There must be reasons why the leaves decay;
> Time will say nothing but I told you so. . . .
>
> Suppose the lions all get up and go,
> And all the brooks and soldiers run away;
> Will Time say nothing but I told you so?
> If I could tell you I would let you know.

I met Auden in the autumn of 1958, but I had seen him before, in the late forties at a publisher's party. Although we did not exchange a word on that occasion, I still remembered him quite well – a nice-looking, well dressed, very English gentleman, friendly and relaxed. I would not have recognized him more than ten years later, for now his face was marked by those famous deep wrinkles as though life itself had delineated a kind of face-scape to make manifest the 'heart's invisible furies'. If you listened to him, nothing could be more deceptive than this appearance. Time and again, when to all appearances he could not cope any more, when his slum apartment was so cold that the water no longer functioned and he had to use the toilet in the liquor store at the corner, when his suit – no one could convince him that a man needed at least two suits so that one could go to the cleaner or two pairs of shoes so that one pair could be repaired, a subject of an endlessly ongoing debate between us throughout the years – was covered with spots or worn so thin that his trousers would suddenly split from top to bottom, in brief, whenever disaster hit before your very eyes, he would begin to kind of intone an utterly idiosyncratic, absurdly eccentric version of 'count your blessings'. Since he never talked nonsense or said something obviously silly, and since, moreover, I always remained aware that this was the voice of a very great poet, it took me years to realize that in his case appearance was not deceptive and that it was fatally wrong to ascribe what I saw and knew to the harmless eccentricity of a typically English gentleman.

I finally saw the misery, somehow realized vaguely his compelling need to hide it behind the 'count-your-blessings' litany, and still found it difficult to understand fully what made him so miserable, so unable to do anything about the absurd circumstances that made everyday life so unbearable for him. It certainly could not be lack of recognition. He was reasonably famous and anyhow ambition in this sense could not have counted for much, since he was the least vain of all authors I ever met, completely immune to the countless vulnerabilities of ordinary vanity. Not that he was humble; in his case it was self-confidence that protected him against flattery, and this self-confidence was prior to recognition and fame, prior also to achievement. ('I am going to be a great poet,' he told his Oxford tutor, Nevill Coghill.) It never left him because it was not acquired by comparisons or winning a race in competition; it was natural, interconnected but not identical with his enormous facility to do with language, and do quickly, whatever he pleased. (When friends asked him to produce a birth-day poem for the next day they could be sure to get it; this clearly is possible only in the absence of any self-doubts.) But even this facility did not go to his head, for he did not claim, or perhaps even aspire to, final perfection. He constantly revised his own poems and agreed with Valéry: 'A poem is never finished; it is only abandoned.' In other words, he was blessed with that rare self-confidence that does not need admiration and the opinions of others and can even withstand self-criticism and self-examination without falling into the trap of self-doubt. This has nothing to do with arrogance but is easily mistaken for it. Auden was never arrogant except when pro-voked by some vulgarity, in which case he protected himself with the rather abrupt rudeness characteristic of English intellectual life.

Stephen Spender, who knew him so well, has stressed that 'throughout the whole development of [Auden's] poetry . . . his theme had been love' (had it not occurred to Auden to change Descartes' *Cogito ergo sum* and to define man as the 'bubble-brained creature' that said 'I'm loved therefore I am'?). And he tells, at the end of the address he gave in memory of the dead friend at the Cathedral Church in Oxford how he had asked Auden about a reading he had given in America: 'His face lit up with a smile that altered its lines, and he said: "They loved me!".' They did not admire him, they *loved* him – here I think lies the key both to his extraordinary unhappiness and to the extraordinary greatness, intensity, of his poetry. Now, with the sad wisdom of remem-brance, he seems to me to have been an expert in the infinite varieties of unrequited love among which the infuriating substitution of admiration for love surely must have loomed large. And beneath these emotions, there must have been from the beginning a certain animal *tristesse* which no reason and no faith could overcome:

> The desires of the heart are as crooked as corkscrews,
> > Not to be born is the best for man;
> The second-best is a formal order,
> > The dance's pattern; dance while you can.

When I knew him, he would not have mentioned the best any longer so firmly had he opted for the second-best, the 'formal order', and the result was what Chester Kallman so aptly has named – 'the most dishevelled child of all disciplinarians'.

I think it was this animal *tristesse* and its 'dance while you can' that made Auden feel so attracted and almost at home in Berlin during the famous twenties, where the *Carpe diem* was practised daily in many variations. He once mentioned as a 'disease' his early 'addiction to German usages', but much more prominent than these, and less easy to get rid of, is the obvious influence of Brecht with whom I think he had more in common than he was ever ready to admit. (In the late fifties, together with Chester Kallman he translated Brecht's *Rise and Fall of City Mahagonny* which never was published – presumably because of copyright difficulties. To this day, this is the only adequate rendering of Brecht into English.) In merely literary terms Brecht's influence can easily be traced in Auden's ballads – as for instance in the late, marvellous 'Ballad of Barnaby' the tumbler who having grown old and pious 'honoured the Mother of God' by tumbling for her, or in the early little story

> About Miss Edith Gee;
> She lived in Clevedon Terrace
> At Number 83.

What made this influence possible was that they both belonged to the post-First World War generation with its curious mixture of despair and *joie de vivre*, its contempt for conventional codes of behaviour and its penchant for 'playing it cool', which expressed itself in England, as I suspect, in wearing the mask of the snob, while it expressed itself in Germany in a certain widespread pretence of wickedness, somewhat in the vein of Brecht's *Threepenny Opera*. (In Berlin one joked about this fashionable inverted hypocrisy as one joked about everything; *Er geht böse über den Kurfürstendamm* – meaning that is probably all the wickedness one is capable of. After 1933, I think, nobody joked any longer about wickedness.)

In the case of Auden as in the case of Brecht, inverted hypocrisy served to hide an irresistible inclination to being good and doing good, something they were ashamed to admit or to proclaim. This seems plausible for Auden because he finally became a Christian, but it may shock at first to hear the same about Brecht; a close reading of his poems and plays seems to me to almost prove it. There are not only the plays, *Der Gute Mensch von Setzuan* or *Die Heilige Johanna der Schlachthöfe*, but there are, perhaps more convincingly, these lines in the midst of the cynicism of *The Threepenny Opera* :

> *Ein guter Mensch sein! Ja, wer wär's nicht gern?*
> *Sein Gut den Armen geben, warum nicht?*
> *Wenn alle gut sind, ist* Sein *Reich nicht fern.*
> *Wer sässe nicht sehr gern in Seinem Licht?*

What drove these profoundly unpolitical poets into the chaotic political scene of our century was still Robespierre's *zèle compatissant*, this powerful urge towards *les malheureux*, as distinguished from any need for action, for public happiness, or the desire to change the world.

Auden, so much wiser – though by no means smarter – than Brecht, was aware early on that, 'poetry makes nothing happen'. To him, it was sheer nonsense to claim for the poet special privileges or to ask for indulgences which we are so happy to grant out of sheer gratitude. There was nothing more admirable in him than his complete sanity and his firm belief in the sanity of the mind; all kinds of madness were in his eyes lack of discipline – 'naughty, naughty', as he used to say. The main thing was to have no illusions and to accept no thoughts, no theoretical systems that would blind you against reality. He turned against his early leftist beliefs because events – the Moscow trials, the Hitler-Stalin pact, also experiences during the Spanish civil war – had proved them to be 'dishonest', 'shamefully' so, as he said in his Foreword to the *Collected Shorter Poems 1927–1957*, when he threw out what he once had written:

> History to the defeated
> may say alas but cannot help nor pardon.

To have said this was 'to equate goodness with success'. He protested that he had never believed in 'this wicked doctrine', which I doubt, not only because the lines are too good, too precise to have been produced for the sake of being 'rhetorically effective', but also because this was indeed the doctrine everybody believed in during the twenties and thirties. Then came the time when –

> In the nightmare of the dark
> All the dogs of Europe bark. . . .
>
> Intellectual disgrace
> Stares from every human face. . . .

– the time, when it looked for quite a while that the worst could happen and sheer evil could become a success. The Hitler-Stalin pact was the turning point for the left, now one had to give up all beliefs in history as the ultimate judge of human affairs.

In the forties, there were many who turned against their old beliefs, but there were very few who understood what had been wrong with them. Far from giving up their belief in history and success, they simply changed trains, as it were; the train, socialism and communism, had been wrong and they exchanged it against the train of capitalism or Freudianism or some refined Marxism or a sophisticated mixture of all three. Auden, instead, became a Christian, that is, he left the train of history altogether. I don't know whether Stephen Spender is right in asserting that 'prayer corresponded to his deepest need' – I suspect that his deepest need was simply to write verses – but I am reasonably sure that his sanity, the great good sense, which illuminated all his prose writings, essays and book reviews, was due in no small measure to the protective shield of orthodoxy. Its demanding and time-honoured coherent meaningfulness that could neither be proved nor disproved by reason provided him, as it had provided Chesterton, with an intellectually satisfying and emotionally, rather comfortable, refuge against the onslaught of what he called 'rubbish', that is the countless follies of the age.

Rereading Auden's poetry in chronological order and remembering him in the last years of his life, when misery and unhappiness had become more and more unbearable without, however, in the least touching either the divine gift or the blessed facility of the talent, I have become more convinced than ever that he was 'hurt into poetry', even more than Yeats – 'Mad Ireland hurt you into poetry' – and that, despite his susceptiveness for compassion, public political circumstances were not necessary to 'hurt him into poetry'. What made him a poet was his extraordinary facility with, and love for, words, but what made him a great poet was the unprotesting willingness with which he yielded to the 'curse' – the curse of vulnerability to 'human unsuccess' on all levels of existence; the crookedness of the desires, the infidelities of the heart, the injustices of the world.

> Follow, poet, follow right
> To the bottom of the night.
> With your unconstraining voice
> Still persuade us to rejoice;
>
> With the farming of a verse
> Make a vineyard of the curse,
> Sing of human unsuccess
> In a rapture of distress;
>
> In the desert of the heart
> Let the healing fountain start,
> In the prison of his days
> Teach the free man how to praise.

Praise is the key-word of these lines, praise not of 'the best of all possible worlds' – as though it were up to the poet (or the philosopher) to justify God's creation – but praise that pitches itself against all that is most unsatisfactory in man's condition on this earth and sucks its strength out of the wound – somehow convinced, as the bards of ancient Greece were, that the gods spin unhappiness and evil things to mortals so that they may be able to tell the tales and sing the songs.

> I could (which you cannot)
> Find reasons fast enough
> To face the sky and roar
> In anger and despair
> At what is going on,
> Demanding that it name
> Whoever is to blame;
> The sky would only wait
> Till all my breath was gone
> And then reiterate
> As if I wasn't there
> That singular command
> I do not understand,
> *Bless what there is for being,*
> Which has to be obeyed, for
> What else am I made for,
> Agreeing or disagreeing?

And the triumph of the private person was that the voice of the great poet has never silenced the small but penetrating voice of sheer sound common sense whose loss so often has been the price paid for divine gifts; he never permitted himself to lose his mind, that is, to lose the 'distress' in the 'rapture' that rose out of it:

> No metaphor, remember, can express
> A real historical unhappiness;
> Your tears have value if they make us gay;
> *O Happy Grief!* is all sad verse can say.

It seems, of course, very unlikely that young Auden, when he decided that he was going to be a great poet, knew the price he would have to pay. I think it entirely possible that in the end, when, not the intensity of his feelings and not the gift to transform them into praise, but the sheer physical strength of the heart to bear them and live with them, gradually faded away, he might have considered the price too high. We, at any event, his audience, readers and listeners, can only be grateful that he paid his price up to the last penny for the everlasting glory of the English language. And his friends may find some consolation in Stephen Spender's beautiful joke beyond the grave – that 'his wise unconscious self chose a good day for dying' – for more than one reason. The wisdom to know 'when to live and when to die' is not given to mortals; but Wystan, one would like to think, may have received it as the supreme reward that the cruel gods of poetry bestowed on the most obedient of their servants.

Oliver Sacks
Dear Mr A . . . .

Dr Oliver Sacks, the author of Awakenings, *was a friend of Auden's during his last years*

'Goethe was an extremely complicated character and, in most Englishmen and Americans, at least, he arouses mixed feelings. . . . Yet, grumble as one may, one is forced in the end to admit that he was a great poet and a great man. Moreover, when I read the following anecdote:

> Goethe suddenly got out of the carriage to examine a stone, and I heard him say, "Well, well, how did *you* get here?" – a question which he repeated. . . .

I find myself exclaiming, not "Great Mr G!" but "Dear Mr G!"'

The closing words of this essay on Goethe epitomize what, for me and so many others, was the central characteristic of Auden, that which was most constant in his complex, agile and often enigmatic character – firstly and finally, the quality of *dearness*. Mr G., for him, was always 'Dear Mr G.', no less than 'Great (and complex) Mr G.'; this was evident in a thousand ways.

Just before Wystan finally left America, Orlan Fox and I were helping him to sort and pack his books, a painful (and I somehow felt, premonitory) task: after hours of shoving and sweating we paused for a beer, and sat without saying anything for a timeless time. (Wystan, among so many qualities, had that rarest and most precious quality – he was a man one could be quiet with; we could sit together over a beer or a fire, not saying anything, not needing to say anything, communing without talking, silently imbibing each other's presence and the silent, eloquent, presence of the now.) After a while Wystan got up, and said to me 'Take a book, some books, anything you want.' He paused, then seeing my paralysis, he said 'Well, I'll decide then. These are *my* favourite books – two of them anyhow!' and he gave me a much-tattered volume of Goethe's letters (which he fetched in from its place on his bedside table), and *The Magic Flute* (his and Chester Kallman's libretto). The old Goethe was full of affectionate scribblings, markings, annotations and comments – as happens only with something as dear and familiar as a bedside book. Every few pages, in an exclamatory hand (very different from his usual minute and methodical hand) he had written 'Dear Mr G!' in the margins of the book; not 'Dear Wolfgang' – that would have been improper – and the sense of what was proper was as strong in Auden as the sense of dearness. Together they formed the corresponding poles of his character.

At the end of the week – it was Saturday, 15 April 1972 – Orlan and I ran Wystan to the airport. We arrived early, about three hours early, because Wystan had an absolute horror of missing trains or planes. (He once told me of a recurrent dream of his: he was speeding to catch a train, in a state of extreme agitation, he felt his life, everything, depended on catching the train. Obstacles arose, one after the other, reducing him to a silently-screaming panic. And then, suddenly, he realized that it was too late, that he had missed the train, and that it didn't matter in the least; at this point there would come over him a sense of release amounting to bliss, and he would ejaculate and wake up with a smile on his face.) Wystan and Orlan and I arrived early then, and whiled away the hours in a meandering conversation (it was only later, when he left, that I realized that all the amblings and meanderings returned to one point: that the focus of the conversation was farewell – to us, to America, to those thirty-three years – an entire half of his life – which he had spent in the USA; a trans-Atlantic Goethe, he would half-seriously, half-jokingly say). Just before the call for the plane, a complete stranger came up to us, a quintessential (almost allegorical) American, intensely shy, sincere and effusive; he stuttered 'Gee! You look like, you are Mr Auden. . . . We have been honoured to have you in our country, Sir. You'll always be welcome back here as an honoured guest – and a friend. Good-bye, Mr Auden, God bless you for everything!' – he stuck out his hand, and Wystan shook it with great cordiality. He was much moved – there were tears in his eyes. I turned to Wystan and asked him whether such encounters were common to him: 'Common,' he said, 'but never common. There is genuine love in these casual encounters. . . .' As the decorous stranger discreetly retired, I asked Wystan how he experienced the world, whether he thought of it as being a very small or a very large place. 'Neither,' he replied. 'Neither large nor small. Cosy, cosy . . . (and, in an undertone) . . . like home.'

He said nothing more – there was no more to be said. The loud impersonal call blared out, and Wystan hurried to the exit-gate. At the gate he turned and kissed us both – the kiss of a godfather embracing his godsons: a kiss of benediction and farewell. . . . As he entered the aisle which led to the plane, he suddenly looked terribly old and frail, but as nobly formal as a Gothic cathedral.

Cosy, cosy – it was one of his favourite words, one of the words he most used when chatting. (He was dissatisfied by its coverage in the great OED, and thought of re-doing this, making an anthology of the cosy, giving the word its full and proper world-embracing power.) Whenever he said 'cosy' in his peculiar voice, it seemed to acquire a special richness of evocation and meaning. Once we saw a bird fly to its nest atop a sooty lamp-post in St Mark's Place: 'Look!,' exclaimed Wystan. 'It's gone home to its nest. Think how cosy it must be in its nest!' For a moment I felt (I fancied I felt) exactly what the bird felt – cosy, protected, at home, in its nest. And Wystan's apartment in the East Village, though squalid and cluttered and dilapidated and dirty, this too was cosy, wonderfully so: it had the cosiness of a human nest. (I greatly regret never having seen his house, his real home, in the village of Kirchstetten – of which he hymned every room in some of his loveliest poems).

Words became palpable, solid, alive, when Wystan used them, both things in themselves and expressions of himself: and this was especially true of the word 'cosy'. He cared nothing for possessions as such; they only had meaning for him as vehicles of personal meaning and feeling. The first time I had tea with him – back in 1969 – I found the teapot in a tea-cosy, and my egg in an egg-cosy; and this was in no sense mere eccentricity or oddity – Wystan put them in cosies because he cared for them personally – they ceased to be mere things, inanimate, and were given a life and reality of their own: he would say 'you' to the teapot, as Goethe said 'you' to the stone. When he saw me out – I had a BMW at the time, with a jacketed tank – he was pleased at the sensible and simple design of the machine (this was Wystan the boy, the lover of models and mines and machines, of good craftsmanship of every kind) but he was especially taken by the jacket round the tank: 'I like that,' he said, 'it shows you care for the bike. I have never seen a bike with a bike-cosy before. But it's absolutely right – it belongs where it is.'

That afternoon sensitized me to the concept of cosiness, and amongst other things, drew my attention to something which runs through all his poems, but which I had never properly seen before then; his delight in the cosiness of language itself, the fitting-together of words and ideas, the way in which phrase is fitted into phrase into phrase into phrase, the way in which every word is embodied, encysted, nested cosily in its right and proper place, where it belongs, at home, in the body of the poem.

The dovetailing and complementary concepts of cosiness – belonging, propriety, place – were perfectly exemplified for Auden in the intricate structure and disposition of the body – the physical body, the social body, the body of the cosmos – bodies made of metaphors incarnate and alive; metaphors intimately, infinitely, entwined; metaphors within metaphors, worlds within worlds; the body, the world, as an infinite metaphor, but a metaphor, above all, of dearness, of home. Wystan felt, in the most literal, tangible, immediate way, that every organ had its place in the body, as every man had his place in the world. The sense of the body as a home, as a landscape, only conscious on the surface, but going deeper and deeper, into the infinite depths of our world-home, the cosmos, is beautifully expressed in one of his last poems – 'Talking to Myself' – which with great generosity he dedicated to me. Wystan had no belief in accident or chance: 'Random, my bottom!', he writes in this poem. Everything, for him, stood in mutual awareness, knowing its place, and that of all others: every body, every organ, every atom, every star, the whole grand prosody of nature itself. In the world as Wystan saw it, there was great aspectuality, and alternatives – without number – but never any hint of arbitrariness or accident; history was a series of significant moments – the union, the unison, of harmony and destiny. This elemental musical sense – musical literally and musical figuratively, musical in the sense of Mozart or Bach, and equally in the sense of Pythagoras or Leibniz – was absolutely fundamental in Wystan's thought and sensibility, as in his technical virtuosity. He was lyrical, he sang, because the world was lyrical and nature was a song (though constantly menaced by noise and disarray). Wystan was passionately fond of hymns, of which he knew an inordinate number (and which, from childhood, he liked to sing in the bath); one of his last reviews was on a new English hymnary, as one of his last poems (in conjunction with Casals) was the composition of a glorious *Anthem*. Hymnody and psalmody to him were as basic as prosody, as basic as melody. Wystan's religion (like so much else in him) was at once intensely private and public: he prayed in a solitary and silent mode, but he also liked to lift up his voice in prayer, in a community, in a church, in a chorus of voices; choirs and choruses, for him, were emblems and microcosms of the choragium of nature.

It was, amongst other things, this musical sense which brought us together, and which formed a constant, tacit bond between us. In his review of my *Migraine*, and again in the last letter he ever wrote to me, Wystan quoted an aphorism of Novalis: 'Every sickness is a musical problem, and every cure a musical solution.' I find, looking back on our correspondence, that Wystan sent me a typescript of his *Anthem* a fortnight after he had published his review of *Migraine*, and that in my reply I wrote: 'Yes, I agree, I feel, absolutely with Novalis. . . . My medical sense *is* a musical one. I diagnose by the feeling of discordancy, or some peculiarity of harmony.'

I came to know Wystan best in the last three years of his life; it seems to me we talked of every subject under the sun, and sometimes of subjects and worlds under suns other than ours – non-existent but imaginable languages and worlds, which he would invent, with a gay, chthonic and child-like abandon.

Wystan was at once the most common-sensical and down-to-earth man I have known, but also the most fantastic and fanciful when he let himself go. When he writes of Pope's 'zaniness' –

> Here living *Teapots* stand, one Arm held out
> One bent; the Handle this, and that the Spout:
> A Pipkin there like *Homer's Tripod* walks;
> Here sighs a Jar, and there a Goose-pye talks. . . .

(as akin to that of Lewis Carroll) he is describing (as always in his essays on others) something very deep and elemental in himself. He never, it seemed to me, imputed to others qualities which were not in them, mere projections of his own rich fancy. But his genius for appreciation – whether in the extraordinary range of his friends or his writings – testifies to the extraordinary range of his own imagination and identity, which allowed him to detect in others, at once, what he knew so well from his experience of himself.

I feel, in many ways, that Wystan understood me better than I understood myself. Certainly, by his extraordinary powers of sympathy and empathy, and his generous and loving maieutic technê, he became a living mirror for me – someone who could detect and encourage the perception of new vistas, images, and trains-of-thought long before I myself was conscious of them. And if he did this with me, he did it with a hundred others. He showed us ourselves, he drew us into greater possibilities of being – 'self-actualization', to use the current, trendy word – by being himself, wise and tolerant and affectionate as Socrates, completely devoid of censoriousness and moralizing, yet deeply, purely and passionately ethical. This, plus a wild, extraordinary and demonic imagination, made Auden – for me, for so many of his friends in America and elsewhere (and he had the power to find or create new friendships, and to enter new fields, at an age when most men have become rigid and dull) – uniquely significant in the discovery and creation of our destiny, our selves. I owe to Auden the realization of certain possibilities whose very existence might otherwise have remained dormant or latent, and hidden from me. Certainly I owe to him much of the unfolding of thoughts which constitute the originality (and eccentricity) of *Awakenings*. Indeed, I feel that had I not known him, had he not encouraged me, with that constancy, gentleness, power and tact of which he was so consummate a master, the book would never have been completed, or would have assumed a different (and much more ordinary) form; and it is for this reason that I dedicate to him its coming edition.

But for all the variety of topics we covered, it seems to me that our conversations would always return to medicine, whatever geodesics it looped through in strange other worlds. Auden was himself the son of a physician, and carried within himself, as part of his patrimony, a deep love and understanding of doctors and medicine – he would, I am sure, himself have been one of our greatest physicians, had he not felt 'elected' or 'ordained' (other favourite words!) from his earliest years, for the wider destiny of a poet and genius. He had the analytic brilliance and vigour of a physical scientist; he had an intuitive penetrating, almost clairvoyant sense of what was going on in people, physically and spiritually, what was amiss and what was aright; and, in addition to these attributes – the attributes of genius – he was a homely, cosy (though never nosey) old body (I am here conflating his own descriptions of Mayhew and Ackerley Senior) of a sort whom everyone confides in and trusts; the very image of a wise and decent, old-fashioned GP. And in this, no doubt, he was the son of his father, as he was a sort of son/father to me and other physicians. It is no mere coincidence that in his last book of poems, Auden dedicates no less than four of them to physicians he has known, who have been significant to him, as he was to them; and I am, at once, happy and sad, grateful and astonished, to find that I myself (though I was not Auden's doctor) am the fourth and last of these, the last-in-line of a generic series.

The amalgamation of accuracy and affection, knowing what is proper and loving what is dear – this is the essence of care, be it medical care, or any other sort of care; care for the body, care for the soul, care for the individual, care for Society, were almost inseparable in Auden's mind. God, for him, was no mere geometer high in the sky, but the cardinal principle of decency and care. It was essential for Wystan that there should be people to care for his needs, in whose skill and goodness he could repose entire faith. He required this, as we all require this, if we are to survive physically, existentially, and to enjoy decent health. Wystan smoked and drank like blazes, but he had a tough constitution and tough common sense. He was both careful and careless about his health – careful because he knew he was precious, that he had work to do which he and he alone could do (however hard he drank in the evening, he was always up and at work by six the next morning), and careless (because worrying about his health would distract his energies and take him away from the call of work).

So long as he had professional caretakers – Dr Protetch in New York, Dr Birk in Kirchstetten – Wystan could put himself in their hands, with perfect confidence that they would care for him. When David Protetch was alive, Wystan was well and lovingly taken care of, protected from '. . . the sadist, the nod-crafty, and the fee-conscious' and from '. . . medical engineers with their arrogance'. With David Protetch's death, there occurred a grave and tragic change in Wystan's situation: he had lost his own doctor, and could find no one to replace him. Why? Because decent, kindly, general practitioners are all but extinct in the United States today, and because the ancient art of healing is itself almost dead. Wystan was maintained in fair health – some bronchitis, some emphysema, nothing too serious – so long as David Protetch was there to look after him. With Protetch's death (and Dr Birk's retirement) Auden no longer had anyone to whom he could turn: he came face-to-face with '. . . the sadist, the nod-crafty, the fee-conscious' . . . 'medical engineers . . . with their arrogance', or 'specialists' with whom no relation was possible.

> . . . The specialist has his function
> but, to him, we are merely banal examples of
> what he knows all about. The healer I faith is
> someone I've gossipped
>
> and drunk with before I call him to touch me,
> someone who admits how easy it is to misconster
> what our bodies are trying to say, for each one
> talks in a local
>
> dialect of its own that can alter during
> its lifetime. . . .

With Protetch's death, and the impossibility of finding anyone to replace him, to care for him properly, Wystan's condition visibly deteriorated. Already, when I first met him, his breathing was laboured and he was blue around the lips – he patently stood in need of good care. At Christmas 1971 he had an attack of severe vertigo, which frightened him and prevented work for a whole day. (Auden, like Goethe, could write poetry even when violently sea-sick: but this vertigo and light-headedness, this was something very different, which he intuitively knew to be serious, perhaps mortal.) Wystan had long ago 'assumed' that he would live to eighty, and *then* drop dead; but he felt differently after this attack. The more so as in metropolitan New York, a city of ten millions, he could find no one to care for him, nobody to undertake his continuing care, nobody really fit to be a doctor amid the swarming regiments of board-certified specialists, sadists and quacks. I saw Wystan the day after his attack of vertigo, found him apparently recovered, but shocked in a fundamental, unprecedented way, feeling or realizing that his days were numbered; that he would not make it to seventy, let alone eighty. Of death itself he had no fear; deterioration he regarded with horror. What shocked him, inexpressibly, was the absence of care, the absence of any prospect of care.

By the beginning of 1972, then, Wystan had resolved, finally and firmly, to leave America, and to spend his remaining days in England and Austria. He found the start of that winter a particularly grim one, with a mixed presiding sense of illness and isolation, and the complex and contradictory feelings aroused by his decision to leave America, where he had lived so long and loved so deeply.

His first real break from this doom-laden feeling came on his birthday, 21 February. Wystan always loved birthdays and celebrations of all sorts, and this one was particularly important and moving. He was sixty-five; it was to be his last birthday in America, and in a sense his formal farewell to it. His publishers had prepared a special and splendid party for him, where he was surrounded by friends from far and wide, friends old and new, an astonishing range and variety of friends, united with him in celebration and dearness; friends who could themselves have constituted an entire academy, an ideal republic, a cross-section of all the richness of life. It was only then, at this extraordinary gathering, that I fully realized the richness of Wystan's aspectuality, personality, his genius for friendship, for friendship of all types, an emblem of his appreciative, receptive, integrating genius. Wystan sat beaming like a great mellow sun, ensconced in the middle of all his friends, all-giving, all-receiving (like his favourite *Hatem*) spacious, at-home, in the centre of perspectives. Or so it seemed to me: I had never seen him happier than he appeared on that day. And yet, interfused with the radiant moment, there was also the sense of sunset, of farewell; and this feeling deepened during the next eight weeks – Wystan's last weeks in the USA – when I saw him more frequently, more intimately, than ever before.

Wystan's departure in April affected me like a sudden darkness, the eclipse of all light and reality from the world. I knew him to be a man mortally ailing, and when he left I mourned his death in advance. I suddenly realized what I had never properly realized or avowed before, that Wystan had been a beacon for me, a reality-bearer, so that his departure subtracted reality from my world . . . and it was only very slowly that the void was filled, and there is a Wystan-shaped space which will never be filled.

In February 1973, I visited Wystan at Oxford, and spent the day with him, in hall, and in his cottage, at Christ Church. It was the last time I was to see him. I had an inkling that both of us, perhaps, were sensible of this, for we spoke of certain things we had never touched on before, and which Wystan would never have spoken of under 'ordinary' conditions.

A few minutes before I left I gave him the proofs of *Awakenings* – he was the only man to see these apart from my publisher. He flipped through the long galley-pages with incredible speed – Wystan could read, or 'scan', almost as fast as his eyes could move. 'It's beautiful', he said. 'A beautiful book. . . . Just one point, however: when you say "Eros" at the end, you don't mean Eros, you mean agape of course.' And these were the last words which Wystan said to me.

He wrote to me on 21 February (below the date he had written 'My birthday') and we wrote to each other several times during the spring and the summer. In his last letter to me, Wystan said he particularly hoped I would be able to come to Kirchstetten – his 'home' – before my return to New York in the autumn. 'It is lovely here now', he wrote, and added that his heart had been 'playing up a little'.

If only I had gone. For there was something unprecedented in the tone of his letter, the sense (I think) that he only had days or weeks still left. Wystan often said: 'I have a sure sense of timing. I always know the next thing to do.'

He knew then, without doubt, that the next thing was death: that the time had come, that dying was the right and proper thing to do. It seems, from what Chester Kallman has since told me, that Wystan composed himself for death with the grace and the deliberation he had shown all his life.

I read of his death in the *New York Times*, on Sunday 30 September: 'W. H. AUDEN DIES IN VIENNA', the legend surmounted by a singularly beautiful and peaceful photograph. There followed a single enormous yet instantaneous flash in which I seemed to see the whole of Wystan's life, its history and pattern, its meaning and destiny, a million moments brought together in one single moment; and in that moment his face was transfigured to an immense edifice – a human cathedral – which a moment later dissolved into dust; but though the building crumbled, something persisted, a sort of living chorus, composed of his works, his words, his memories and friends.

There was a funeral in the little village churchyard of Kirchstetten. For us, in New York, there was a memorial service in the Cathedral Church of St John the Divine. It was a motley crowd which gathered there on that long, unforgettable Wednesday evening: many faces were familiar – faces I had seen in public places, faces I had seen at his great birthday party; but there were also many faces of strangers, yet not strangers, who had somehow heard of the memorial service, and who had ventured in to pay their last respects, to a man they had never seen or met, but whom they felt as a personal friend.

We wept unashamedly – I don't think there was a dry eye in the place. All of us were experiencing particular memories, our own particular sense of loss, and yet there was something shared, uniting, between us. Wystan would have spotted the feeling in a moment, and reminded us of the words we all half-remembered:

Such, Echecrates, was the end of our comrade, who was, we may fairly say, of all those whom we knew in our time, the bravest, the wisest, and the most upright of men.

POSTSCRIPT SEPTEMBER 1974

Receiving an advance copy of *Thank You, Fog*, Auden's final and posthumous poems, I find clarification and confirmation of what I had half-known, half-guessed, with regard to the final year of his life. I believe that Wystan was markedly depressed during his first months at Oxford, so much so that he wrote scarcely any letters, and no poems at all – none, at least, that he cared to publish. I believe that he experienced a deep change of mood and creative renewal in February of 1973, turning simult-aneously to the fullest possible affirmation of life, and the fullest possible acceptance of death. I say this for three reasons: first, my own impressions of our unforgettable last meeting; second, his sudden burst of letters to friends at this time, following an epistolary blank of several months; third, a tiny but crucial clue which indicates that *Thank you, Fog* (the opening poem of his final cycle) could not have been written before this month. Wystan, in his affectionate, playful, and sometimes riddling way, loved to insert 'hidden' messages and references to his friends in some of his poems. Now, a year after his death, I find that *Thank You, Fog* contains the words 'festination' and 'volant' in close conjunction – and these are favourite words of *mine*, and key-words in *Awakenings*. I cannot help thinking that they constitute Wystan's play-ful (and now, alas, posthumous) 'Hello' to me. But it was only in February that he saw the proofs of my book. . . .

I have said that a genius for appreciation, for affection and gratitude, lay at the very centre of Wystan's whole being. I think this shines through his last poems with radiant force, scarcely admixed with any other emotion: gratitude is the express theme of 'Thanksgiving', and most of its fellows; gratitude is the theme of the poet's farewell. 'Let your last thinks all be thanks', he writes in the last poem of all. Wystan's mind and heart came closer and closer in the course of his life, until thinking and thanking became one and the same.

John Hollander
Under Aquarius

John Hollander is a poet and a critic, whose first book Auden chose to be published in the Yale Series of Young Poets

When there are so many who have to mourn, and from so many times and places, one can perhaps do no more than speak for his own city. The New Yorker Wystan Auden – the presence in the American metropolis during the forties and fifties – was a deeply and dearly important figure for my whole generation. He was our exemplary man of letters. His public and private conscience were manifested in exemplary ways. His sallies of encounter, his refusals of the fugitive and cloistered virtue were exemplary as well, and not merely because our coming of age could find congenial what continuities we felt persisted between an unorthodox Marxism and a personal form of crisis theology. For young poets he was a living precursor, a constant teacher of poetic craft and a devoted guardian of the power of the magic of language, rather than the machinations of ideology, to yield true poetic thought. To those of us who were students at Columbia University at the end of the Second World War, poets whose work would eventually diverge so widely like Louis Simpson, Daniel Hoffman, Allen Ginsberg, Richard Howard – he was an unofficial teacher, as well as the resident poet of our city. The poets whose work he caused to be introduced to the public – Hoffman, Rich, Merwin, Ashbery, Wright among them – testify not only to the wisdom and generosity of his judgements, but to a flourishing literary moment shaped by his presence, rather than by trivial and stultifying imitation.

The following verses, written for Wystan Auden's sixty-fifth birthday, were framed in the stress-accented elegiacs of Goethe's *Römische Elegien* (from which the quotations) that he so loved, in – and trying to speak in some measure for – the city, at a time of intellectual failure of nerve.

> Strained and worn, the winter sunlight refuses our windows'
>   Invitations and waits hovering, under the shade
> Afternoon still distributes; this is the moment before what
>   Warm renewals there are light up the lengthening days –
> Promises rather than cold regrets, a time when familiar,
>   Craggy formations of rock, looking as if they were built
> Up through the course of the years, not undergoing erosion,
>   Come to count for more. Obsolete cadences, too –
> And if these lines should fall with less mechanical footsteps
>   Down the corridor's dark stretch to the end of the hall,
> Yet, the longer ones yours, the shorter ones ours, they may manage
>   To serve an occasion of love, gratitude, blessings and praise.

The Sixties

72 TOP Poets' corner: (*left to right*) Spender, Auden, Hughes, Eliot and MacNeice at a party
given by Faber & Faber in London in 1961.
73 ABOVE Auden with T. S. and Valerie Eliot at the same party

74 BELOW Auden on his return to Iceland in 1963. (See Basil Boothby's contribution.) (*Left to right*) the then Minister of Education and Culture, Gylfi Gislason, Auden, Thomas Gudmundsson, Iceland's national poet.
75 OPPOSITE Auden with his sister-in-law Sheila Auden in Florence, 1968.

76 ABOVE Auden at his niece's wedding reception in Florence, with Matthew Spender.

77 RIGHT Chester Kallman, Auden's friend and collaborator.

Something, at this time of year, demands a more measured cadence,
    Backs a little bit more straightened than ones we would trust:
Outside the door, in the street, the high, millenarian voices,
    Hailing the spring's delay, solemn, unserious, rise
Over the din of their feasting. Languid and unregimental,
    Hand in hand but, alas, thereby thus somehow in step,
Young people drift in the square, the evening's readying early
    Still, and the quiet shade daubing the pavements with dim
Colours of doubt, and of colder shadows awaiting their moment.
    Distant curfews wail wanly on circling winds.
Here as if light were in disrepute, now that darkness is falling,
    Some of the sadder ones huddle along the arcades,
Glaring at lamps that begin to twinkle out of our windows,
    Staring upward instead, looking for some kind of sign,
Eyes finally lighting upon the tired zodiacal emblem
    Rising, penultimate now, over the nights of our years.
Back under other signs, as chattering schoolboys, we revelled
    Hopefully on the ground your way of speaking prepared
(Froh empfanden wir uns auf klassischem Boden begeistert) :
    Only our sense of sound first was awakened, and then,
Echoing through the open halls that we quarried to hide in,
    Faintly, the sound of sense: trustworthiness of a voice
Carrying over an ocean; if, like a clever young uncle,
    Helping us over the few gurus we'd ferreted out
Back at the end of the forties, then like a wise old aunt who
    Knew much more than the ropes, holding our hands in the dusk,
Pointing across the fields at other old candlelit houses,
    (Then they only looked strange) where a few guardians sat:
Half-silent Wittgenstein, who listened to all the retreating
    Hoofbeats of a remark, trying to follow it home;
Hunchback Lichtenberg, hanging over his puddle of language,
    Glimpsing the mirrored sky crowning his unimproved shade;
Deep Sarastro's priest, assessing Tamino's prognosis
    ('Er ist ein Prinz,' he said; *'Er is ein Mensch,'* he was told)
Guarding a region of beauty where the loftiest pitches
    Resonate to the bad, keeping the bases of notes
Thoroughly good, where the golden needles of fire reflected
    Brightly from clear and cold water unravel the dark.
Ganymede, certain ancient writers remark, was this water-
    Bearer, the lovely boy stooping intently to pour
Rivers of nectar (not into an empty jug out of a full one,
    Emblem of Temperance, lip kissing the levelling lip)
Filling the bowl of space to more than mere overflowing,
    Instances of his light flooding the generous dark.
(Knaben liebt ich wohl auch, doch lieber sind mir die Mädchen:

One might therefore have glossed differently, and the clear
Figure in outlined tunic comes to have been a soprano
   Role for some college girl, singing along to some Gluck
Only discovered last summer, moistening gently the arid
   Air of these cold, dry days.) Surely a sign hanging high
Over the rubble of nonsense built in the glimmer of starlight
   Over the disarray mental brutalities make,
Even with gentle touching, out of the loveliest landscape,
   Signifies that its own shining cannot be assigned
Values that range over more than mighty distances from us.
   Space, beyondness and light give us what meanings we need.

Even these minims of light from the setback skyscraper towers
   Glistening south of the park, winking in late-thirties films,
Wheeled in the sky you discoursed on, visions of what in a Fallen
   City's highest rise wisely acknowledge their own
Partial failure. And now the constellation that night has
   Dropped into water's chill, dark in this pool in a square,
Ringed with those crystals of light and giving them back to our silence,
   Rises: *Der Dichter* – if not seasonal, then all the more
Present continuingly, and *Alpha Poetae*, the brightest
   Star, the one whose name everyone always recalls,
Burns away knowingly, used to having been steered by, and glowing
   Up among us and our worlds turning in darkness around.

David Luke
Homing to Oxford

David Luke is Tutor in German at Christ Church, Oxford

Not many months before his death on 29 September 1973, Wystan had written a poem called 'Lullaby' ('Poets keep writing lullabies to people,' he had said; 'Why shouldn't I write one to myself?'). It had been published on 6 August, but in a manuscript copy, left among his things in the empty cottage in Christ Church which he had only recently begun to occupy, I first read it on 30 September.

> The din of work is subdued:
> another day has westered,
> and mantling darkness arrived . . .

Now you have licence to lie
naked, curled like a shrimplet.
jacent in bed and enjoy
its cosy micro-climate . . .
snug in the den of yourself,
Madonna and *Bambino* . . .
Sleep, Big Baby, sleep your fill.

What came across was not only the sense of a premonition – naturally enough there had been a number of references to death in his latest work – but also yet another confirmation of what many of those who knew him well had sensed: the deep-rooted-ness of his homing, nesting instinct, of his nostalgia for a family situation, a secure snug place, a mother and child relationship which in the end, he had felt, could be completely introjected (his theory of old age as a kind of return to primary narcissism is explicitly repeated in the same poem). It was clear that in returning from New York to England and Oxford in 1972 he was moving from a situation in which he had been free, alone, and vulnerable, into one in which he hoped he would be surrounded and enclosed, back into a ritualistic social context, a place of regular feeding-times. At the same time, once back, he was increasingly withdrawing into himself and into his own process of dying.

Wystan's conception of Oxford and of Christ Church in particular was inevitably moulded by the impressions of earlier and happier years – his undergraduate days in the 1920s and his tenure of the Professorship of Poetry from 1956 to 1960. In the formation of his decision to return here in 1972 there can be little doubt that his memories of the late fifties were especially significant. Life in college as it was then suited his needs exactly. One of his many strict self-imposed rules about time and its allocation was that he would never work in the evening, and the hour or so that elapsed between the end of dinner and his moment for going to bed was a time for sitting and drinking and talking in congenial company. Christ Church was one of the few colleges that performed every night the after-dinner ceremony known as 'Common Room': dessert, port, coffee and brandy served and circulated in the inner sanctum of the senior members' club – an oak-panelled room hung with portraits of distinguished predecessors, furnished and decorated in a hideous but venerably traditional manner. Common Room in the 1950s was a very flourishing and well attended affair, and Wystan promoted not only its social geniality but also its practical amenities: having found to his astonishment that our pantry contained no refrigerator, he presented Cyril Little – the Admirable Crichton of that domain – with a blank cheque to buy a large and expensive one. Another gift he made to the college was a discreetly designed public address system for the Hall, with the result that it became for the first time possible to hear all the speeches made at Gaudies and similar occasions. He himself, at the Gaudy of June 1960, made his farewell for the time being by proposing the Toast of the House in verse, a Betjemanesque piece combining faintly scurrilous reminiscences of his undergraduate days in Peckwater Quadrangle with appreciative allusions to present personalities. He had in particular formed a close personal friend-ship with the former Regius Professor of Hebrew, Cuthbert Simpson, Dean from 1959 until his death in 1969; Wystan described him as the only person over here who, as a fellow-American, could mix dry martinis properly. He made a habit of revisiting us for a night or two nearly every year, when in transit from Austria to New York, early in each Michaelmas term, staying regularly at the Deanery. In 1962 the Governing Body of Christ Church, by a massive and unopposed vote, elected him an Honorary Student; he wrote to me after hearing this news that it had 'absolutely overwhelmed' him. I think it may well have been in the late 1960s that he formed the idea of returning here on a more permanent basis. It became known that this was what he would like, and in due course the Governing Body, again by a massive and unopposed majority, voted for the principle that an immediate attempt should be made to find for Dr W. H. Auden (the University had recently made him an Honorary D.Litt.) suitable accommodation in or near the college. After this there were still practical problems of detail to be solved, and Wystan, unfamiliar with the internal administrative complexities of so unusual an institution as Christ Church, found the whole process a little puzzling. He was alleged to have remarked that a possible alternative to returning to Oxford might be to settle in Iceland; as a move to the country of his remoter ancestors I suppose that would have been another kind of homing. Eventually, to his great delight, we were able to offer him the tenancy of a small quaintly shaped sixteenth-century brewhouse cottage in the garden of one of the Canon-Professors: an enclosure within an enclosure, very near the Hall, the Old Senior Common Room and the New Senior Common Room. He would pay a reasonably economic rent (the amount of which, by some misapprehension, was grotesquely understated in the press) and occupy it during the winter terms, spending his summers as hitherto in Austria. (We came to think of him as 'the inverted swallow'.) He arrived punctually at the beginning of the Michaelmas term of 1972, met at Oxford station by a battery of press photographers. For a few weeks, during completion of some necessary modifications to his intended dwelling, he stayed at All Souls College as the guest of his friend and publisher, Charles Monteith. At the end of November he was able to install himself in the Brewhouse (as it is commonly known). Since he had last been a regular diner and luncher in Christ Church twelve years earlier, there had been a marked increase in the number of senior members of the college; both main meals were now more populous and less intimate. Wystan was clearly rather disconcerted by this. 'What a lot of us there are!' he would mutter. He would protest, with some reason, at the apparently uncontrollable noise during dinner in Hall, where, like the rest of us, he had to make himself heard to his neighbours not only against general vocal clamour but also over the crash of crockery and cutlery onto the stone floor or into wooden boxes and waggons hallowed by centuries of misuse. He approved deeply, as before, of the impressive and relentless punctuality with which the dinner ritual had always begun; 'Why are you *late*?' he would demand, more in amazement than in anger, if one arrived at 7.20½ instead of 7.20. But he was saddened by the fact that in recent years, for a complexity of reasons, the Common-Room ceremony after dinner had been falling if not into disuse, at least into more sporadic use. He found Common Room attended often by only a small group, varied in composition and not regularly containing many members of the central tutorial body. He had probably not foreseen clearly the effect of the insertion of a very famous creative writer, with his particular work-pattern, into a society of increasingly hard-pressed academics. He nevertheless clung to what was left of the past, and insisted on sitting down to a glass or two of port after dinner every night of the week – even when, rather pathetically, he was the only person doing so – while the rest of us swallowed coffee, glanced at a newspaper and hurried off. Yet it must also be said that in this matter Wystan himself, as so often, did not greatly help his own cause. In order to overcome his essential loneliness and shyness he needed not only the assistance of a well-defined social structure but also a rather special kind of cooperation and sympathy from those with whom it brought him into contact. Moreover, in these later years his creative energies needed to be husbanded for his literary work during the day: in the evenings he was usually exhausted and, to quote his own words in the Toast at the 1960 Gaudy, 'not overly sober', and therefore could not often give the best of himself as a conversationalist. Instead he would adopt a restricted repertoire of lines of small-talk which had the character of recurrent nervous reactions, did not represent his real intellectual personality and were not always well adjusted to the needs and susceptibilities of those who happened to be there. It seemed that he had returned not fully reckoning with the entrenched force of English reserve, although being at heart both English and reserved himself.

As is well known, the outstanding and indeed unique feature of his tenure of the Chair of Poetry had been his practice of simply being present between certain hours at the Cadena coffee-house in the Cornmarket, which still existed in the fifties; during these sessions numerous undergraduates would come and go as they pleased, showing him their work and discussing it and other matters with him. He could always be sure of finding himself in a more or less coherent group of congenial younger persons. It was a remarkable venture in informal communication, of incalculable pedagogic value. His attempt to repeat it in 1972, to take up again where he had left off, was for a number of reasons not conspicuously successful. As a substitute for the vanished Cadena, since he now needed a *Stammkaffee* very close at hand, he chose not altogether fortunately one more or less opposite Tom Gate, adjoining and associated with an Anglican bookshop: the St Aldate's Church Bookshop and Coffee House. It was made known that he would be there between four and five on every weekday afternoon, but the undergraduate response to his availability at this particular venue seems on the whole to have been disappointing. It may be that, by comparison with about fifteen years earlier, there were fewer young men in Oxford of sufficient talent and taste to interest him and be interested in him. A number of those who visited the café came for the wrong sort of reasons. He seems chiefly to have been beset by post-graduates from overseas, some perhaps seeking thesis material, others having read little or nothing of his work but anxious to view him as tourists might view a curious monolith. Too often, looking rather formidable, he would be sitting by himself, watched from other tables. Some sensitive undergraduates felt inhibited from approaching him by the mere fact that it had become the craze and the fashion to do so. Then there were the representatives of experimental trends in writing with which Wystan was entirely out of sympathy, and his condemnations of which tended to be dogmatic rather than tactful.

The impact of his return to Oxford on the present younger members of the university is in general a matter for speculation and controversy. He belonged for them to the remoter past, to their grandfathers' rather than to their fathers' generation, but in spite or perhaps because of this he was to many still a very noteworthy figure: a poet on whom essays were written for tutors and examiners but who was nevertheless still alive and now physically present. Under the auspices of the undergraduate Poetry Society, he had given a public reading of his work at the Oxford Union in October 1970 and after his return he gave another, in December 1972, in the hall at Balliol (he of course never charged a fee for reading in Oxford; in America the going rate for one reading or lecture by Auden was two thousand dollars). The Balliol servants, hearing that there was to be a recital of poetry, put out about thirty chairs; about six hundred people turned up, of whom about two hundred had to be turned away after queuing in the rain. This reading as such was not a great success; Wystan was in poor form and fluffed his lines. (By contrast, the reading in 1970 had been highly accomplished and exciting.) His public appearances in the two terms after his return to Oxford were rare. One of the difficulties confronting dining clubs and others who wanted to ask him out in the evening was that if he came he was liable to leave again at nine o'clock in order to go to bed. This had long been one of his known social eccentricities, in England, America, and Austria – he had even been known to leave immediately after dinner – but in this last Oxford period he was tired and ill and the bed-time rule was hardening. He did not, and evidently just could not, engage in active social contacts to anything like the same extent as in the fifties. At that time, with those whom he met in the Cadena, he would quite often propose further weekly meetings in his rooms at a fixed time; in 1972–3, to be invited to the Brewhouse at all was a rare privilege for a few.

Fortunately, the record of Wystan's last period in Oxford is not wholly a sad one, and it is its happier and more positive consequences that we should note. Some of these are of course quite imponderable. We do not know how many young people who were not already interested readers of his work began to read it, or to read more of it, because they had met him or seen him or at least knew that he was around; or how many for the same reason became interested, or more interested, in poetry generally. But there were a certain number of valuable and valued creative encounters, some new friendships and informal mentor-pupil relationships started, there were promising pointers and hopeful beginnings which might well have developed further had not the whole story ended after a mere six months. There was still a nucleus of serious and talented young writers to be found here and with some of them, in the course of these two winter terms, he made genuine contact. Some were from Christ Church, some from other colleges, some he met for the first time not at the St Aldate's café but in other social contexts. I did not hear much about any of this from Wystan himself, but after his death there were reports, direct or indirect, from those concerned. One of them wrote to one of Wystan's older friends in whose house he had met him: 'I shall be eternally grateful to you for introducing me to Auden. Over the few times that I went to see him I grew so fond of him; as I had expected he was a wonderful critic, but he was also a most rare and compassionate human being. The field of letters is barren without him.' I talked myself during the Michaelmas term of 1973 to some of them: to Andrew Motion, Andrew Harvey, Edward Levy, Fram Dinshaw, Mark Morris. Several weeks after Wystan's death most of these, and one or two others representing the Poetry Society (Neil Sowerby, Adrian Ward) joined me in a kind of informal evening seminar, a symposium concerned with recollections of Wystan and estimates of how younger members of the university generally had reacted to him in the period after his return. I am grateful to them for what they told me and for their willingness to let me attempt to report it here.

Naturally, the views of the poet's work and personality expressed on that evening were not all uncritical, and if they had been it would have been a duller occasion. I was impressed above all by the animation of the discussion, by the general sense that here someone and something of exceptional and exciting importance was being talked about and recalled. There was a consensus that in order to get through to the real Auden one had had to be patient, stand one's ground and work fairly hard, beginning from the right initial attitude, from an appreciation of who and what he was. If one could penetrate his carapace of dogmatic self-quotation one could be rewarded by moments of sudden spontaneity, informality and warmth, and by a sense that he himself was happier to be talking like that instead of giving the standard verbal performance. It was agreed that one of the disadvantages of the St Aldate's café had been its smallness: if one went and sat at Wystan's table one would be embarrassingly aware of other undergraduates within earshot listening perhaps rather cynically to every word one exchanged with him. Occasionally, if one had met him before, it would be Wystan who came across to the table where one might be sitting with a friend arguing about poetry. I heard of how he once umpired a lexical wrangle ('Termagint? What's termagint? No one'll understand that . . .'). The master, whose latter-day love-affair with the multi-volume Oxford English Dictionary is well known, had listened rather crossly, then suddenly got up to go, uttering as he rose a single syllable: 'Osse'. In the ensuing silence his uniquely disarming smile had returned. 'It means to portend or augur; "it osses well" for "it seems to be starting well". I've used it in my last poem. Good afternoon.' If one wished to receive the coveted summons to the Brewhouse ('Will you come for a drink at six-seventeen, please') the café was not necessarily the best place to meet him, and it was a good idea to send him one's poems in advance, especially if he had heard about them already from some other intermediary whose judgement he respected. He was still curious to encounter new talent more particularly if he was told that so-and-so shared, for example, his passionate interest in the revival or importation of unusual prosodic conventions. 'Have you ever tried writing a *cywydd*?' he would ask. 'It's the classic medieval Welsh metre, consisting of . . .' and he would then explain this highly complex verse-form. Or he would comment: 'At your age, what matters is not what you say in your writing but how you say it.' Some doubted the pedagogic wisdom of this insistence on technicalities, or at least of its timing as the master's very first reaction to a newly-fledged work; others thought it encouraging, as implying an assumption that since one was writing at all the 'what' of one's poem was sincere and significant in any case. On the 'how', certain absolute rules had been firmly enunciated: there was a list of words that might under no circumstances be used, or of 'imperfect rhymes' which were strictly and utterly banned. Might one rhyme 'Auden' with 'modern', or 'greyness' with 'penis'? Certainly not. (The fact that half-rhymes of this kind were to be found even in his own later work made no difference at all.)

The most successful and enjoyable public event of Wystan's two final terms was certainly the production at the Playhouse by the Christ Church and St John's Dramatic Society of *The Dog Beneath the Skin*. The director, Mark Morris, had clearly been on excellent terms with the poet, and what had impressed him above all was that Wystan had given him a free hand to make updating amendments to the dialogue of this early play, and even to rewrite whole passages. (The alterations were sufficiently extensive for Edward Mendelson, Auden's meticulous bibliographer and literary executor, to have asked to see a copy of the acting script, as representing an authorized variant text of the work.) *Dog-skin* (as Wystan called it for short) drew full houses and received favourable comment in the national press; one of my colleagues who had had reservations about the poet's proposed return to Christ Church ('We have his portrait on the wall of the SCR, we can't have *both* the man *and* the portrait and the portrait got here first . . .') was observed to be in the audience and clearly as enthusiastic about the show as the rest of those who saw it. Wystan attended the first night and was delighted, though he insistently criticized one detail: 'The surgeon,' he said, 'ought to have appeared in a white coat.' During interval drinks in the manager's office he dissolved the slight strain in the atmosphere by congratulating everyone warmly on 'a swell job' and adding: 'But the surgeon must wear a *white* coat; after all my father was a doctor, so I know.' He was assured that the proper attire had been ordered but delayed (it arrived in time for the remaining performances) yet in the forty seconds it took him to get from his seat in the front stalls on to the stage to make his bow at the end, he muttered as he climbed the steps: 'It should have been a *white* coat.' In the course of the play the director had interpolated a short scene in which a corpulent poet with a heavily lined face shambled on in bedroom slippers, sat down and in a comically elaborate manner lit a cigarette. The actor had been sent along to the St Aldate's café week after week to study his subject's gait, gestures and mannerisms meticulously, and the pastiche had been rehearsed for hours. 'Do you think this is supposed to be me?' Wystan asked me unnecessarily and with relish. The whole occasion betokened a happy and unembarrassed relationship with many undergraduates, reminiscent of earlier days.

While the enterprise of Wystan's resettlement in Oxford lasted, a number of us felt that there were signs of readjustment on both sides – that things (as he himself might have put it) were ossing well. The tutors in English at Christ Church hoped that although he had no contractual obligations to do so (he had simply been made a tenant in the curtilage of the House, with no strings) he would in due course involve himself more positively and regularly with at least those who were studying English at his own college. By the time he left he had already attended a party for graduates in the subject, and sat in at one seminar; it was planned that he would take part in another, on Shakespeare, in the Michaelmas term of 1973 for which he did not return. The rate at which his illness would progress was not even medically predictable; it could not be foreseen how much or how little time there was at his and our disposal, and with hindsight it is hard to judge whether those hopes would have been realized. All that is clear is that among junior and senior members there was a whole spectrum of reactions to him. He could be outrageous, tiresome, amusing, lovable. One undergraduate said to me: 'To us he was such a fantastic figure that it didn't matter two

W. H. AUDEN

POEMS

S. H. S. : 1928.

78 The title page of Auden's first published work, printed privately by Stephen Spender.

79 The title page of the first printing in 1933 of Auden's first published dramatic work for the Group Theatre, which featured Rupert Doone as the dancer.

80 The cover of the issue of *The Criterion* containing Auden's *Paid on Both Sides*, his first major piece published commercially. T. S. Eliot wrote to E. McKnight Kauffer, 'I have sent you the new *Criterion*, to ask you to read a verse play *Paid on Both Sides*, by a young man I know which seems to me quite a brilliant piece of work. . . . This fellow is about the best poet that I have discovered in several years.'

W.H.
AUDEN

•

THE
DANCE
OF
DEATH

•

FABER &
FABER

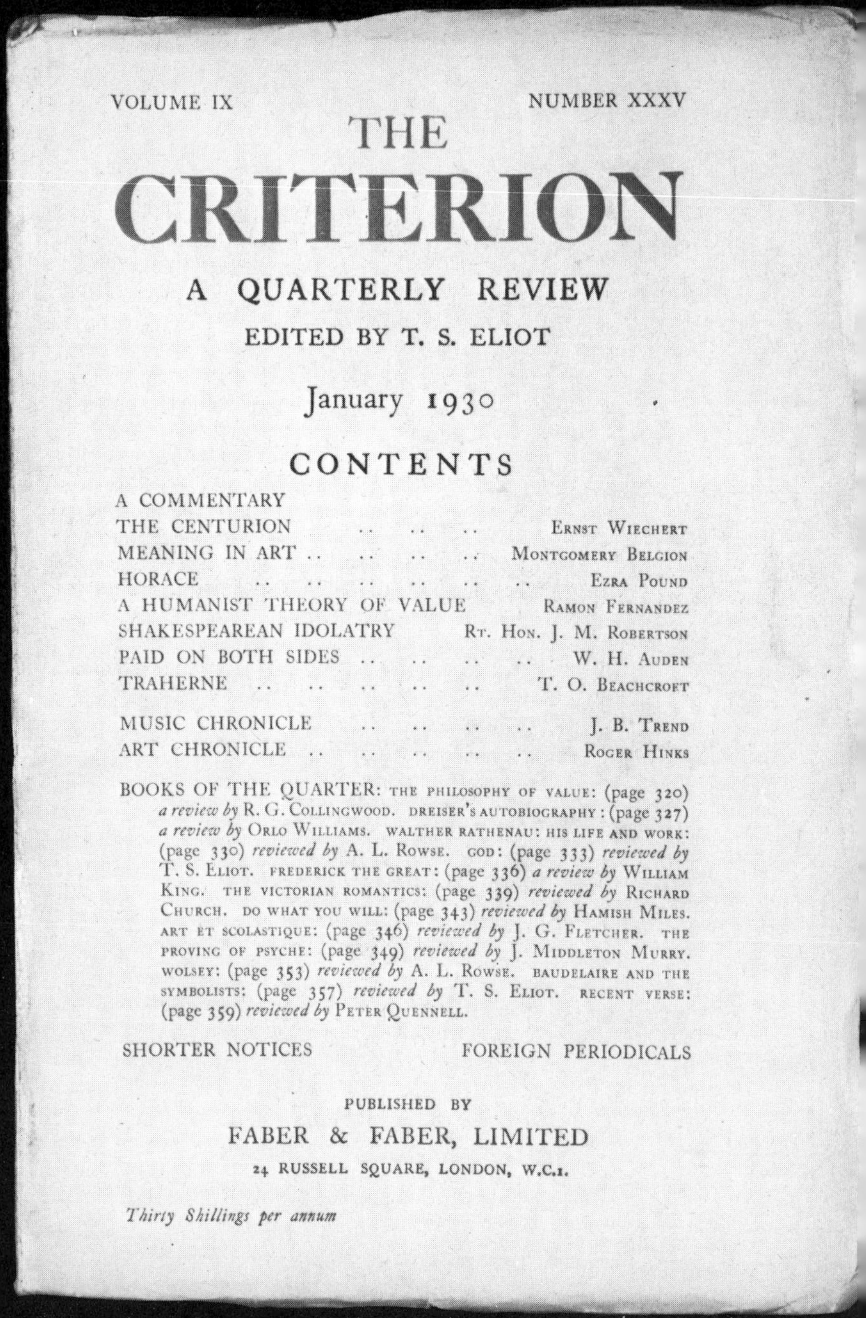

VOLUME IX   NUMBER XXXV

THE

CRITERION

A QUARTERLY REVIEW

EDITED BY T. S. ELIOT

January 1930

CONTENTS

PUBLISHED BY
FABER & FABER, LIMITED
24 RUSSELL SQUARE, LONDON, W.C.1.

Thirty Shillings per annum

81 TOP The dust jackets of the three major collections of Auden's work, published *from left to right* in 1962, 1966 and 1968 respectively; the first by Random House, the second and third by Faber & Faber.

82 BELOW Three special tributes for W. H. Auden. *Left to right* a booklet produced by Random House, Auden's American publishers, in a limited edition of five hundred copies, to celebrate his sixty-fifth birthday; a special issue of the magazine *Shenandoah*, dedicated to Auden on his sixtieth birthday; and the famous double number of the magazine *New Verse*.

83, 84 Photographs of two of Auden's manuscripts, now in the possession of the Lockwood Memorial Library in Buffalo, New York.

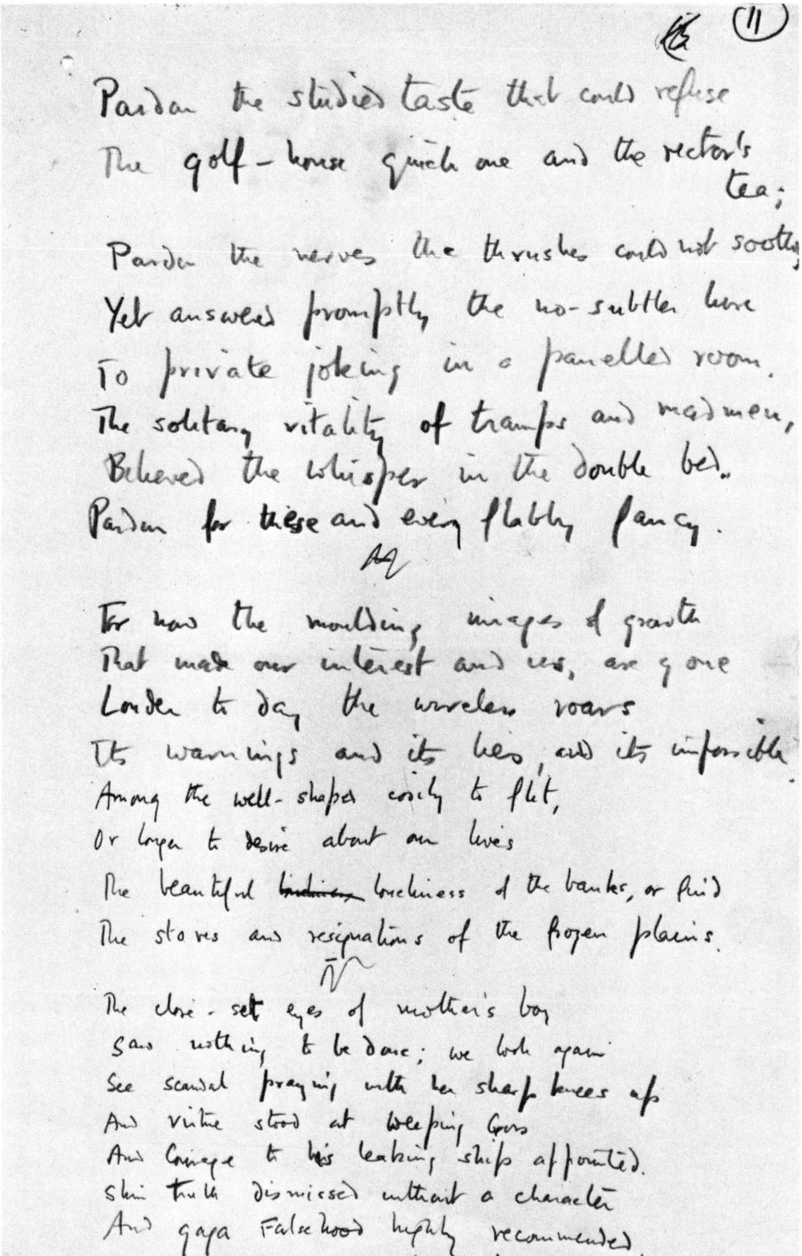
(11)

Pardon the studied taste that could refuse
The golf-house quick one and the rector's tea;
Pardon the nerves the thrushes could not soothe,
Yet answered promptly the no-subtler lure
To private joking in a panelled room.
The solitary vitality of tramps and madmen,
Believed the whisper in the double bed.
Pardon for these and every flabby fancy.

For now the moulding images of growth
That made our interest and us, are gone
Louder to day the wireless roars
Its warnings and its lies, and its impossible
Among the well-shaped cosily to flit,
Or longer to desire about our lives
The beautiful ~~[illegible]~~ loneliness of the banks, or find
The stores and resignations of the frozen plains.

The close-set eyes of mother's boy
Saw nothing to be done; we look again
See scandal praying with her sharp knees up
And virtue stood at weeping Cross
And Courage to his leaking ship appointed.
Slim truth dismissed without a character
And gaga Falsehood highly recommended.
The green thumb to the larger knuckled down.

Poem

O who can ever praise enough
    The world of his belief?
Harum-scarum childhood plays
In the meadows near his home,
In his woods love knows no wrong,
Travellers ride their placid ways,
In the cool shade of the tomb
    Age's trusting footfalls ring.
O who can paint the vivid tree
    And grass of phantasy?

But to create it and to guard
    Shall be his whole reward.
He shall watch and he shall weep,
All his father's love deny,
To his mother's womb be lost,
Eight nights with a wanton sleep,
But upon the ninth shall be
Bride and victim to a ghost,
And in the pit of terror thrown
    Shall bear the wrath alone.

W. H. Auden

HANS WERNER HENZE

The Bassarids

Opera Seria with Intermezzo in One Act
based on "The Bacchae" of Euripides
by W. H. Auden and Chester Kallman

Text

B. SCHOTT'S SÖHNE · MAINZ

W. H. AUDEN and CHESTER KALLMAN

THE
RAKE'S PROGRESS

Music by
IGOR STRAWINSKY

BOOSEY & HAWKES

*Elegy
for Young Lovers*

Opera in three acts

Textbook

B. SCHOTT'S SÖHNE · MAINZ

85 ABOVE The covers of the first printings of the three best known opera librettos written by Auden in collaboration with Chester Kallman.

W·H·AUDEN

The Double Man

"We are, I know not how, double in ourselves,
so that what we believe we disbelieve, and
cannot rid ourselves of what we condemn."

MONTAIGNE

RANDOM HOUSE · NEW YORK

THE
COLLECTED
POETRY OF
W. H. AUDEN

RANDOM HOUSE · NEW YORK

88 Japanese, Macedonian, Hungarian and German translations of Auden's work. *Worte Und Noten* contains Auden's inaugural address to the Salzburg Festival in 1968, printed in English, French and German versions.

86 OPPOSITE LEFT The title page of the first printing, in 1941, of the first of Auden's works written entirely after he had settled in the USA, known in Great Britain as *New Year Letter*.

87 OPPOSITE RIGHT The title page of the first major collection of Auden's poetry, published in 1945, it included many revisions and dropped many of his earlier poems, but was never published in England. Auden disliked the finality of the title.

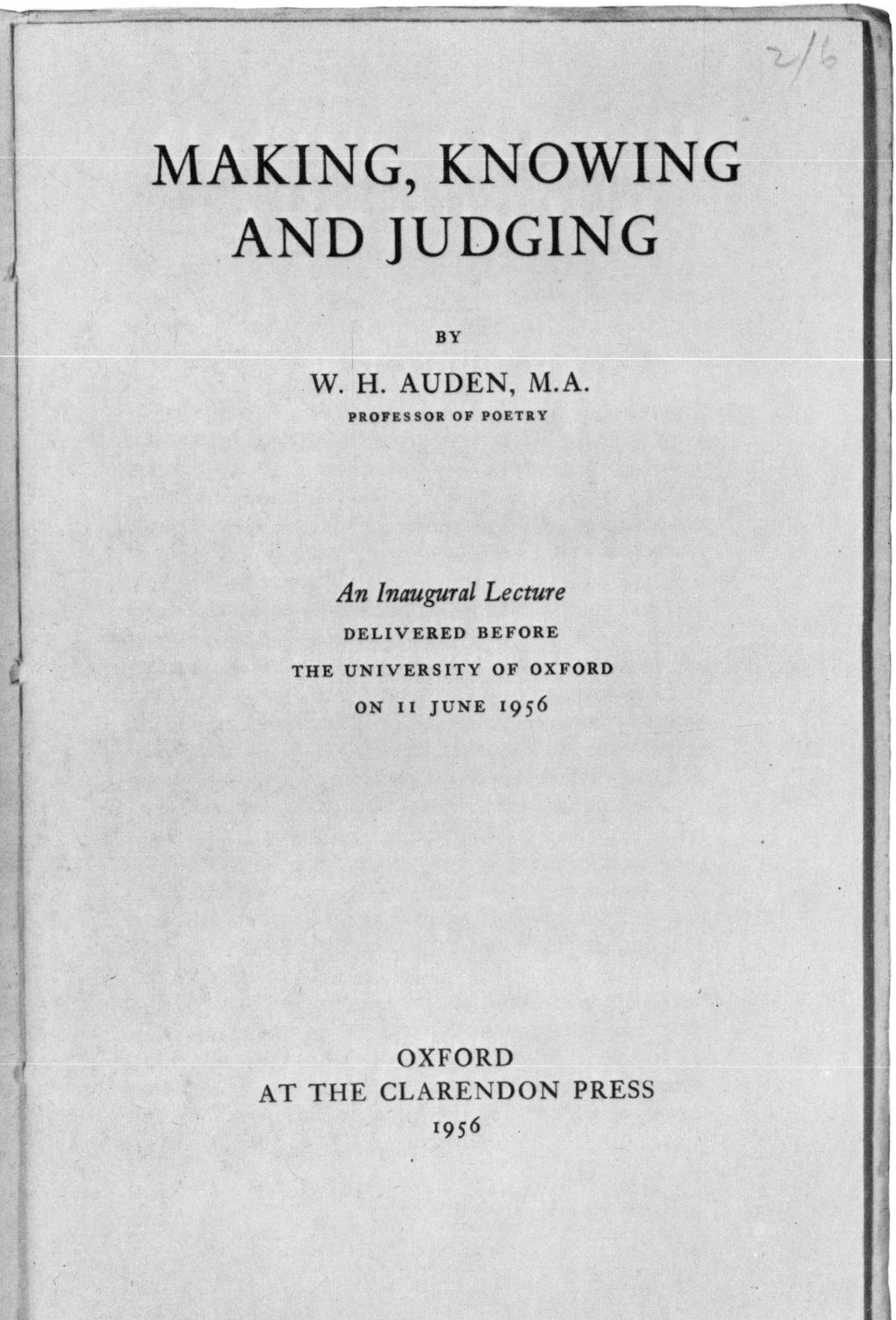

2/6

MAKING, KNOWING AND JUDGING

BY

W. H. AUDEN, M.A.

PROFESSOR OF POETRY

An Inaugural Lecture

DELIVERED BEFORE

THE UNIVERSITY OF OXFORD

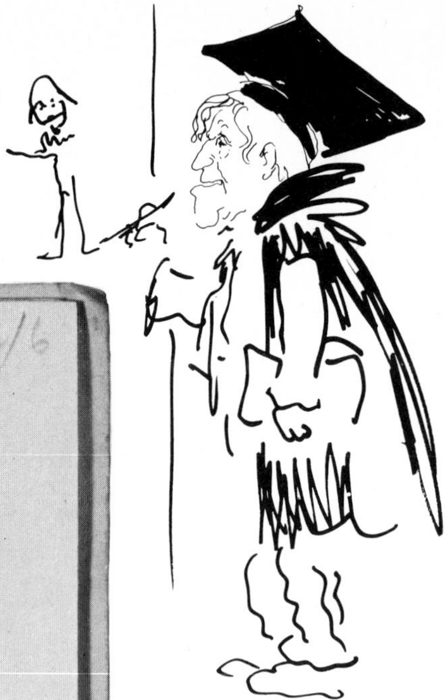

ON 11 JUNE 1956

OXFORD

AT THE CLARENDON PRESS

1956

89 BELOW Title page of Auden's first lecture as the Professor of Poetry at Oxford, a famous professorship which includes in its duties the delivery of three lectures a year. While he was at Oxford, Auden made a point of making himself available to the students at a certain time every day.

90 ABOVE The frontispiece to *Academic Graffiti*, published by Faber & Faber in 1971, which reveals Auden's fondness for 'clerihews'. In this case the clerihew runs:

My First Name,
Wystan,
Rhymes with *Tristan*,
But – O dear! I do hope
I'm not quite such a dope.

shits what he did – he could have stood on his head in the quad talking Serbo-Croat, and we'd have still thought him great.' Another: 'I wasn't the least interested in Auden, any more than I am in Picasso or Stravinsky or Casals or Shostakovitch; our inspirations and models are different nowadays.' Another: 'Having him back here was somehow like that scene in the film *2001*, about the space-ship – you know, where they destroy the main computer: one of those last few perspex relays was being pulled out. He was a last link between us and the thirties.' With two at least of our younger colleagues, whose research fields (scientific in the one case, stylistic in the other) happened to fascinate him, he achieved some real communication. He also became very friendly with the new Bishop of Dorchester, Canon Peter Walker, who told me once that the more he saw of Wystan the more affection he felt for him; and Wystan, on the way to Heathrow after his final departure from Oxford, specifically mentioned this friendship as one of the things that had made his whole homecoming worthwhile. Our organist and choirmaster Simon Preston was another kindred spirit, with whom he could talk constantly about music ('You could usually tell what line Wystan was going to take, but there were always ways of getting him to add something new every time'). During his later years, when in Oxford, Wystan had always been seen regularly in Christ Church Cathedral, and had preached two or three times at the College Evensong on Sundays, drawing very large congregations, though the only service he would attend habitually, as being still untouched by the liturgical reforms he anathematized, was the short 8 am mass (from which, immediately after receiving the sacrament, he would shuffle out without further ado to buy the Sunday papers). In 1966, at the suggestion of Dean Simpson, he and William Walton (another Honorary Student of the House) had together written for us *The Twelve: an Anthem for the Feastday of any Apostle*, a piece which Simon Preston much admired. It was the latter's idea that Wystan's own words should also be used for the memorial service on 27 October 1973, at which the Cathedral and the college took their official farewell of the poet: the two anthems were two of his poems set to music long ago by Benjamin Britten, the famous *Hymn to St Cecilia* (1942) and the extraordinary *Shepherd's Carol* (1944):

> O lift your little pinkie and touch the evening sky:
> Love's all over the mountains where the beautiful go to die.

The fact that the poet and the composer had not met for many years made this choice all the more appropriate and moving. Britten was prevented by ill health from coming to the service; he wrote to the Dean that he wished he could have paid Wystan this tribute and that he had been deeply shocked by his death. The cathedral was filled with Wystan's mourners and admirers, members of his family, the religious and the irreligious, friend and old enemy alike, from Oxford and London and further afield. In 'Lullaby' he had said to himself, as we said to ourselves now:

> Let your last thinks all be thanks.

Charles Rosen
Public and private

Charles Rosen is an internationally famous pianist and essayist

Auden strongly disapproved of revelations of the intimate lives of poets. This in no way spoiled his delight in reading them. Perhaps his belief that the enjoyment was sinful added to the pleasure. His love of decisive moral distinctions made the sinner who knew he was doing wrong more acceptable to him than one who sinned ignorantly or – even worse – indifferently. He himself was quite happily ashamed of his interest in posthumous gossip about private lives (just as he frowned upon wicked book reviews of other writers' works, and read them with enthusiasm – 'Chester and I very much enjoyed your article,' he said, sternly and reproachfully to the writer of one such review, adding, 'Very bitchy').

The division of public from private was of the greatest importance to Auden. In this distinction lay for him the foundation of literary morality, and he tried without success to make it consistent. His own poetry attempts to wear a public face: even the love lyrics avoid that air of mystery which hints at a private interpretation. Their meanings lie open on the surface: the mystery is hidden, lies in regions more profound. In the same way what is most idiosyncratic and most personal about Auden's poetry seems at first sight to be merely a matter of technique, a part of his craft. The elaborate technical mastery has, as one of its functions, the erection of a barrier.

But no poem could ever become completely public for him. He refused to admit the public nature of publication. His poems always remained his private property, he felt, to withdraw as he pleased, to alter, to suppress. No one has ever taken so ethical a view of copyright as Auden.

I once told him about going up to speak to Marianne Moore (whom I had never met) after she had given a reading of some of her poems, to tell her that I regretted a poem she had left out of her collected poems: it had a beautiful comparison of the swan to the mathematician's sign greater-than bearing its point upon the lake, and it ended with 'An arrow turned inward has no chance of peace' (a line I am no longer certain I care for so much). 'I am glad you liked that poem,' said Miss Moore, 'I liked it too, but James Laughlin didn't, so I left it out.' When I told this to Auden, I had forgotten that he was sensitive about the revisions and suppressions he had performed on his own work. He was very indignant at my story, and curiously, most indignant at Miss Moore's reaction, which he must have felt had compromised her fellow poets.

When I said that there were writers and composers, like Schumann, whose revisions fell below the standard of their original inspiration, he replied that quality had nothing to do with it: the work belonged even after publication to the author. He felt I had gone beyond what was permissible in playing Schumann's original versions. A suppressed version had no right to exist: to read it was almost to pry into the author's life, to force into light that which he had chosen to hide. Public and private were absolutely separate for Auden, but each could be transformed into the other by an act of will, which was always a moral decision.

Having made this apparently absolute distinction, Auden was able to play light-heartedly with the relation between the public and private. Towards the end of his life it became clear that it was the forbidden, the private aspects of a writer's life that interested him: he reviewed editions of letters and diaries with greater relish than anything else. Would I have liked him? is a question he asked himself before any other about poets and novelists of the past.

Nowhere was this ambiguity more important than in his attitude to his own brilliantly pornographic poem, *The Platonic Blow*. He was outraged by its unauthorized printing in an underground publication in America. 'That poem ascribed to me . . .' he started by calling it, and a few sentences later was discussing it as his own with justifiable pride. Every poet except Wordsworth has written some verse that was either obscene or scatological, he claimed. But most verse of this kind in the work of other major poets is satirical or comic, and *The Platonic Blow* is neither. It is as straightforward and dispassionate as Leonardo's drawings of sexual intercourse, except that in Auden's case the intention is clearly to excite.

The Platonic Blow was private, never intended for publication; it presents itself, however, as public. A first-person narrative of complete impersonality and complete indiscretion, nothing would identify it as Auden except its virtuoso style; only the extraordinarily detailed realism creates the illusion – as in Defoe – that the author was there.

Auden was pleased to have been the first (not only in this poem, but also in some signed reviews) to introduce certain out-of-the-way homosexual slang expressions into written English. This insurgence of his private world into the public one is the obverse of his play with words in the published poems. There he sometimes used words that he appears to have invented for their onomatopoeic value: 'sossing through seamless waters'; 'shrunk to a soodling thread'. But both 'soss' and 'soodle' are public, to be found in the OED, a book Auden read in the large thirteen-volume edition until his copy fell apart. (He was looking for a new one when he left New York for Oxford.) There are, in fact, no neologisms in Auden.

His distinction of public and private was – like most of his views on ethics – a game played with the utmost seriousness in which he decided all the rules. What was important to him was not to cheat once the rules were made. Having classified unpunctuality as a serious crime (along with speeding and drinking before five o'clock), he once turned up an hour early for Christmas dinner, explaining apologetically that cabs were difficult to find in his part of town and he had started to look for one well in advance in order not to be late.

Morality is always a public affair, but for Auden it had to be the result of a directly personal, private, even arbitrary decision. Perhaps this is why in his poetry his grand public manner has such an oddly personal tone, and can speak to us so intimately.

Stuart Hampshire
A look back at the Collected Poems

Stuart Hampshire is the Warden of Wadham College, Oxford. This article is based on a review which originally appeared in the New York Review of Books

It has sometimes been claimed that for several hundred years without interruption there has always been a major poet writing in the English language. Perhaps there have been some dull decades, for which the word 'major' would need to be stretched a little, when the already established resources of the language were just being steadily mined, without any new discoveries being made. Auden began to publish in a decade that was very far from being poetically dull. He was almost immediately recognized as likely to prolong the necessary line into the future, which, after Eliot, he did.

The mature poetry of Eliot and Yeats surrounded Auden's beginnings more than forty years ago, when the first bright-jacketed Faber volumes began to appear. He was an intruder with a harsh voice, and, in *The Orators* and elsewhere, dramatized himself as an enemy of established poetical good manners. In his Preface to the *Oxford Book of Modern Verse*, Yeats showed his distaste for Auden's new reductive style, like a metaphysician of that time deploring the logical positivists. There was a respectful, veiled hostility between the generations. In the thirties every English undergraduate who cared at all for contemporary writing kept those early Auden volumes with him, because they were the living, and also lyrical, language of restlessness and dissent. One stands in a peculiarly intimate relation to a poet, and even perhaps to a philosopher, whose work develops in parallel with one's own experience. A two-way running commentary is established, and one is either grateful to the poet for expressing what needs to be expressed at the right time, or one is censorious because he has failed to rise to some occasion (unknown to him), and because he has perversely taken a path of his own and failed to understand what was expected of him.

Auden had always left his followers behind. He looked back to his own public history in a disclaiming spirit, with a mild and elderly gaze and with some surprise. He seemed to dislike some of the ungentlemanly opinions and political prophecies in his early verse, and he had repudiated the untidy involvements of the thirties. But having been, for good reasons, the poet laureate of one dishevelled generation, at least in England, and having so far found no successor in full possession of the title, he could not easily slip away into an eccentric privacy even if he was no longer representative and was no longer a public voice.

The original reasons for his dominance are not too difficult to understand. It seemed that in his poetry he never allowed fine fictions and believable truths to be divided only by a blurred and disputed line. He wanted always to be strictly truthful. For a generation made literal-minded by new political brutalities and by the probability of war, it was no longer possible to give license to half-serious beliefs which seemed poetic playthings and which, taken by themselves, were just incredible. The whole apparatus of spell-binding and critical mystery, of hints and ironies, of allusions to Church and State, in Eliot's magnificent middle manner suddenly seemed to many heavy-handed and irrelevant. The vulgar, obvious question had been carefully kept in the background for too long: Can I believe a word – a magnificent word – of what the poet is indirectly saying? Must I care for the integrated society, for poetry's sake? So much reverence, so much disdain of contemporary thought and experience, and so much fine Bradleyan philosophy, disguised as criticism, had sooner or later to yield to plain speaking.

Auden was never reverent. Conjuring tricks with thought and language were left in his verse to look just like conjuring tricks. When he cast a sudden spell in his famous opening lines, he adopted at the same time the pose of the magician, undeceived. When he juggled with his beliefs, Marxist or Freudian, the jugglery depended upon metrical exuberance, upon a delight in verbal traps and in figures of speech and in imaginary landscapes. Whatever the play with his lyrical flights, it was open and above-board. So, following in the wake of the grand old pretenders, he seemed immensely modest, direct, and without pretences.

> . . . It's as well at times,
> To be reminded that nothing is lovely,
> Not even in poetry, which is not the case.

Perhaps most new turns in poetry, which capture a strong allegiance, have this aspect of a new literalness, of the restoration of poetry to a common light, and of a kicking away of stilts. A hard intelligence which respects contemporary realities restores the authority of poetry, at least for a time. One is grateful for the speaking voice, for a closing of the gap between reader and writer, and for an easier tolerance of common concerns. After the grand old men, the soothsayers and oracles, Auden seemed the first of the post-modern writers in England, assimilating journalism, slogans, the slag-heaps and waste-matter of political minds, the boys' games and imaginary conspiracies of middle-class Englishmen, the jumbled notions of Freudian new thought, the decaying railway lines and semi-urban landscapes of Baldwin's England. He made poetry out of unmasked lies and mere propaganda, and in *The Orators*, began a kind of literary pop art of his own which no one had seen before. He eliminated the Parnassian mode altogether, and borrowed the jerky rhythms and syncopations of musical comedy for the sake of a contrived vulgarity and catchiness of a kind of anti-poetry. His lyrical gift was never used to justify a claim to a superior imaginative truth which cannot bear the test of prosaic doubt and of mere common sense. The moral didacticism is just left to show, undisguised, through his play with verse forms.

> My problem is how not to will:
> They move most quickly who stand still:

I'm only lost until I see,
I'm lost because I want to be.

If this should fail, perhaps I should
Content myself with this conclusion;
In theory there is no solution.

All statements about what I feel,
Like I-am-lost, are quite unreal:
My knowledge ends where it began;
A hedge is taller than a man.

In his didactic verse, the message is often mocked by the manner, and he will see how thin, flat and unpretending he can be and still succeed. In other early poems, which still seem as startling in their assurance and air of command as when they were first read, the reminiscence of Yeats is broken into fragments. The myths and esoteric philosophies have disappeared, and the imagery conveys psychological truths, a diagnosis.

'I see the guilty world forgiven,'
Dreamer and drunkard sing,
'The ladders let down out of heaven,
The laurel springing from the martyr's blood,
The children skipping where the weeper stood,
The rivers natural and the beasts all good.'

So dreamer and drunkard sing;
Till day their sobriety bring:
Parrotwise with deaths reply;
From whelping fear and nesting lie;
Woods their echoes ring. . . .

'From whelping fear and nesting lie' – this was the characteristic Auden topic. 'The Paysage Moralisé' became his original style:

Hearing of harvests rotting in the valleys,
Seeing at end of street the barren mountains,
Round corners coming suddenly on water,
Knowing them shipwrecked who were launched for islands,
We honour founders of these starving cities,
Whose honour is the image of our sorrow.

This was the more or less political poetry of its time.

Look there! The sunk road winding
To the fortified farm,
Listen! The cock's alarm
In the strange valley.

> Are we then the stubborn athletes?
> Are we then to begin
> The run between the gin
> And bloody falcon?
>
> The horns of the dark squadron,
> Converging to attack;
> The sound behind our back
> Of glaciers calving.

As one reads to the end, from 1927 onwards, neither the mastery of verse forms nor the use of poetry as moral comment in an imaginary landscape seems greatly to change. The fact that many of the surviving early poems counted as politically inspired and were written in the context of a supposed social revolution, seems to make little difference either to their meaning or their value. The Eden of congruity and justice that he constructs from disordered images of northern landscapes is the same all the way through, and the same kind of obsessional, or sacred, objects stand for sanity, order and calm. Even when Auden turns most strongly, in his later verse, against political prophecy, and against political anxiety as a theme, one can still shuffle the poem back into the first third of this book and find no great unfittingness. He dominates his own beliefs so completely that they seem never, or rarely, to take him off course, or to make him untrue to his own temperament. In this respect he is, and intends to be, more like an Augustan poet than any of his contemporaries. The canons of good sense are already fixed in the real obvious world, and he does not grope or flounder in his published work. As far as a modern writer can, he has made the idea of his own development seem critically irrelevant. His development, he implies, is simply his getting older, and must not be turned by his readers into some exemplary spiritual progress, as if he were Goethe. The famous poems of so many years ago –

> Look, stranger, on this island now
> The leaping light for your delight discovers. . . .

or:

> As I walked out one evening. . . .

or:

> About suffering they were never wrong,
> The Old Masters. . . .

or 'Lullaby' or 'A Summer Night' – do not seem to be exploratory, or to be a preparation for anything beyond themselves. Nor do the more controlled and less ambitious later poems, from the age of Empson, seem later poems.

> Time will say nothing but I told you so,
> Time only knows the price we have to pay;
> If I could tell you I would let you know.

If there is a discernible line of development at all, it is simply that the proportion of song to epigram diminishes. But even so one might not be able to guess whether these lines are late or early:

> A sentence uttered makes a world appear
> Where all things happen as it says they do;
> We doubt the speaker, not the tongue we hear:
> Words have no word for words that are not true.

Auden used the discoveries of Blake, Lear and Hardy, as well as of Yeats and Eliot, with a peculiar detachment. He takes the letter and experiments with it, and leaves the philosophical spirit behind. He uses his predecessors, as a musician may, for the forms that they suggest to him for variation and development.

He is the first English poet, and one of the first major writers of any kind, whose way of thought had from the beginning been formed by an early knowledge of clinical psychology, and therefore by an amused understanding of the wild mechanisms of imagination. If Eliot sometimes seems a sidesman in a surplice, suspecting heresies, Auden's natural, and perhaps inherited, attitude is that of a clinician in a white coat, expecting epidemics of madness and hypochondria, the slow poisons that affect the whole political body and are natural disturbances of the mind. Anxiety, taken as a pathological symptom, is an unexpected theme for poetry, and he had made it his own. He is particularly the poet of the imaginary threat which becomes real, of a creeping political madness, of an epidemic of distraction and fear. One might crudely have expected that so much self-consciousness would undermine the power, and even the will, to invent. But it is characteristic of him to swerve from the most abstract and pedantic reflection to concrete imagery, and, in a sense, to swerve from prose to poetry within poetry. He likes to represent and to control panic by drawing up lists of its obsessional signs, and he sometimes uses poetry as an incantation that disinfects in a mocking spirit. He ensures that his own words are clean and that they carry no secondary infection of doubtful meanings.

He had the habit of revising his earlier work, and one finds that familiar passages have disappeared. Any speck of mere rhetoric which he had noticed has been removed. Like a philosopher of the analytical school, he did not want to be taken to mean more than he actually says, even by the narrowest margin; for he did not want to be an oracle, indeterminate in meaning. There cannot be both science and oracles or we shall be either mad or just frivolous, or at least half-serious, in assertion. If poetry and philosophy are different from the natural sciences and from religion, in their attitude to truth, the difference cannot be that they do not really mean what they seem to say.

Auden's attitude to poetical philosophizing is parallel to G. E. Moore's attitude to McTaggart, whom Yeats revered. If there is no literal sense in which time is unreal, there ought to be no poetical or philosophical sense either, except as a pretence. If poetry is an intricate game, which, through an obsessional delight in formal rules, sometimes reveals hidden connections, the hidden connections must be there, visible even to a prosaic eye. If no hidden connections are discovered, or even attempted, poetry is just an intricate and absorbing game with images and signs, 'a contraption', a variant of nursery rhyme, or of song or nonsense verse; and so much the better: anything rather than literary egoism and home-made metaphysics. It is too late for these indulgences, which have in any case proved themselves insanitary and dangerous.

Auden had in later years called for gentlemanly restraints upon men of letters who vulgarly claim too much for themselves. Whatever their eccentric skills, they know no more than they can rationally prove, and they have no sense that is superior to common sense and to the traditions of good manners and worldly prudence. They must not look for acknowledgement as legislators of the world: quixotism was finished, finally exposed, in the thirties. A middle and modest style is appropriate to an age of fanaticism and public indignities. Poetry may perhaps revive the virtues of the music of the eighteenth century, before the silly confusions (as he believes) between art and religion, or between art and ethics, began. It can illustrate a proper sense of scale and of measure, a respect for moderate moods, and a decent confinement of wild ambitions within clear and difficult forms. In the later pages of this collection the anxiety and the hint of madness in the air, the sense of panic, that runs through the early verse can only be heard from much farther away. There is a natural ageing in the volume and the poet is, as usual, entirely self-conscious about it.

The weight and variety of achievement are dazzling. The combination of lyricism and epigram, the controlled strangeness, the wit, the genius in formal invention, are a perpetual pleasure. Auden has become and will surely remain one of the most quotable of poets, typically perhaps more in single verses and even phrases rather than in whole poems. He seems often to be checking and curbing his own cleverness and his own artifices in case they should go too far. He expresses, both in verse and in prose, a restrained and careful confidence in literature, kept in its proper place which is on the surface of things. His most vivid writing refers to a natural order, a remembered landscape of suitable rock and soil and water, which is as easily lost or spoiled now as when he was first published in Baldwin's England.

Chester Kallman
The Dome of the Rock [1970]

Chester Kallman was Auden's collaborator in the writing of the librettos.

May my tongue cleave to the roof of my
*   mouth. . . .*

With the farming of a verse
Make a vineyard of the curse. . . .

After the Holy Sepulchre, the souks
And the Wailing Wall, we stand here
Before another work of man's wit,
Wystan, Alan and I. Nobody smokes
Nor thinks of smoking: six Arabs bathe
    their feet
And hands preliminary to prayer.
The Temple Mount like the Acropolis
Undoubtedly is a holy place:
Lavish, untended, bare.

I think of Yannis whom I loved,
Killed more than a year ago
Now and as entirely present as though
Like the present he had nothing more
Urgent to do than be survived.
So it is. I need no assurance here;
Nor as an afterthought could resent
The patched-up survival of this monument
God knows beautiful enough
For any faith to reverence and/or love.

I speak for myself alone,
For a second only unbereft.
Here, as back in our hotel
Too far, too dear, too overstaffed
With Arabs overanxious to oblige,
Two Jews by birth, one practicing Anglican,
Confine our elation to a state of siege,
A heavenly surround, as usual;
That much we can afford.
Through air clean of thought now and eyes

Stung over during a half-remembered
    prayer
At the Wailing Wall, clear
(Damn my eyes! I've always seen too well
To train a vocabulary of detail;

Easy recall sufficed me and undoes
The vision it refers to,
My present task; you will have to take my
    word),
I take in wonder, spellstopt, amateur:
Here is the Mosque with an arched portico,
    called
The Scales, to counterpoise humanely its
    upreared
Imposition topped by a dome of gold;
Ardent blue tile surrounds Mount Moriah's
    peak,
Paling the heaven it swears to.
No fear: the oath is kept; belief requires a
    rock.
Here my Ur-father, daggered Abraham,
Wearing his Sabbath best, awe-struck,
Brought his dear son and, finding a scape-
    goat ram,
Gratefully made sacrifice
The center of the universe for his race,
Then took the good news home;
    Mohammed riding
El Burak, his horse, galloped to Paradise
From here, Solomon's Temple here long
    down
To Rome's levelling; and here I applaud
    Solomon
Foresightedly providing
A court for money-changers to confirm,
Ever recalled in exile and in trading,
His choice of focal sanctity

Through every change of hands.
Dear souls of the departed, gathered in
    prayer
Under this rock forever, I pray you be
Forever faithless of your charm
To wheedle Charon's fare so, have your
    funds
In deed well grasped, knowing how much
    David paid
To work your shelter as a threshing floor,
When you are herded out here to be
    weighed,
As once you lived by reckoning day by day
Sporadically, on Reckoning Day. (I come
By all this info from a good cheap Guide.
Am I convinced by it? I am.) I am
Single-minded in duplicity,
My natural preoccupation with getting my
Money's worth, that is, what I expect;
It sets me up altogether taken in
By what responds to a live touristic yen
For picturesque authenticity
Outsoaring shade, outlasting doubt,
Believing all even as I half suspect
All true believers apostate
At heart; and heart I question if we dare
Set this all down as Mythic Architecture,
That poetry we called pure.
I wonder. Whatever mind or eyes
Can learn from knowing that the vexed
Design around the Mosque is Holy Text,
I am unready for such certainties,
However they thread my spelled captivity
With gold, an artistic bent. 'And Nature's
    own,
What's in it for them?' I ask when through
My kenning two misguided bees
Worry from ruined rose to ruined rose,
From garden-plot to garden-plot with
    gapped
Rusty palings, powdery soil, as though
Their one cycled glory were to symbolise
The fruitless nature of change. 'I won't
    accept
That for myself or them or any-thing or
    man,'
I shrug at our surround. Alan counters me,
Exhorting, 'Let the Heathen reign!
Look at Constantinople: the Turks

Have blessed it with neglect; how
    misbegotten
Greek effort would be, and in time
    redundant,
To tidy out the worst. They would
    overwhelm
The best in doing so. It never works!'
True enough, dear, and non-partisan,
But it argues a free, always dependant
Duchy, Criticism; here is a Realm
However blotted and rewritten
Where words fail, as the saying goes,
To serve with what we feel
And how believe, absolute laws.
We remained infidel
Chattering in the cab to our hotel,
Eternal tourists, never quite at home,
Three good New Yorkers, our one scope
'As obscure as that heaven of the Jews,'
In being here is simply to be here;
Saved, we would like to hope,
From the eternally addressed
Gyrations of a tourist hell
Not by Saint Christopher
But by unminted, hence superior
Personal Saints, Leisure and Taste;
Nor ever about, good God! like some
Whose every trip, I gather, is taken to muse
And winkle out another stale new poem.

Wystan is gone; a gift of fertile years
And now of emptiness: I found him dead
Turning icy-blue on a hotel bed.
Yannis had worshipped him; Alan reveres
Him and his work with studied irreverency;
I shared his work and life as best I could
For both of us, often impatiently.
So it was; let it be:
I say, yet cannot leave it blank,
That overplus of bedrock and of good,
And try to think what I have learned of
    him,
A teacher born. I never learned to think
As passionately and dispassionately
At once, nor feel the world a personal
    affront.
And personal joy, preoccupied as I am

With taking sporadic scrupulous account
Of personal feeling; but if I sometimes
        feel
That I feel nothing, he has taught
My hands to spell it out,
Trusting the heart's recall.

Everything changes, nothing does,
Eroded wisdom puts it, as the river flows
Love too, if you will, answers the paradox,
Or the belief in love; so watch your step,
        lover,
Keeping the just balance of a true believer:
A home-made love of justice raged
Round this old City, once again besieged,
Entered and levelled all the Synagogues;
Much truth, much love and much belief
        recall
Mea Shearim Jews to the Wailing Wall
A differing truth and its companion love
Had made a public convenience of,
With tears of joy; they kiss their apostate
Army who shed blood and fought
On Sabbath to allow them back,
Then bulldozed every house in sight
To spare them any less than just attack
From snipers. Let them live to bargain:
        like those
Who cram the Churches with their votaries;
Like Arab villagers who flock over
The Jordan with produce and take home
        their well
Grasped wages of fly-blown meat; like
        affable
Israeli boys in uniform who must race
Into the Holy Sepulchre whenever
Orthodox Armenian and Russian
Fraternally clash on orders of procession,
To haggle a peace at any price;
Like them off-duty, tourist conquerors,
Ritually frowning in an Arab shop
Through the exchanges of money asked
        and offered
Lest they be jewed for souvenirs:
Here's your Esperanto faith, your river
Fertilising non-stop
Your feeling purity recovered!

Old enemies practically embrace;
They muster and relish their loves
With daggers up their sleeves
Like true lovers; they throng the narrow
        streets
As thick as May-flies on nuptial flights
Dying, dying, the eternal gift of life.
What is the name of the month
In Hebrew and Arabic? Good grief,
What will guide us living from this
        labyrinth?
Where runs the Via Dolorosa not?
Where is the Rest-room? At the Dung
        Gate.
How are we doing? God knows. Alan grew
Dizzy, I dim, Wystan ploughs through
Blindly as ever, as ever making
Chaos good soil and bearable.
Things look up. There improbable
And visible hover atremble
Our patron Dioscuri, half human flesh,
Half papier-maché, outspokenly celestial,
Invoked by his presence, gardant, real,
Wired with love, putti gracing a crèche:
It was too incredibly heartbreaking;
I made myself note how they resemble
Our passing selves perhaps a shade stouter
Alas. Alas, I note too, my tenses fall
Into improper sequences; no matter,
When I have gathered and have as
        undertaking
To picture it elementary to outlast
Verbal conveniences like *The Past*.

Thus I stand here then:
I question and would recall
My ancestral tears at the Wailing Wall;
I question the Holy Sepulchre, a gaud
Of pi gimcrackery; I am afraid
Of the eternal questing appetite of men
After the bloody reek of lamb
Lining the souks; I cannot give a damn
For their questionable yen
To worship something somewhere; and I
        pray
Dear Yannis and dear Wystan pray for me.

John Bayley
Only critics can't play

John Bayley is Fellow and Tutor in English Literature at New College, Oxford

Even more than with most poets there is a gap between Auden and his critics, or rather between the way his poetry works and the things that we find to say about it. From its earliest beginnings the iconography of his poetry has always depended on a seeming system of correspondences – abounding intellect, theory and appetite for metaphysical and scientific systems transforming themselves in and through the poetic scene into fantasy and play, the fashionable and the sociable. But to get inside the poetry by winding it back, as it were, into this world of theory and abstraction, does not help.

For the fact is that Auden's poetry can no more be 'serious' than life can be, and thus it resembles life far more than its author thought it ought to, or could. There is no need to labour Auden's almost obsessional preoccupation with the difference between art and life – 'we *may* write, we *must* live', and his stress on the divided self of the artist, the man who must sit apart, wrestling with the glum realities of existence, while the poet can enjoy himself as he pleases, giving tight-lipped orders to imaginary underlings (his crafts and vocabularies), arranging sensational displays and explosions, and 'spending, what would otherwise be a very boring evening indeed, planning how to seize the post office on the other side of the river'. But in fact, just as the formidably 'with it' iconography of his poetry melts into its social and performing being, so its 'contraptive' aspect, its 'halcyon structures', bring us by the best route into the middle of the ordinary human scene, the lives that poets and ourselves have to lead. Yeats wrote, 'in dreams begin responsibilities'. In spite of Auden's specific denial that life is in any sense a game, there is no doubt that in his poetry morality begins in the games of fantasy.

This is as much as to say that Auden's poetry, like that of other great poets, not only *is* a world but joins on at every point to the open world – the *civitas* or *res publica* – in which the literate and responsive are dwelling or attempting to dwell. The point was admirably made by John Fuller in his *Reader's Guide*, when he stressed the comprehensiveness of the Auden microcosm; and the same emphasis is given in two very recent American academic studies – Frederic Buell's *Auden as a Social Poet* and Richard Johnson's long essay called *Man's Place*, which explores Auden's anthropomorphization of the world of nature. Both are scholarly attempts to integrate the Auden canon, demonstrate the processes of development and assess comparative achievement. To these one might add François Duchene's *The Case of the Helmeted Airman*, which, in spite of an appalling misquotation in the actual epigraph of the first two lines of 'Consider this and in our time', has some pertinent things to say about the change in poetic attack and meaning which began in *New Year Letter*.

Yet since in order to make their critical points they have to take the poetry seriously, these, with other critics, are bound to remain outside the curiously intimate and Alice-in-Wonderland world of its logic and impact. And I can think of no other poet in whose case this particular phenomenon is so marked. Keats is perhaps the nearest parallel, for Keats too has critics who concentrate on what might be called the projectional side of his poetry – the attempt at working out, or at least the adumbration, of important Romantic myths in *Endymion* and *Hyperion* – and are silent on its extraordinarily complex, vulnerable and in some ways almost embarrassingly sensuous realities. There is nothing embarrassing about Auden's poetic world, at least not to most people, and as a poet he has little in common with Keats, except this elusiveness – this tendency to by-pass in the act what is implied in the project.

Professor Johnson speaks of the 'apparent failure' of *The Age of Anxiety*, 'which attempts to treat the phylogenic and ontogenic history of man both as a series of landscapes and as a series of narratives growing out of a dramatized situation'; and he concludes that the work 'suffers from a confusion of spatial and temporal form'. It shows the way Auden's poetry works that Professor Johnson follows this up in a footnote with an odd afterthought – that the 'allegorical expansion of images and plot requires a more complex metrical unit than the alliterative line, perhaps the Spenserian stanza?' – and then comes to the disarming conclusion: 'Yet I am far from certain *The Age of Anxiety* is a failure'. Neither am I, but I wholly sympathize with Professor Johnson's feeling as a critic that it ought to be. His comments reveal, in passing, something of real interest: the difference in Auden between craftsmanship – always immaculate – and the almost slickly throwaway conception, like 'phylogenic and ontogenic history', which is indeed in some sense there, but as kind of distraction and an earnest of magic, the mystic passes of the conjuror's hands.

If *The Age of Anxiety* is, so far from being a failure, among Auden's most dazzling achievements, it is not because of its powers of 'phylogenic and ontogenic' diagnosis but because Auden hit on a new way of using a metre – and for English alliterating and accentual rhythm a totally unexpected one – to convey dramatically the interplay of daydream, self-deception and self-awareness. Rosetta's daydreams of English landscapes and country houses are extraordinarily funny and touching – they surprise us into feeling: yes, this is what we feel, our inchoate selfhood is rendered with all the precision, economy, and humour of great art. I want to offer two critical ideas on this aspect of Auden's poetry, particularly in the development of his later poetry.

First, taking a hint from Auden's essays, I would try to join up the family aspect of the poetry with the deliberately monsterish – high camp monsterish – techniques which it latterly cultivated. The directness and common sense of the essays often conceals, I believe, a more subjective relevance than their apparently objective judiciousness would allow. Reflecting on Max Beerbohm in an essay called 'One of the Family' Auden wrote:

The great cultural danger for the English is, to my mind, the tendency to judge the arts by the values appropriate to the conduct of family life. Among brothers and sisters it is becoming to entertain each other with witty remarks, hoaxes, family games and jokes, unbecoming to be solemn, to monopolize the conversation, to talk shop, to create emotional scenes.

This constitutes a real threat, he goes on, to art 'which cannot be governed by the rules of social amenity'. Nonetheless, in some curious and remarkable way, Auden did so attempt to govern his own art, and increasingly so as time went on. Horace, true, was one of his background models, but another – both for his art and the effect it has on us – was Wagner:

> If we are to get the full benefit of Wagner's opera, we have simultaneously to identify ourselves with what we hear and see on the stage – 'Yes, all that is me' – and to distance ourselves from it – 'But all that is precisely what I must overcome'. If we can do this then we shall find that, just as Milton was 'of the devil's party without knowing it', so Wagner, equally unknowingly, was on the side of Reason, Order and Civilization.

Now, of course Auden 'knew it' perfectly well; but the point is that he understood that the kind of art he had at his command works on us in extremely oppositional, divided and devious ways. No one is a better example of the total moral effectiveness of an art which is not only not didactic but actually uses didacticism as a plaything, a family gambit. In an essay on Walter De la Mare, whom he deeply admired, he quoted Santayana's comment: 'Every artist is a moralist though he needn't preach.' Though Auden works on us very differently from Wagner it is equally by remote control. His Wagnerian properties, so to speak, are assertions and arguments, dogmas and distinctions; he seems to harangue and even to hector us by a kind of double bluff: 'the more assertive I am the more we both know it is a game, with the rules of the game, and as you come both to perceive the point of the rules and to relish them – so you will find yourself on the side of Reason, Order and Civilization. . . .'

And so in spite of his caveat about art and family life, Auden's art really depends on something very like it. But it is, let me hasten to add, family life on an international scale – there is nothing provincial about it. Not only can any number play, provided they have a proper knowledge of and enthusiasm for the English language, but the rules of the game, which are in many ways eccentric, extensible and unexpected, are actually designed to favour those who have no instinctual or socially conditioned grasp of them. No artist has known so well the secret of mixing what might seem the irredeemably cosy, with what is ageless and confident, with unindulgent authority – the authority of the Maker in the compelling late poem of that title. It would not be out of place to compare this remarkable gift for international intimacy, which Auden as an artist possessed, with the powers of Tolstoy for achieving intimacy with the reader, especially in *Childhood* and in *War and Peace*. In *Boyhood* Tolstoy has a category of persons who *understand*: they may not be very good or clever (indeed Nekhlyudov, the future hero of *Resurrection*, who is both good and clever, is not one of them) but they have instinctively grasped the rules and seen what the game is about. One does not have to be of the English upper-middle class to see the point of Auden's game and to play it with him.

One does, perhaps, have to cherish a dislike for the grosser aspects of modern realism in art. The television play, the modern drama, much modern beat or pop-art verse exert in common a brusque dismissal of anything resembling family understanding, appealing instead to some sort of peer group ethos or, more characteristically, to the solitary ego who has no time for the conventions and rules which are required by a family's need for privacy and forbearance.

This brings me to my second point. It is often said that while early Auden was very influential with other poets, his later poems were usually considered by them (Berryman remarked as much) as isolated, eccentric, fuddy-duddy, and off the beam. Some kind of defensive stance may indeed have been important to such poets, because the continuing potency and authority of Auden affected them more than they knew or were prepared to admit. For Lowell and Berryman turned themselves into American family poets, a different species from the English kind, but none the less owing practically everything to it.

Of course Auden was not in their sense a confessional poet: he never gave us any revelations about his schooldays, sex-life, intimate friendships or relations with mother and father, all of which, and especially the last, have been Lowell and Berryman's stock-in-trade. So what is Auden's relevance to poets who wish to tell us how things are with themselves, and to reveal the modern dilemma by showing how they personally in their lives have coped or failed to cope with it? I think the short answer is that he continued up to the time of his death to give them a sort of confidence, and a convention to operate in, which, however they modified it, would not have existed without him.

My point is that just as 'naturalism' is itself a particular use of selective conventions, so this confessional and personal poetry is really a question of tone, a scale whose whole range Auden explored before it was used by confessional poets for their purposes. Auden created a completely authoritative and idiosyncratic world, loaded in the thirties with private menace and public dread, where the political, social and personal anxieties of an age were mimed by agents and portents who 'talk to your admirers every day'.

> By silted harbours, derelict works,
> In strangled orchards and the silent comb
> Where dogs have worried or a bird was shot. . . .

The naturalism here is of course in that mixture of dread and desire which is the almost universal human response to imagined catastrophe, and which makes Auden's poetry of the thirties seem in retrospect as comprehensive and accurate in reflecting its time, as Tennyson's poetry reflected his. From this authority everything in later Auden naturally follows: the method remains the same. As I remarked in a book called *The Romantic Survival*, Auden showed how an intensely private world 'could be brought right out into the open, 'eclecticized', and pegged down to every point of interest in contemporary life'. No wonder the influence was so great, not only showing the way to a poet like Berryman but making it difficult for him to escape. (Berryman reminisces in one of the *Love and Fame* poems that he didn't want his poetry to sound like Auden, but in that case what was it to sound like?) There is no doubt that the right use of

The Last Years

91 Auden on his return to Oxford in 1972, where he rented a cottage in the grounds of
Christ Church. (See David Luke's contribution.)

92 OPPOSITE Auden after his return to Oxford giving a poetry recital.
93 Auden in Peckwater Quad, Christ Church. The fifth and sixth windows in the middle row from the left belong to the rooms he occupied as an undergraduate from 1925 to 1928.

94 Auden with his godson, Philip Spender, in 1972, to whom he wrote *Epistle to a Godson*.

95 Auden at the Poetry International Festival in London, 1973, with Allen Ginsberg.

96, 97 ABOVE and RIGHT Two photographs of Auden at his summer home in Kirchstetten, a village south of Vienna. The one on the right was taken a few weeks before his death and shows him engaged in one of his favourite pastimes – the crossword.

98 ABOVE A scene from the last production of *The Dog Beneath the Skin*, performed at Christ Church in 1973 with Auden's approval. The text on this occasion contained variations sufficiently at variance from the original for Edward Mendelson, Auden's literary executor, to request a copy.

99 RIGHT The funeral at
Kirchstetten on 4
October 1973.

100 BELOW Choristers at
the memorial service at
Christ Church, Oxford on
27 October 1973. '*The
death of the poet was
kept from his poems.*'

Auden enabled him to be infinitely contingent and infinitely personal, while at the same time making of the *Dream Songs* a 'halcyon structure' which was pure art and not actuality, however totally it appeared to imprison itself in the actual.

Founded as it was on Auden's genius, the paradox is yet not one of which we are conscious in Auden's own poetry. It may be the very completeness of the naturalism in which Berryman set about grounding his personal myth that makes us feel in the end boxed in by him, and that, meticulous as his art's awareness of common and contingent living seems to be, it is not in fact 'earthed'. By demonstrating its art so openly, on the other hand, and asserting its bonds of metre, its curiosity of phrase and search of vocabulary, Auden's later poetry joins itself effortlessly to life, shows us that it is indeed the game which counts most as the basic human activity, not personal myth or private confession.

A light masterpiece like 'The Fall of Rome', in *Nones*, illustrates this as well as anything. Its appeal begins instantly in incantation and image, and goes on to reveal meaning that is both sharp and heavy with common sense and open to public verification – a meaning ultimately outside the poet – in a sense in which the historical fantasies of Lowell's *Notebooks*, for instance, do not strike us as being. The games and devices invented by Auden as a poet are played by us as members of the public, whom they can both delight and instruct, in the daily world and not in the world of poetic vision, the world into which the flower-bells of Rilke 'endlessly prolong themselves'. Such a world as Rilke's is of course the critics' joy: their exegesis matches his myth in taking itself seriously, and it was because of this that Auden had characteristically mixed feelings about him. Rilke is a poet of the elsewhere, as Lowell and Berryman in their different ways are too; and for Auden, as for Hardy, that was always only a region to be desired and imaged from outside, as happens in the concluding stanza of 'The Fall of Rome'.

> Altogether elsewhere, vast
> Herds of reindeer move across
> Miles and miles of golden moss,
> Silently and very fast.

Stephen Spender
Auden at Milwaukee

This is a note from my diary written on my sixty-first birthday, 28 February 1970, after dining with Auden in New York

Dined with Auden. He'd been at Milwaukee
Three days, talking to the students.
'They loved me. They were entranced.' His face lit up the scene.
I saw there the picture of him, crammed into
Carpet bag clothes and carpet slippers,
His face alone alive alone above them.
He must have negotiated himself into the room
Like an object, a prize, a gift that knows its worth,
Measuring his value out to them on scales
Word weighed by word, absorbed in his own voice.
He knows they're young and, better, that he's old.
He shares remoteness from them like a joke.
They love him for it. This because they feel
That he belongs to none yet gives to all.
They see him as an object, artefact, face that time
Has carved criss-cross with all these lines, and has opacity
And yet a core inside that burns,
Alabaster-like light through amber.
Surrounding him with all their eyes and ears,
They know a tenderness that's hewn.

Joseph Brodsky
Elegy

Joseph Brodsky visited Auden at his house near Vienna after being exiled from Russia by the Soviet Government

The tree is dark, the tree is tall,
to gaze at it isn't fun.
Among the fruits of this fall
your death is the most grievous one.

The land is bare. Firm for steps,
it yields to a shovel's clink.
Among next April's stems
your cross will be the unshaken thing.

Seedless it will possess its dew
humiliating grass.
Poetry without you
equals only us.

The words are retreating to the stage
of lexicons, of the Muse.
The sky looks like an empty page
which you did not use.

The tree is dark, the tree is tall,
pleasing its Maker's scheme.
The thing I wish to talk
of least of all is Him.

Crossing horizons objects shrink;
it's hard to realize
there is someone for whom the thing
gains its previous size.

Stephen Spender
Valediction

The following is the address Stephen Spender gave on 27 October 1973 at Auden's memorial service in Christ Church

This gathering of friends to honour and remember Wystan Auden is not an occasion on which I should attempt to discuss either Wystan's personality or his place in the history of English literature. It is, rather, one on which to recall his presence, and express our praise and gratitude for his life and work, in these surroundings where, intellectually and as a poet, his life may be said to have come full circle.

He was a citizen of the world, a New Yorker with a home in Austria, in the little village of Kirchstetten, where he is buried, for whom Christ Church, 'The House', had come to mean his return to his English origins. For making this possible, the Dean and Canon and students are to be thanked.

I knew Wystan since the time when we were both undergraduates, and saw him at intervals until a few weeks before his death. It is impossible for me, in these surroundings, not to juxtapose two images of him, one of forty years back, and one of a year ago only.

The first is of the tow-haired undergraduate poet with the abruptly turning head, and eyes that could quickly take the measure of people or ideas. At that time, he was not altogether quite un-chic, wearing a bow-tie and on occasion wishing one to admire the suit he had on. He recited poetry by heart in an almost toneless, unemotional, quite unpoetical voice which submerged the intellectual meaning under the level horizontal line of the words. He could hold up a word or phrase like an isolated fragment or specimen chipped off the great granite cliff of language, where a tragic emotion could be compressed into a coldly joking word, as in certain phrases I recall him saying. For instance:

> The icy precepts of respect

or

> Pain has an element of blank

or perhaps lines of his own just written:

> Tonight when a full storm surrounds the house
> And the fire creaks, the many come to mind
> Sent forward in the thaw with anxious marrow.
> For such might now return with a bleak face,
> An image pause, half-lighted at the door. . . .

A voice, really, in which he could insulate any two words so that they seemed separate from the rest of the created universe, and sent a freezing joking thrill down one's spine. For instance, the voice in which, one summer when he was staying with me at my home in London during a heat wave, and luncheon was served and the dish cover lifted, he exclaimed in tones of utter condemnation like those of a judge passing a terrible sentence:

Boiled ham!

The second image of Wystan is of course one with which you are all familiar: the famous poet with the face like a map of physical geography, criss-crossed and river-run and creased with lines. This was a face upon which experiences and thoughts had hammered; a face of isolated self-communing which reminded me of a phrase of Montherlant's about the artist's task of 'noble self-cultivation'; a face, though, which was still somehow entertaining and which could break down into a smile of benevolence or light up with gratified recognition at some anecdote recounted or thought received. It was a face at once armoured and receptive.

It is difficult to bring these two images – spaced forty years apart – together. But to do so is to find reason for our being here to praise and thank him.

His fellow undergraduates who were poets when he was also an undergraduate (Day Lewis, MacNeice, Rex Warner, and myself) saw in him a man who, instead of being, like us, romantically confused, diagnosed the condition of contemporary poetry, and of civilization, and of us – with our neuroses. He found symptoms everywhere. *Symptomatic* was his key word. But in his very strange poetry he transmogrified these symptoms into figures in a landscape of mountains, passes, streams, heroes, horses, eagles, feuds and runes of Norse sagas. He was a poet of an unanticipated kind – a different race from ourselves – and also a diagnostician of literary, social and individual psychosomatic situations, who mixed this Iceland imagery with Freudian dream symbolism. Not in the least a Leader, but, rather, a clinical-minded oracle with a voice that could sound as depersonalized as a Norn's in a Norse saga. Extremely funny, and extremely hard-working: always, as Louis MacNeice put it, 'getting on with the job'. He could indulge in self-caricature, and he could decidedly shock, but he did no imitations of other people's speech or mannerisms, though he could do an excellent performance of a high mass, including the bell tinkling. His only performance was himself.

He was in no sense public and he never wanted to start any kind of literary movement, issue any manifestoes. He was publicly private.

> Private faces in public places
> Are wiser and nicer
> Than public faces in private places.

We were grateful for a person who was so different from ourselves, not quite a person in the way that other people were. His poetry was unlike anything we had expected poetry to be, from our public-school-classical-Platonic-Romantic English Literature education at that time.

He seemed the incarnation of a serious joke. Wystan wrote somewhere that a friend is simply someone of whom, in his absence, one thinks with pleasure. When Wystan was not there, we spoke of him not only with pleasure and a certain awe, but also laughing. People sometimes divide others into those you laugh at and those you laugh with. The young Auden was someone you could laugh-at-with.

I should say that for most of his friends who were his immediate contemporaries, the pattern of his relationship with them was that of colleague; with his pupils that of a teacher whom they called 'Uncle Wiz'. During the years when he was teaching at prep school, he wrote his happiest poetry. But in those days of exuberance, merging into the vociferous and partisan 1930s, he almost became that figurehead, concerning whose pronouncements he grew to be so self-critical later on: the voice of his generation. Or, rather, its several voices, under which his own voice sometimes seemed muted. For it was not true to his own voice to make public political noises. His own voice said:

> O love, the interest itself in thoughtless Heaven,
> Make simpler daily the beating of man's heart.

Nevertheless he did speak for the liveliest of the young at that time: those who wanted to throw off the private inhibitions and the public acquiescences of a decade of censorship and dictatorship and connivance with dictatorship, those who were impassioned by freedom, and some who fought for it. He gave to them their wishes which they might not have listened to otherwise. They were grateful for that. He enabled impulses to flower in individuals. All that was life-enhancing.

Thinking now of the other face, of the later Auden, a great many things about him, quite apart from his appearance, had changed. He now mistrusted his past impulsiveness and rejected in his *oeuvre* many lines and stanzas which had been the results of it. His buffoonery was now sharpened and objectified into wit. His eccentricities had rigidified into habits imposed according to a built-in timetable regulating nearly every hour of his day. This was serious but at the same time savingly comic. He never became respectable, could always be outrageous, and occasionally undermined his own interests by giving indiscreet interviews about his life. These tended to disqualify him in the eyes of members of committees dedicated to maintaining respectability.

He had also perhaps acquired some tragic quality of isolation. But with him the line of tragedy coincided almost with that of comedy. That was grace. One reason for this was his total lack of self-pity. He was grateful that he was who he was, namely W. H. Auden, received on earth as an honoured guest. His wonderfully positive gratitude for his own good luck prevented him from ever feeling in the least sorry for himself. Audiences were baffled and enchanted by this publicly appearing very private performer, serious and subtle and self-parodying all at the same time. They could take him personally and seriously, laughing at-with-him.

He had become a Christian. There was a side to this conversion which contributed to his personal isolation. Going to Spain because he sympathized with the Republic during the Spanish civil war, he was nevertheless – and much to his own surprise – shocked at the gutted desolation of burned-out churches. Later, he had some signal visionary experiences. These he did not discuss. He was altered in his relations with people, withdrawn into his own world which included our world, became one of those whom others stare at, from the outside.

In his poetry Christianity appears as a literally believed in mythical interpretation of life which reveals more truth about human nature than that provided by 'the healers at the end of city drives' – Freud, Groddeck, Homer Lane, Schweitzer, Nansen, Lawrence, Proust, Kafka – whom Auden had celebrated in his early work as those who had 'unlearned hatred'.

> and towards the really better
> World had turned their face.

For throughout the whole development of his poetry (if one makes exception of the undergraduate work) his theme had been love: not Romantic love but love as inter-preter of the world, love as individual need, and love as redeeming power in the life of society and of the individual. At first there was the Lawrentian idea of unrepressed sexual fulfilment through love; then that of the social revolution which would accom-plish the change of heart that would change society; then, finally, Christianity which looked more deeply into the heart than any of these, offered man the chance of redeeming himself and the society, but also without illusions showed him to himself as he really was with all the limitations of his nature. Christianity changed not only Auden's ideas but also in some respects his personality. Good qualities which he had always had, of kindness and magnanimity, now became principles of living; not prin-ciples carried out on principle, but as realizations of his deepest nature, just as prayer corresponded to his deepest need.

Of all my friends, Wystan was the best at saying no. But if asked for bread, he never produced a stone. Young poets who brought him their poems were told what he thought about them. (Though, in their case, if he gave them a discourse on prosody, they may have thought that, instead of bread, he was giving them a currant bun.) He no longer believed in the efficacy of any political action a poet might undertake: but that did not mean he had no social conscience. A few years ago I told him that some writers in Budapest had said to me that if he would attend a conference of their local PEN club which was soon to take place, the name Auden would impress the authorities, and their lives perhaps become a bit easier. Wystan left Vienna almost immediately and attended their meeting in Budapest.

Still, he no longer believed that anything a poet writes can influence or change the public world. All a poet can do perhaps is create verbal models of the private life; a garden where people can cultivate an imagined order like that which exists irresistibly in the music of Mozart, and perhaps really, within eternity.

Much of his later poetry was a long retreat from his earlier belief in the feasibility of healing literature, into the impregnable earthworks and fortresses of language itself, the fourteen-volume Oxford dictionary, the enchanted plots of poetic forms in George Saintsbury's book on English prosody, the liquid architecture of Mozart, and the solitaire of *The Times* crossword puzzles.

Wystan died a month ago now. How long ago it seems. In the course of these few weeks much has happened which makes me feel he may be glad to be rid of this world. One of his most persistent ideas was that one's physical disorders are reflections of the state of one's psyche, expressing itself in a psychosomatic language of spots and coughs and cancers, unconsciously able to choose, I suppose, when to live and when to die.

So I am hardly being superstitious in joking with him beyond the grave with the idea that his wise unconscious self chose a good day for dying, just before the most recent cacophonies of political jargon blaring destruction, which destroy the delicate reduced and human scale of language in which individuals are able to communicate in a civilized way with one another.

We can be grateful for the intricate, complex, hand-made engines of language he produced, like the small-scale machinery he so loved of Yorkshire mines, or like the limestone landscapes of that northern countryside of hills and caves and freshets where he spent his childhood. He made a world of his imagination and had absorbed into his inner life our outer world, which he made accessible to us in his poetry as forms and emblems to play with. His own inner world included his friends, whom he thought about constantly.

He also had a relationship, which one can only describe as one of affection, with an audience, wherever that happened to be. He could project the private reality of his extraordinary presence and voice on to a public platform when he gave a public reading. He provoked some uniquely personal reaction from each member of his audience, as though his presence had dissolved it into all its individual human components.

The last time we met in America I asked him how a reading which he had given in Milwaukee had gone. His face lit up with a smile that altered its lines, and he said: 'They loved me!' At first I was surprised at this expression of unabashed pleasure in a public occasion. Then I thought, how right of him. For he had turned the public occasion into everyone's private triumph. One reason why he liked writing – and reciting – his poetry was that a poem is written by one person writing for one person reading or listening – however many readers or listeners there may be. So as a public, an audience, a meeting of his friends as separate individuals here gathered together, may each of us think separately our gratitude for his fulfilled life and our praise for his completed work.

APPENDIX

Edward Mendelson
A Note on Auden's text

Edward Mendelson is Auden's literary executor

THE POEMS

Auden's drastic revisions – and often complete renunciation – of much of his early work creates problems for his readers and his editors. No one supposes that Yeats, for example, damaged his early poems through his late revisions, but the changes that Auden made in many of the poems that established his reputation have been both denounced by readers who lament the loss of youthful energy and excitement, and defended by others who welcome the perfected polish and technique.

From the start of his career Auden published his poems in magazines shortly after finishing them, and then gathered them, often in revised form, in volumes that he published about every five years, beginning in 1930. (The new poems in the 1945 *Collected Poetry* take the place of that year's quinquennial volume.) Three times, however, Auden made large-scale revisions and winnowings for retrospective collections. The first such occasion was *The Collected Poetry of W. H. Auden* – a title he disliked for its implied finality – published in America in 1945. (The 1950 British volume *Collected Shorter Poems 1930–1944* is essentially based on this first collection but restores four poems rejected earlier.) Many poems were further revised for a selection published by Penguin in 1958, and by the Modern Library in America the following year. Finally, even more drastic changes occurred in the *Collected Shorter Poems 1927–1957*, published in 1966. (The *Collected Longer Poems* of 1968 has only minor variants.)

Through all these progressive revisions Auden altered his early poems in a manner different from that he applied to his later ones. In the poems written before around 1945 Auden often revised by dropping stanzas, re-arranging whole poems as parts of other works, and in general making massive changes: and he did this even when revising the poems between their magazine appearances and their first publication in book form. On the other hand, the poems written after 1945 never endured more than minor verbal tinkering, perhaps because Auden had their final shape more firmly in mind when first writing them. While many of the early poems disappeared from later collections, after 1945 Auden never published a poem which he later rejected.

Complicating Auden's text are some revisions that were made for legal reasons – or were not made by Auden at all. (One critic became especially heated about changes that resulted from typographical errors.) The final paper-bound proofs of *Letters from Iceland* printed the following lines in the first part of 'Letter to Lord Byron':

> I must remember, though, that you were dead
> Before the four great Russians lived, who brought
> The art of novel writing to a head;
> The Book Society had not been bought.

In the published book the last line was changed (by Auden?) to avoid libel:

> The help of Boots had not been sought.

A rather bizarre change came about because Auden first offered *The Double Man* to John Lehmann for the Hogarth Press, who proceeded to announce the book in their advertisements. Faber and Faber pointed out that they had contractual rights to all of Auden's books, and T. S. Eliot seems to have negotiated an amicable transfer of the manuscript. Apparently not wishing to publish a title that had been announced by another publisher, Fabers changed the title to *New Year Letter*, taken from the central poem in the book. Then, while reading the proofs, Eliot noticed that the suppressed title survived in a line of 'Prologue':

> And neither a Spring nor a war can ever
> So condition his ears to keep the song
> That is not a sorrow from the Double Man.

Without consulting Auden, Eliot quietly changed this to:

> the song
> That is not a sorrow from the invisible twin.

The American edition, however, retained the proper title and text. And for a note on Auden's reaction to the title *Look, Stranger!*, which Fabers invented while Auden was safely inaccessible in Iceland, see the entry for 22 October 1936 in the 'Chronology' at the beginning of this volume.

Auden hoped to publish a further collection of his shorter poems during his lifetime, and had made some relatively minor corrections and changes which would have appeared in the new edition. He also decided to restore four poems ('James Honeyman', 'Crisis', 'Canzone' and 'Kairos and Logos') that he had omitted in 1966. In place of this projected volume of shorter poems, the Auden Estate plans to publish in 1975–76 a single edition of the shorter and longer *Collected Poems*, with the final revised versions of all the poems that Auden wished to preserve. As for the rejected and altered early work, Auden forbade reprints *during his lifetime*. A selection of early writings in prose and verse, using the texts of the first editions as well as some unpublished pieces, is planned for publication simultaneously with the *Collected Poems*. In the mid-1980s the Estate plans to publish a complete edition of all of Auden's poems, including the rejected work and juvenilia, using the first-edition texts, and with a full apparatus of variant readings.

THE PLAYS AND LIBRETTOS

Most of these are collaborations: the plays, except for *The Dance of Death*, with Christopher Isherwood; the librettos, except for the unpublished *Paul Bunyan*, with Chester Kallman.

The published texts of the plays usually represent versions that were extensively altered in production. At the end of the published text of *The Dog Beneath the Skin*, Sir Francis Crewe walks proudly away from his bourgeois enemies, 'to be a unit in the army of the other side'; on stage, he was unheroically shot by a crazed villager. (A lost 1947 revision for a New York production, by Auden alone, seems to have had Sir Francis stabbed instead.) *The Ascent of F6* enjoyed three or four different endings within three years of publication, and in 1945 Auden reworked the ending once more, this time in rather incongruously Jungian terms, for a production at Swarthmore in which he played the silent cowled monk who holds the crystal before the climbers.

The Auden Estate plans a complete edition of Auden's plays and librettos, including the radio plays and narratives for documentary films. The edition will also print *Paul Bunyan* and a 1949 prose sketch for an unwritten Auden-Kallman libretto, *On the Way*. The texts used will be the final revised versions – although the 1945 ending of *F6* will be relegated to an appendix – together with an account of earlier texts.

THE PROSE

Some four hundred essays, reviews and introductions remain uncollected, and some lectures are entirely unpublished. The two collections of essays that Auden published in his lifetime, *The Dyer's Hand* and *Forewords and Afterwords*, will remain in print. The first of these includes Auden's lectures as Professor of Poetry at Oxford, most of which were previously unpublished; many of the other essays in the book are extensively revised. *Forewords and Afterwords* has only slight revisions and corrections.

A complete edition of Auden's prose, probably in four volumes, is planned. This will print the first published text of each piece, including those later revised in the two collections, and will print for the first time any unpublished prose that Auden left in finished form.

Auden's plaque in Poets' Corner, Westminster Abbey, unveiled by the Poet Laureate, Sir John Betjeman, on 2 October 1974. (*Photo:* Mark Gerson.)

Acknowledgements

'Siegfriedslage' by Lincoln Kirstein is copyright 1967 by *Shenandoah*, reprinted from *Shenandoah*: The Washington and Lee University Review, with permission of the Editor. 'Under Aquarius' by John Hollander first appeared in *For W. H. Auden*, an edition of five hundred copies published by Random House in 1972. Louis Kronenberger's contribution is based on 'Stray Notes for a Memoir', which also appeared in *For W. H. Auden*.
The Editor and Publishers wish to acknowledge the invaluable assistance of B. C. Bloomfield and Edward Mendelson, authors of *W. H. Auden: a bibliography, 1924–1969* 2nd ed. Charlottesville, University Press of Virginia, 1972.

The Editor and Publishers are grateful to Faber & Faber Ltd, who were Auden's Publishers in the UK, and to Random House Inc., who published him in the USA, for their kind permission to quote from the following works:
From *Collected Shorter Poems* 1927–1957: 'Dear though the Night is Gone', 'In Memory of W. B. Yeats', 'A Summer Night', 'Who's Who', 'Sonnets from China', 'At the Grave of Henry James', 'A Healthy Spot', 'Lullaby', 'If I Could Tell You', 'Death's Echo', 'Miss Gee', 'Precious Fire', 'The Truest Poetry is the Most Feigning', 'Plains', 'The Maze', 'The Bonfires', 'The Fall of Rome', 'Musée des Beaux Arts', 'As I Walked Out One Evening', 'Words', 'Consider'; from *Look, Stranger!*: 'Birthday Poem' and 'Epilogue'; from *Epistle to a Godson*: 'The Garrison', 'Dedicatory Poem', 'Talking to Myself', 'The Art of Healing'; from *City Without Walls*: 'Marginalia', 'Elegy'; from *Thank You, Fog*: 'A Contrast', 'Lullaby'. Also quoted are lines from 'Spain', *For the Time Being*, *The Age of Anxiety*, *The Orators* and *The Dog Beneath the Skin*.

Photographs and illustrations were supplied or are reproduced by kind permission of the following:
Associated Press 35, 51; John Auden 1, 2, 4, 5, 6, 7, 9, 10, 11, 13, 75; Steve Bamford 98; Cecil Beaton 52–64; B. C. Bloomfield 47, 48, 78–82, 85–89; BBC Library 28; Rosamira Bulley 8; Camera Press 100; Sir William Coldstream 71; Cyril Connolly 15; Robert Craft 40; Ray Daffurn 95; Durham University Library 12, 14; Maurice Feild 66; GPO 26; Mark Gerson 72, 73, 94; David Hockney 65; Matthias Johannessen 74; John Johnson 20; Lincoln Kirstein 34; Lockwood Memorial Library, Buffalo New York 16, 83, 84; Frank Lyell 30; Mander and Mitchenson Theatre Collection 19, 21, 22, 23, 24, 25, 41, 42; Lennox and Anita Money 76; Charles Monteith 3; Henry Moore 70; Ursula Niebuhr 37, 44, 45; Bill Potter 91, 92, 93; Radio Times Hulton Picture Library 27, 37; Stephen Spender 39; James Stern 29, 31, 32, 33, 34; Topix 99; Michael Yates 43, 46, 77, 96, 97. 68 and 69 are from *Auden Poems/Moore Lithographs*, by courtesy of the Petersburg Press. Jacket illustration by Jill Krementz.
Picture research by Philippa Lewis and Simon Dally.

Index